Welcome To...

INTERNET

From Mystery to Mastery

Tom Badgett
& Corey Sandler

MIS:
PRESS

A Subsidiary of
Henry Holt and Co., Inc.

First Edition—1993

ISBN Book 1-55828-308-0
Printed in the United States of America.

10 9 8 7 6 5 4 3 2 1

MIS:Press books are available at special discounts for bulk purchases for sales promotions, premiums, fund-raising, or educational use. Special editions or book excerpts can also be created to specification.

For details contact: Special Sales Director
                MIS:Press
                a subsidiary of Henry Holt and Company, Inc.
                115 West 18th Street
                New York, New York 10011

ACKNOWLEDGEMENTS

No book is the work of the authors alone. This book on Internet, perhaps more than many, required the work of many people.

We can't mention everyone who helped with this book, but we'd like to extend special thanks to these:

Niels Jonker, networking expert, programmer, and international consultant based in the Netherlands. Niels read this book as it evolved, offered regular and valuable suggestions, and put us in touch with numerous other resources.

Holly Towne, computer skills teacher at Vine Middle School in Knoxville, TN, and driving force behind Operation Uplink, an international education and community project on Internet. Holly first introduced us to the Internet and to her students, whose school lives are changing because of their Internet activities. We learned a lot from the students while they learned about the Internet.

Jack Lail, Metro Editor of the Knoxville News Sentinel, and dozens of others around the world who answered questions, found resources, put us in touch with other people, and in general helped to make our travels fun and interesting.

Debra Williams Cauley, Project Development Editor at MIS:Press, who struggled with us to fine tune the book design, edit the manuscript, and do all the hundreds of other jobs that have to be done before a book can get to you.

Steve Berkowitz, Publisher at MIS:Press who saw the wisdom of this book and arranged for us to write it.

We'd also like to thank The Well, an on-line conferencing service, who arranged for us to experience their services and the Internet from a different perspective. And, there are countless other people on the Internet and at MIS:Press who worked behind the scenes to bring this book to you.

CONTENTS

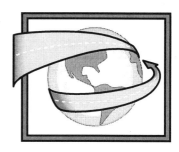

INTRODUCTION

The Internet is a telecommunications superhighway, picking up information from corporations, government institutions, private individuals, and universities over branch roads leading into nearly every corner of the globe.

Like a superhighway, it beckons potential travelers with its promise of faraway places, exotic destinations, and interesting people. Like a superhighway, Internet can take you from one major destination to another quickly, then introduce quiet back roads and quaint locales for leisurely exploration. Like a superhighway, Internet carries holiday and family traffic, people who know precisely where they are going or those who are wandering, government and educational traffic as well as business and commercial traffic. In short, Internet is there for anyone interested in short journeys or lengthy treks, for users who need a quick shortcut across town or across the country.

Unlike a regular superhighway, Internet does all this electronically—you need never leave the comfort of your home, office, or classroom.

A few years ago the concept of sitting in front of a computer terminal and reaching out to other people across the country or around the world would have seemed impossible or at least foreign to most of us. Businesses were doing it, of course, using the expensive resources at their disposal to connect workers around the world. And a relatively small cadre of individuals—computer gurus or engineers, mostly—were doing it. But for the average person, accessing a global electronic network such as Internet was out of the question.

Most of us didn't know about the Internet for one thing, and the cost was more than most individuals were willing to pay. No, global networking was for the big companies.

That has changed, of course. The Internet is only one of a group of fascinating and useful networks that are linking people in all walks of life into a giant, global community without walls:

✦ A group of middle school students from underprivileged neighborhoods in Knoxville, TN, log on to the Internet daily to chat with other students in California, Kentucky, New York, and Canada. They also are on a first name basis with company presidents and college professors from Chicago, The Netherlands, and England.

✦ A college professor in Gettysburg, PA, logs on to Internet several times a week to update colleagues on his latest discoveries working with computer-based testing of hand-eye coordination timing. He finds out what others in his field are doing and gets suggestions directly from other experts.

✦ A West Coast software developer uses Internet during the final stages of writing a custom application to upload programs to his client in England and to get progress reports and early implementation.

✦ A range of users from executives and managers to sales persons and secretaries at companies such as J.P. Morgan, IBM, Coca-Cola, and Walt Disney check Internet electronic mailboxes several times a day to keep in touch with far-flung members of their corporate community, to send proposals and quotes to clients, or to confirm travel schedules.

✦ The curious and the expert, the young and the old, male and female, keep Internet wires humming well into the night from the darkened corners of bedrooms, dens, and offices at home. What are they doing? Talking with each other, working late, finding recipes, reading poetry, searching for news, playing games, and more.

The Internet is like a diverse community of millions of people, divided and subdivided into close groups of intimate strangers where everybody knows your name. Little wonder that as computer technology drops in price and moves onto nearly every corporate and home desk that we naturally seek a way to come together even as we sit apart in the privacy of our own logical worlds. And the list of users is growing and growing. One estimate, from Merit, Inc., an Ann Arbor, MI company that tracks such things for the National Science Foundation, predicts that there will be at least 100 million users by 1998.

In this book we'll show you how to tap into the captivating world of Internet, giving you "news you can use," whether you already are using Internet, or are merely fascinated by the prospect. We'll take you along the Internet superhighway in a travel guide that shows you how to get on board, how to explore the opportunities it presents, and how to bring back souvenirs from your journeys.

You'll find information that addresses your business and educational needs, as well as how to enjoy and benefit from Internet as an individual user. There's also a survey of available databases and services along with easy-to-use information on how to search them fruitfully. And, we'll introduce you to the hundreds of conferences and libraries available on-line.

This is a hands-on book that you can use to learn about Internet from scratch, to establish your own personal or business account, to find software to help you access the system, and most importantly to navigate this electronic maze on your own. But this book goes beyond the "how" of Internet access. We want you to know the "what" and the "why." Why use one database or the other, why travel down this road or that one, what can you expect from this conference or the other one?

The idea is to take you as far as you need to go but to travel only along comfortable roads. You are ready for this book if you know how to turn on your computer and type a little on the keyboard. Sure, some of Internet is couched in technical terms, and the procedures for using some features seem esoteric and befuddling.

Don't worry. We don't expect you to be a computer expert or to have any real experience with computer communications as you read this book. We will take you through the steps and show you what's required at every crossroads. If you'll take this promise on faith—then be willing to read on, even when things seem complex—you can learn enough about Internet to explore on your own. And soon you'll be expert enough to venture off to go where you want, and as far as you want.

CONVENTIONS WE USE

Before we get started, let's agree on some terms and some ways of doing things. We'll try to keep the format of this book as simple and as straightforward as possible while, at the same time, making clear the various commands, files, and structures we need to discuss.

NOTE

TIP

WARNING

First of all, in addition to plain text, you'll find throughout this book some icons (small pictures) designed to draw your attention to one section or another. When you see the Note icon, for example, you know we have some special information that applies to the main text in that area, but we feel it is important enough to point it out. Likewise, if you see the Travel Tip icon you'll know there is information that can save you time or trouble on your journey. Finally, if you see a Warning icon, we are telling you about something that is potentially confusing, could cause you to lose data, or information that is really significant for you to notice.

Beyond icons, we have other ways of presenting data in this book that will alert you to important ideas. These include:

✦ New terms are *italicized*. These are words we are introducing for the first time and likely will use later in the book. You probably will find them described in the glossary.

✦ Keystrokes, file names, commands, and specific options are presented in **boldface**. Information you enter from the keyboard is shown in boldface, but you won't enter everything you see in boldface. We'll show you specifically when to type something on the keyboard.

As you begin reading this book, you should be familiar with the communications software and modem you're using with your machine. As we describe modem command procedures, we will use the Hayes-compatible convention. If your modem isn't compatible with the Hayes "AT" command set, you'll have to refer to your modem manual to learn how to conduct the same commands with your hardware.

WHAT'S IN THIS BOOK

We've already hinted at some of the things we'll cover in this book. Here's some more detail on what you will find.

In Chapter 1, we'll give you a little Internet background and history. Don't worry. It's not much, but it will help you understand why the Internet is the way it is.

Chapter 2 shows you how to get onto Internet. This is at once the hardest part and the easiest part of using Internet. You have to find a pathway, a road, to take you to where you want to go. Depending on where you work, how much money you have, and your level of computer experience, this part of the journey can be easy or a bit difficult. Either way, we'll take you by the hand so you can take this step with as little hassle as possible.

In Chapter 3 we'll handle what we like to call the "housekeeping" part of using Internet. There are file, node, and addressing conventions that you need to be aware of, and we'll show them to you in this chapter. Also, you need to understand something of the physical and logical structure of the Internet; we'll cover that as well.

Chapter 4 is where we really start getting to the things you bought this book for in the first place: tools for using Internet. We'll show you how to find searching and file tools to help you locate other fun stuff to play with and how to get it over to your own system.

Chapter 5 is really a continuation of Chapter 4. We'll cover additional Internet tools and procedures—like talk and send, the IRC (Internet Relay Chat) facility, who you're likely to find on the Internet and how to interact with them. In addition, we'll show you how to find games and other fun things to play with.

Chapter 6 is a detailed reference section that shows you how to find files and conferences about specific topics. You'll use this chapter as a quick reference to get you started with your own searches, then you'll likely return to it again and again, when you need to find something specific on the Internet.

In Appendix A we give you a quick reference to UNIX and some of the important UNIX commands you're going to need to make Internet travel a little easier. Even if you've never used a computer from an operating system prompt before, this reference will help you with the little bit of UNIX you need to know on the Internet.

Appendix B discusses an unsavory topic, but one you need to know about: computer viruses. As you attach to foreign systems and download files and programs, you need to be aware of the possibility of a virus infecting your system. This appendix shows you what viruses are, how to detect them, and how to rid your system of one should you get infected.

Appendix C is a fun reference to some of the on-line emotions you're likely to encounter. The smiley face is just one example of the many ways Internet travelers sometimes show how they feel about a topic or another traveler's comment.

Use Appendix D as a reference on some of the common file types you may encounter on the Internet. We can't possible cover them all, but this reference will at least show you some conventions used and point you toward understanding what you have found in some of those obscure corners of the Internet.

Finally, we include a glossary to help you understand the terms we use in this book and others you may encounter on the Internet.

ON TO INTERNET!

OK. Enough preparation. If you've stayed this long, you're ready to start our journey of learning and exploration. Turn the page and take an exploratory trip on the Internet. Then we'll look at some Internet history and background—so you'll know why the Internet is what it is. Finally, we'll start traveling the Internet superhighway together.

Let's have some fun. . .

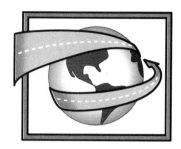

Chapter One

JOURNEY INTO THE INTERNET

You must have heard some of the excited talk and seen printed rhetoric about Internet, or you wouldn't be reading this book. However, the best way to begin learning about the Internet is to try it for yourself. Prepare to embark on a guided electronic exploration.

In this chapter you will expand your understanding of the Internet—what it is, how it operates, and what it can do for you. Among the topics we'll cover are:

✦ Hands-on Internet practice

✦ An Internet definition

✦ Internet history and background

✦ Getting on Internet

✦ Who is on Internet?

Right now we're going to show you how to get a hands-on, brief introduction to the type of services you can find on Internet. This is only an excursion but every long journey must start somewhere.

Ready? Let's go.

WHAT IS THE INTERNET?

Internet is more than a network of computers—it is really a network of networks. Beyond that, Internet is also a network of services and resources, a library, a database, and a community of people from all walks of life ready to answer questions, listen, and share.

To get a sense of the nature and personality of the Internet, we want you to log on to an Internet *node* (a computer connected directly to the Internet and which offers at least some Internet features) and begin to explore some of its resources. In fact, to help you get a feel for the Internet environment, we'll show you two separate nodes, each with different services and different personalities.

Initially you will learn how to access The Well, an on-line conferencing system, and UUNET, an e-mail and conferencing system. Then we'll explain how these two services are different and how you can try them out for yourself. You won't actually be traveling the Internet during these demonstrations because you will use a direct dial number to talk only to one host at a time. Both of these services offer access to the Internet, but you have to be a paid subscriber to use the Internet from either of these nodes. You will log on to these computers and see some Internet-like screens, but your experience will be confined to one system at a time. If you were on the Internet itself you could hop from one system to another, send mail across the network, and download files from multiple systems.

Exploring The Well

The first service you'll access is The Well, a computer conferencing system and Internet access node. The Well was started by the Whole Earth Catalog folk. (You *do* remember the Whole Earth Catalog, don't you?) Well stands for Whole Earth 'Lectronic Link. The on-line information about The Well describes it this way:

19.40 TOTAL
1.44 SALES TAX
1.99- TOTAL DISCOUNT
19.95 SUBTOTAL
1.99- 10 PCT. DISC.
BOOK$AVER 1263105619 12/95
19.95 1558283080

B.DALTON BOOKSELLER SPOKANE, WA
71 610.02.02.10 01/22/94 17.03 1776

were an eclectic mixture of nbers from the Farm, tele- dently minded people.

nferencing system. This e in Sausalito with a whole f networks connected to it. their own computers and ther, without having to be

y other similar systems h degree of personal con- the WELL have met each ged by the fact that the e) in-person parties every

he WELL is people using places to meet and discuss with one another.

You can enter The Well through the Internet if you are connected to Internet from somewhere else. You can also access The Well directly through a telephone exchange in Sausalito, CA, or through the CompuServe Packet Network. Whatever method you use, as a member of The Well you are charged a monthly fee ($15 per month as this book is written), plus an hourly access fee ($2.00 per hour or about 3.3 cents per minute, currently). However, we're going to show you how to sneak a peek at The Well for free and get a flavor of the Internet in the bargain.

Remember, you can access The Well three ways: via Internet, by calling a Sausalito telephone number, or via *CompuServe Packet Network* (*CPN*). For direct access, dial **415-332-6106** on a modem. (We'll show you how to log on in a moment.)

We're assuming you aren't already on Internet at this point, but if you are, you can access The Well with telnet at **well.sf.ca.us**. (If you don't know what that means, don't worry. We said we are assuming you aren't on Internet yet anyway, remember?)

The third method of access is via CPN. If you're not already using CPN to access CompuServe or another on-line service, you can find out the telephone number of your local node by dialing

800-848-8980. That connects you with CompuServe network client support. Simply tell whoever answers that you're looking for a local access number for CPN. They'll ask you some questions and give you a local phone number. This is the number you'll use to get onto The Well.

Whether you are dialing directly into The Well at the 415-332-6106 number, or you are using a CPN connection, set your communications software for the highest speed your modem supports and configure it for seven data bits, even parity, and one stop bit. Enter your communications software's terminal mode where you can issue commands directly to the modem. If you are not sure whether you are in terminal mode, type **AT** on the keyboard (assuming your modem is Hayes or AT-command compatible). You should see the modem response, **OK**, on your screen.

Type **ATDT** (but don't press **Enter**) if your modem is an AT-compatible model and you are using a tone dial telephone line. If your modem uses another command set besides the AT command set, consult the modem manual for the proper command to dial a number on a tone dial line. If you are using a pulse dial line (you have rotary dial telephones instead of push buttons), then use the **ATDP** command (but don't press **Enter** yet) instead of **ATDT** (Again, if you are using a non-AT-command modem, substitute the proper command for dialing a number over a pulse tone line).

To dial The Well directly, enter the direct dial number after the dialing command and press **Enter**. At the login: prompt, type **guest** and press **Enter**. Your screen should look similar to the one in Figure 1.1.

Again, if you are using a pulse dial line, then your command on the first line of this figure would be **ATDP 415-332-6106** instead of **ATDT 415-332-6106**. And, if yours is a non-AT-Command modem, you will have a different dialing command on the first screen. After you have read this initial screen, press **Enter** again and you will see The Well opening menu, shown in Figure 1.2. If you are using the CPN network, then use ATDT (or ADTP) and the local access number for CPN. When CPN answers, press **Enter**, and you'll get this prompt:

Host Name:

Type **WELL** and press **Enter** at the prompt. You should see the screen shown in Figure 1.2 almost immediately.

```
ATDT 415-332-6106
Type     trouble    if you are having trouble logging in.
Type     guest      to learn about The WELL.

If you already have a WELL account, type your username.
login: guest
Erase character is ^H (control-H)


Welcome to The WELL Guest Account.

This account is designed to provide you with some information about The
WELL, and to let you read some samples of the discussion from some of
the conferences on The WELL.

Over the years The WELL has become known as something of a "virtual
community" - people come here to build and maintain relationships with
interesting people.

If you have any questions about what you find here, or about other
aspects of The WELL please let us know.  There is a menu choice to send
us a note.


Press [Return] to continue...
ALT-Z FOR HELP|VT100|FDX|57600 E71|LOG CLOSED|PRINT OFF|ON-LINE
```

```
02KTP

Host Name:  WELL
============================================================
    You are reaching The WELL through CPN - There is usually a
    surcharge of between $4 and $12/hr for using this access method,
    and some gateways involve per-kilo-character charges as well.
    For almost all people within the 48 contiguous United States
    the charge is $4/hr.  Please call The WELL office for
    details (415) 332-4335 or e-mail (support)

    If you get a "Host WELL is inoperative" message you may wish to call
    our status report line:  1-800-326-8354 or 415-332-4627.

    The WELL goes off-line for backups every Sunday morning from  0200
    until 0500  Pacific time.

    ==> European users:   CPN has increased connect charges from some
    ==> cities.  Please read topic #18 in the  sysnews  conference
    ==> for details.
    ==> The new prices took effect on July 1st

Connected to 08WELL


This is The WELL

DYNIX(R) V3.1.0  (well)

Type     newuser    to sign up.
Type     trouble    if you are having trouble logging in.
Type     guest      to learn about The WELL.

If you already have a WELL account, type your username.

login:
```

At the **login:** prompt, type **guest** and press **Enter**. The Well displays the menu shown in Figure 1.3.

Figure 1.3

The Well Main
Guest menu

```
                    WELL GUEST MENU


        1 - What is The WELL? (4K)

        2 - What is a WELL Conference?/

        3 - READ SAMPLES FROM THE WELL CONFERENCES/

        4 - Access Information, Brochure, etc./

        5 - Leave a Note for The WELL Staff*

        6 - Register for The WELL*



    q=Quit menus     d=Download file     m=Mail file     p=turn Pager OFF
    _____

    What do you want to do?
```

You may want to turn on a *capture file* or log file inside your communications software at this point to capture the screens you see as you browse. We will suggest that you capture screens regularly throughout this book. If you aren't sure how to do this with your communications software, find out now. The ability to capture information to disk as it appears on your screen is an important part of using Internet. Now, just follow your fingertips around the guest area of The Well. The entire procedure is menu-driven, so you should have no problems. To get out of The Well, simply return to this main menu and type **Q** to quit.

Remember, accessing The Well as a guest doesn't get you on the Internet, but it gets you on an Internet access node that is typical of some of the hosts you'll encounter in your Internet journeys. A *host* is a computer system attached to the Internet and which you can use to access the Internet, send and receive e-mail, converse with others users, and more. The Well is easy to use, with (mostly) menu access. It offers conferencing and other fun opportunities, as well as providing a gateway to the Internet if you want to use it. We'll discuss how to get you on the Internet in the next chapter, but remember The Well. For many readers of this book, The Well accessed through CPN is a low-cost, easy method for getting on-line with Internet.

Exploring the UUNET Archive

Next, we'll show you how to log on to UUNET (Unix to Unix Network) through a public port, browse around inside some library archives, and then download a few files. Though this isn't a direct Internet trip, UUNET provides a lot of Internet access. For instance, the archive section we'll access contains hundreds of files from this and other Internet nodes. As with The Well, you normally access UUNET via the Internet or by dialing a local UUNET node. Either way you will pay several hundred dollars a month for full UUNET access (for information on UUNET, call 800-488-6384).

However, the archive area we're going to use is available on a pay-as-you-go basis via a 900 telephone number: **900-468-7727**. In this sample logon, you will use this 900 number to access the UUNET and $0.50 per minute of on-line time will be charged to the telephone number you use to make the call. That's $30 per hour, so don't stay on too long—but you can get on, experience a "UNIX platform" style of Internet node, browse around, download some files, and get off without spending too much money. Just don't get carried away and forget the $0.50/minute ticking time clock as you work.

Set your communications software to the fastest speed your modem supports, and for seven data bits, even parity, one stop bit. Use the **ATDT** command (or **ATDP** for pulse lines) to dial the 900 number listed above. (You will need another modem command if yours is not a Hayes-compatible model.)

When the host modem answers, you should see the login screen shown in Figure 1.4.

At the **login:** prompt, type **Anonymous** and press **Enter**. The next UUNET screen, shown in Figure 1.5, is displayed.

```
atdt 1 900 468 7727
CONNECT 9600/V42BIS
UUNET Communications Services (uunet)
     Use of this 900 number costs $0.50 per minute.  This
will be billed on your regular phone bill. If you don't wish
to pay this, hang up now. No additional transfers are
allowed after 30 minutes of connect time.

     login:
```

```
             Welcome to the UUNET archive

     A service of UUNET Technologies Inc, Falls Church,
Virginia.  For information about UUNET, call
+1 703 204 8000, or see the files in /uunet-info

     Use 'cmd-help' for a list of available shell commands,
or 'xfer-help' for a brief synopsis of available file
transfer methods.

     To terminate this session use 'exit' or 'logout'

     bash$
```

The **bash$** characters on the last line of this screen are the UUNET archive prompt. This prompt returns after every display of files or other information. It's the computer's way of saying, "I'm through. Now it's your turn." By the way, the "bash" in this prompt shows you that you are using something called the "Bourne Again Shell," the UNIX equivalent of the MS-DOS Command.COM. You probably don't care about this right now, but it is interesting anyway to know how much information the computer provides as you learn to read the signs.

Notice the difference in this screen and the Well screen we showed you earlier. The Well guest account is a menu-driven system, whereas the UUNET system provides a command-driven interface. You'll see both of these *user interfaces* on the Internet, with the command-driven type perhaps more common. There is a definite trend to move Internet toward a WIMP interface (Windows, Icons, Menus, and Pointers). With a dial-up connection it is more difficult to get this without third party software, but look for it in the future.

So what do you do when an Internet host just waits until you type something? That depends a little on the type of host computer you're talking to. Among the common machines you'll encounter on Internet are Digital Equipment Corporation VAXs, Sun and other UNIX workstations and perhaps IBM mainframes. However, UNIX is a common operating system, even across multiple platforms, so you usually are safe trying UNIX commands at an Internet host prompt.

When you get the first **bash$** prompt, type **cmd-help**, as the welcome screen suggests. This will list some of the commands available at this prompt. You should see the display in Figure 1.6.

NOTE

UNIX systems are case-sensitive. Most commands are entered in all lower-case. If you receive an error message while entering commands, first check that you used all lower-case characters.

Notice that the command **cmd-help** is presented in all lower case letters. This is the norm for UNIX, unlike MS-DOS and other systems that either don't care or prefer all upper case. Anytime you access a UNIX system, pay particular attention to how commands are presented. Most commands are all lower case, but directories and file names may be all upper, all lower, or a combination. Unless you enter information exactly as the system expects to see it, you'll get an error message.

Figure 1.6

cmd-help screen
in **UUNET**

```
Supported commands (via this shell or kermit's 'remote host'):
cat        HLP        ln         rb         RZ-        sz
chmod      index      ls         rm         sb         SZ-
compress   kermit     mkdir      rx         split      uncompress
du         KERMIT-    mv         rz         sx         xfer-help
CMD-HELP   MAN        MORE

Use "man COMMAND" for more information on any commands listed.
bash$
```

These are UNIX commands that are available on many Internet nodes. One command, **man**, stands for "manual." Use it to get more information from the on-line UNIX manual about any available commands. For example, try this command: **man sz**. You should see the display shown in Figure 1.7.

Figure 1.7

man sz command at UUNET bash$ prompt

```
SZ(1)              USER COMMANDS                    SZ(1)

NAME
     sx, sb, sz - XMODEM, YMODEM, ZMODEM file send

SYNOPSIS
     sz [-+labdefkLlNnopqTtuvyY] _f_i_l_e ...
     sb [-ladfkqtuv] _f_i_l_e ...
     sx [-lakqtuv] _f_i_l_e
     sz [-loqtv] -c COMMAND
     sz [-loqtv] -i COMMAND

DESCRIPTION
     Sz uses the ZMODEM, YMODEM or XMODEM error correcting protocol to send one
or more files over a serial port to a
variety of programs running under PC-DOS, CP/M, Unix, VMS,
and other operating systems.
--More--(4%)
```

Notice the **--More--(4%)** at the bottom of Figure 1.7. This indicates that only 4% of the information on **sz** has been displayed. The **--More--** prompt tells you that there is more information to follow. You can press **Return** or (**Enter**) to get the next line; press the **space bar** to display the next screen, or press **q** to quit the display. This convention is used extensively in the Internet.

Use the **man** command to explore other commands listed on the first UUNET screen, if you wish (just remember: $0.50/minute!). This is a good way to learn your way around this particular system and to learn something about UNIX in general.

Now try this. At the **bash$** prompt, type this command: **ls**. That's the UNIX list files command. It should produce the screen shown in Figure 1.8.

Figure 1.8

File List (ls) command at UUNET

```
bash$ ls
ClariNet        doc          languages     opinions      unix-world
admin           etc          library       packages      usenet
applix          faces        lost+found    private       usr
archive         ftp          ls-lR.Z       pub           uumap
bin             graphics     ls-lRt.Z      published     uumap.tar.Z
clarinet        help         ls-ltR.Z      sco-archive   uunet-info
compress.tar    index        mail          systems       uunet-sites
court-opinions  inet         networking    tmp           vendor
dev             info         news          unix-today
```

This is a list of files and directories located in your current directory on the UUNET system. What is your current directory? Type **pwd** to find out. The system should tell you that yours is the **/** directory.

In UNIX the root directory is shown with a forward slash instead of the backslash (\) used on PCs running MS DOS.

NOTE

You can change to another directory with the **cd** command. Just type **cd**, a **Space**, and the name of the directory you want to make current: **cd usenet**. Now you are in a new directory, **usenet**, with a whole new set of files and subdirectories at your disposal. For a really impressive list of directories and topics, use the **ls** command again. Get ready to use the **Ctrl-S** key combination to stop the display and give you time to view the names. Use **Ctrl-Q** to start the display again. **Ctrl-S** and **Ctrl-Q** may not work for you, depending on what kind of system you are using and the type of communications software. In this case, use a different form of the **ls** command:

ls -C | more

You can use **cd** again to change to one of these directories, then use **ls** to show what files and directories are there. As you list files, note which names end in **.Z**. These are archive files that have been compressed using a UNIX-based compression utility. To use these files you'll either have to use UNCOMPRESS on a UNIX system, or locate a version of it for your machine. There are MS-DOS versions available, for example, that will uncompress these and other compressed file formats. We'll show you more about these later in this book.

If you *do* have access to a UNIX system but you don't have the compression utility, you can download it from UUNET. Follow the procedure we describe below for downloading files to get a copy of **compress.tar**, located in the root (**/**) directory. This is the source code for a C program that you will have to compile on your UNIX system to use it. Ask your system administrator for help if you need it. You may also be able to find programs to uncompress these files on your MS-DOS, Macintosh, or other desktop machine.

There are some files on UUNET that you *can* use, however. Return to the original directory by using the **cd** command by itself: **cd**. Now change to the index directory: **cd index**. If you use **ls** at this directory, among the files you'll see is **README**. Let's download this file so you can access it with a local editor or print it out on a local printer. Use this command: **sz README**.

This launches the UUNET *ZMODEM* transfer protocol and gets it ready to send the file **README** to your computer. If necessary, start the ZMODEM protocol on your local machine, specify a file name and wait for the completion of the transfer. Notice that most UNIX systems are case sensitive, so if you specify **readme** instead of **README** the transfer won't work.

This is a *text file* (ASCII characters), so when the transfer is over, you can use the DOS EDIT utility or whatever text utility you have at your disposal to view text files. Most word processors that run on desktop computers can load, display, and edit text files. A text file is one composed only of 7-bit characters. You can display a text file at the operating system prompt and edit it with the simplest of text editors. It doesn't include any special characters beyond the alphabet, numbers, and some punctuation.

Want to try another? Transfer to the **/info** directory and use **sz** again to download the file **archive-help**. This file offers hints on using some of the UUNET features and also gives you some additional practice in file transfer.

With some ZMODEM systems, the local (destination) file is named automatically, based on the name of the source file. If you are transferring from a UNIX system to a DOS system, the file names may not be compatible. In this case, the destination file name won't be the same as the source file. If you have problems saving a file with a name incompatible with your system, use another protocol or turn off automatic naming in ZMODEM. Then you can specify a name for the destination file. For example, if you use *XMODEM* (the **sx** command), UUNET responds:

bash$ sx README

Sending README, 43 blocks: Give your local XMODEM
receive command now.

This gives you an opportunity to enable local XMODEM transfer and specify a file name for your computer.

When you're through experimenting with UUNET, type
BYE or **exit** or **logout** at the **bash$** prompt. You will be logged
off of the system and your $0.50 per minute charges will end.

INTERNET BACKGROUND AND HISTORY

By computer standards, the Internet is ancient, created in 1969 by
a branch of the federal government's Department of Defense.
The original network, called *ARPAnet*, was started by the
Advanced Research Projects Agency, or *ARPA*). It was intended
for use as a research vehicle for the military—a way to find out
how to build *persistent networks* that could withstand the wages
of war. (In computer jargon something "persistent" is able to
withstand unusual conditions or unforeseen events and keep on
working.)

This was the beginning of *peer-to-peer* computer communications. At first, as users experimented with this form of networking, many kinds of data were transferred. Local sites tried
different ways to "packetize" information for efficient and error-
free transmissions. This is where encapsulated *packets* of data are
sent from a source machine to a destination machine along with
information about what should be in those packets. Ultimately, a
protocol evolved over the Internet that was called the *Internet
Protocol*, or *IP*, used in conjunction with *TCP*, or *Transmission
Control Protocol*. You frequently will see this communications
standard mentioned as TCP/IP. We will give you more information about TCP/IP later in this book.

This was a military project, remember, so the assumption
during design of the IP was that the only known aspect of the
network at any given moment is the fact that two computers, a

client and a server, are communicating. If these two entities are exchanging data, then the link between them is sound. Beyond that, nothing about the integrity of the rest of the network is assured or assumed. In addition, even though client A is right now communicating successfully with host B, that link could be broken at any time.

Therefore, TCP/IP and the physical structure of the network itself is such that temporary interruptions or even catastrophic destruction of some Internet facilities won't necessarily destroy the network itself. Moreover, the computers attached to the network are—and were—a disparate mix of different capabilities from different vendors. Standards had to be established that would allow this potentially confusing and incompatible mix of hardware and software to talk to each other.

As it evolved over the first few years, this electronic highway (it wasn't really a *super* highway then) was aimed at providing a pipeline for *electronic mail* services and on-line libraries for universities and government agencies. These users could provide excellent tests for the network integrity that the government wanted to establish, and this network (it wasn't the Internet yet) could provide these agencies a useful vehicle for data exchange.

In the beginning, Internet was like a strain of bacteria that was alive and healthy but which lacked the medium it needed to multiply. Twelve years after its establishment, in 1981, there were 213 computers registered on Internet. Over the next ten years real growth started. But even in 1991, when there were 376,000 computers registered, the "critical mass" required for exponential growth had just barely been reached.

Then things began to happen. One year later, in 1992, the number of registered Internet computers had doubled to 727,000, and today there are probably 1.5 million or more computers connected to the Internet. Currently, there are more than 8,000 *networks* (networks, not computers) attached to the Internet, providing direct access for millions of people. If you take into account the people who use Internet as a carrier only, sending and receiving messages via Internet from other networks, there are probably 25 million people exchanging electronic mail and other on-line information over Internet.

The Internet is made up of *Local Area Networks, Metropolitan Area Networks,* and huge *Wide Area Networks.* The systems are hooked together with everything from standard dial-up phone lines to high-speed dedicated leased lines and satellite, microwave, or *fiber optic* links.

From ARPANET to Internet

In the early 1980s the original ARPAnet split into two networks, the ARPAnet and *Milnet*, but connections continued between the two networks as something originally called the *DARPA* Internet. (The original Advanced Research Projects Agency had now become the *Defense Advanced Research Projects Agency.*) Within a short time, common usage shortened the name to simply the Internet.

However, you can't really think of Internet as a single entity that started small and grew. Actually, Internet had multiple beginnings, like the tributaries of a great river that start small and alone in the dark, cold recesses of a hidden mountain pass. As we mentioned, Internet is really a network of networks, and that's how it got its start. As you might imagine, during the time ARPAnet was getting started, other groups outside the military and government establishment also were seeing the need for decentralized, reliable communications, and these groups started their own networks in parallel to ARPAnet.

Among them were *UUCP* (from UNIX to UNIX Copy Program protocol), an international UNIX communications network, and *USENET*, which stands for User Network. As with Internet in the beginning, USENET started as a network for the university community and later branched into commercial services. USENET and UUCP came into being in the late 1970s. By the early 1980s, we saw the rise of larger networks, including *CSNET* (Computer Science Network) and *BITNET*, both of which were targeted, again, at the university and research community.

Changes in computer technology and networking technology came together in 1986 with the establishment of *NSFNET*, a National Science Foundation link that tied together users with five national supercomputer centers. The growing strength of this network, as it expanded to connect mid-level and statewide academic networks, began to replace ARPANET for research networking until, in 1990, ARPANET was dismantled. It didn't matter that ARPANET ceased operations, however, because all of the interconnections growing out of other networks easily replaced it.

The backbone (the main links or Interstate-like portion) of the current Internet network belongs to the National Science Foundation, but it is managed by Advanced Network and Services, Inc. (ANS) in a partnership among IBM Corp., MCI Communications Corp., and a consortium of universities in Michigan. Since 1989, commercial Internet access providers have been able to lease *interchange points* from ANS and offer electronic mail, file transfer, and database services to individuals and corporations.

In addition, the 35 regional networks connected to the Internet backbone are moving to become more independent of government funding by selling Internet connections. CompuServe, MCI Mail, and GEnie are among commercial on-line services that offer electronic mail gateways to Internet, and Sprint Communications Co. launched SprintLink as an access to Internet in 1992.

Today you have many choices for connecting to the Internet yourself, either as a corporation or as an individual. In the next section of this chapter we'll look at an overview of the Internet structure itself, and show you some of the ways you can access the power of Internet.

Internet Road Map

Now from the hands-on trial at the beginning of this chapter you know what Internet *looks* like, and you learned about the history and background of Internet. We will provide more information about who and what are on Internet soon. In this section, you will develop an overview of Internet that shows what's there and how it all fits together. This is a road map, if you will, of the Internet structure and makeup.

Before you start a vacation trip you probably learn about your proposed destination by viewing a tape or reading an article about the area's history and background. Often you want to know more details of the area's attractions and what is the best way of getting to them. That's what we'll try to show you here about the Internet.

Surely you have guessed by now that Internet is an extremely complex piece of physical and logical architecture. The good news is you don't really have to understand it all to venture into its streets and highways, or to visit the vendors you find along the way. However, a high level view of this amorphous concept might help you find your way.

The drawing in Figure 1.9 shows a conceptual view of Internet hardware. There is a lot of software inherent with this hardware, of course, but for now we don't need to consider it.

Figure 1.9

Internet Hardware interconnection overview

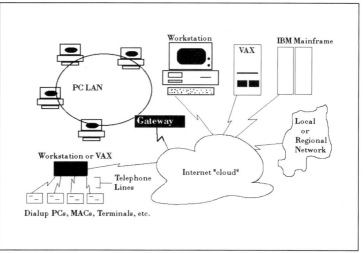

This drawing shows the many types of hardware components that make up the Internet. Notice no component is marked "Central Server" or "Internet Headquarters." That's because there is no such entity on Internet. Although mainframe computers certainly are on the network, these aren't necessarily any more powerful or strategic, from an Internet view, than the PC-based LANs (Local Area Networks) or minicomputer nodes that also are part of Internet.

The Internet itself is shown as a cloud because it is all but impossible to say what is there. Remember that the Internet itself is made up of other networks which include additional computer systems.

In fact, the most accurate drawing of the Internet would be just one big cloud! Even the PC LAN, the Workstation, and other components we have shown here are themselves part of the Internet, so they are inside the cloud. The dial-up computers shown could be outside the cloud if they are simple dial-up connections to a host. Or, they could be part of the Internet itself with special software that lets PCs, Macintoshes and other dial-up desktop units share the Internet directly.

That's the bad news—Internet is a complex arrangement of LANs and individual computers. The good news is that to you, the traveler along this electronic superhighway, all this matters very little.

When you look at a map of, say, the Southern United States to plan a trip from Atlanta to Miami, do you concern yourself with all the little roads that connect to Interstate 75, or do you decide where to get on I75 and how to follow it to Miami? The important part of that map is how to get onto the main interstate, and where to get off at the other end.

The same is true of Internet. We'll show you how to arrange to get on the Internet in your home town, and some of the main routes you can follow. The underlying technology and complexity don't need to concern you, until you are interested enough and have enough knowledge to start learning about it.

Internet is a peer-to-peer network, which means that nearly all of the facilities that make up the network have equal importance and conduct themselves with respect to each other as equals. This isn't strictly true, because the type of connection being used to access the Internet just naturally gives more status to some hardware than to others, but basically Internet hardware is created equal.

Here are the basic types of Internet connections:

✦ **Dial-up** This is the simplest and least expensive method for an individual user to access the Internet. (unless you can get it free through your company or someone else's company, of course). This is an indirect Internet connection because your computer isn't really part of Internet, even when you are logged onto Internet. This is because a dial-up connection is handled through another computer that *is* a part of Internet. You dial a phone number for the "remote" computer (this is a remote computer even if it is located in the same room with your machine; it is not your machine, so it is a remote machine), answer a few questions, and then you can use that computer's Internet connection to get what you want from Internet. This is the way you attached to Internet at the beginning of this chapter, through a remote dial-up connection.

✦ **SLIP/PPP** One step above dial-up is a telephone-line-based node connection that uses SLIP or PPP Internet software. You can use dedicated voice-grade telephone lines or a dial-up connection (most frequently a dial-up connection rather than a dedicated connection) for this level of access. Either way you will use a conventional v.32bis or other high speed modem for the attachment to the wire. This type of connection is like using dial-up Ethernet to your company host. It makes your computer a node on the network, but through a temporary telephone connection from a remote location rather than through a dedicated link onsite. This mode of connection is superior to conventional dial-up because your local computer actually becomes a part of Internet; you aren't using another Internet node as an intermediary between your system and the network. If you're considering SLIP/PPP, shop carefully for a host provider. This method can be considerably cheaper than a conventional logon to a remote host, or it can cost many times more, depending on the arrangement you have with a particular host. This is the next best thing to using a direct connection.

✦ **Dedicated Connection** This is top of the line Internet. Dedicated network access means you have a high speed communications line attached directly through a high speed communications interface to your computer. This is the way minicomputer, mainframe, and relatively large local area networks usually are connected. A dedicated link is always up. Your computer is part of the Internet all the time and anyone with access rights to the dedicated computer can reach Internet. Terminal users, PC-based network members, and dial-up users can all access Internet via the dedicated link attached to your computer. This level of connection is designed to service a large number of users with a relatively large amount of traffic. This type of link is relatively expensive, with sign-up fees of $2,000 or more and thousands of dollars a year in fees. When you use a dial-up link to an Internet provider, you're probably using that provider's dedicated link to access Internet.

✦ **Remote Network Access** If you are a member of CompuServe Information Service (CIS), GEnie, BITNET, MCI Mail, or another on-line service, or if you have access to a BBS system using FIDOnet, you can access Internet to exchange electronic mail and perhaps use a few other limited services. Depending on how your FIDOnet is set up, you may even be able to join news conferences. The process is similar (but different) for each network, so contact your network representative for information about exchanging electronic mail over Internet.

You'll find more detailed information about arranging your own Internet connection in Chapter 2.

INTERNET RESOURCES

We've already talked about what Internet is and who it is. In this section we'll give you a brief list and summary of Internet facilities just to give you a better idea of what you might find on this fascinating resource.

Computer Systems and Centers

Quietly sitting on the Internet are thousands of highly sophisticated computers that form the hub of various local and wide area networks. These systems are on dedicated lines, so they always are on the Internet. Part of their Internet offering is the wealth of information their users have in their heads and are willing to share with other Internet users. Such centers hold a wealth of research data waiting to be tapped. You can't get to everything on these machines, of course, because a lot of the information is proprietary to the company, government agency, or university that owns the machine. But you'd be surprised at how much information is available to Internet users.

Databases

In one sense, the entire Internet is one huge database. You can use Internet to find out about almost anything you can imagine from a wide range of sources, so that's a database. However, in a more formal sense, you can access a variety of databases via Internet—you just have to know where to go.

What's a database? It is a repository of similar or related data. One type of database is a list of databases, and you can find that on Internet. You also can find databases you can search on such topics as:

+ Legal information (The Columbia Law Library on-line catalogue, for example)
+ Medical information (MEDLINE, for example)
+ National education BBS
+ Molecular biology
+ Food and Nutrition
+ Alcoholism
+ Miscellaneous data (Ham Radio Callbook, for instance)
+ Kidsnet, an international interchange for students
+ ERIC, the educational database

- Periodicals
- Federal Information Exchange, a place for the higher education community to interact with various governmental agencies

That's just a sampling, but you get the idea. These databases are created and maintained by the people attached to full-time Internet nodes. In general they were conceived and created with another market in mind—perhaps an in-company project or the work of an organization—then made available to the Internet as an afterthought. Database access is one of the most fruitful aspects of the Internet and reason enough to avail yourself of the opportunity. However, once on Internet, you get so much more, such as conferences...

Conferences

An Internet conference is just what the name implies. Like a conference held at a downtown convention center, Internet conferences attract experts, would-be experts, and the just plain curious to a central location to discuss and learn about a specified topic. There are Internet conferences on about every conceivable topic and if you have an interest for which there isn't already a conference (that's a little hard to believe), you and your group can start one.

When you participate in a conference on Internet you may or may not participate interactively, in real time. You can log on to a conference at any time and read the past discussions about a particular topic, add your own comments to a general audience or respond directly to one of the other participants, then log off. In this example, you haven't actually "talked" to anyone. Rather, you have read what other people had to say, posted your own comments for people to read later, then gone about your business. A few hours later or a few days later, you may log on again to see what has happened since you left.

There are also interactive conferences or discussions (or talks or chats) where you talk directly to other people as if you were on a party line or Citizen's Band radio channel. These conferences or discussion groups also can range across a wide list of topics and may include people from all over the world.

Conferences frequently are accessed through a particular group, association, or service provider. One popular conference area is The Well (did you try The Well as we suggested at the beginning of this chapter?), which is really a conference of conferences. The Well is an independent service provider that offers access to Internet and can be accessed from Internet, but it is known for its conferences. There are about 200 public conferences and 100 private ones going on through The Well at any given time. Here's a brief sample of some of the topics:

Apple Library User's Group (ALUG) Conference
Biosphere II
Grateful Dead Conference
Internet Conference
Movies
Oakland Conference
Scientific Computing
Singles Conference
Spanish Conference
Telecommunications Conference
Veterans Conference
Virtual Communities

That's just a start, of course, and these are just the conferences available on a single resource. If you like to share ideas and learn from other people's expertise and experience, Internet is a good place to do it.

Electronic Mail

There are probably more users of the Internet electronic mail than any other single Internet resource. You can send short letters or lengthy files via Internet e-mail. One reason Internet e-mail is so popular is that you can access it from a variety of non-Internet facilities through mail gateways. If you use CompuServe Information Service, for example, or MCI Mail, GEnie, America On-line, or one of any number of on-line services, you have access to the Internet mail system through a gateway, a computer system that carries information to and from the Internet, but which won't give you direct access to the Internet itself.

Mail is sent and received across Internet in much the same way you send mail with the U.S. Postal Service across the country or around the world. Once you know the Internet address of the recipient, you simply prepare the message with a text editor (or use one of the available on-line editors) and send the message to the proper address.

One of the convenient features of electronic mail is that you can create mailing lists of individual recipients. You can send a letter to many people at the same time by sending it to everyone on the mailing list. There also are mailing lists used by various companies and organizations that you can join. Once your name is on one of these lists, you receive "broadcast" mail designed for a general audience within a specific topic area, and you also receive more specific information addressed to you or a subgroup within this interest area. Unlike a conventional postal mailing list, electronic mailing lists are two way: you can post information to other members of the list (like a conference).

Because electronic mail is usually posted within a few minutes anywhere in the world (though it sometimes takes several hours or even a few days, depending on the routing you use and the destination), you can exchange information almost interactively, with very little delay in getting a response. In most cases your access to Internet is through a local connection, so there are no long distance telephone charges associated with the e-mail service. We show you in Chapter 3 how to use e-mail on the Internet.

Interoperability

Another key feature of the Internet is its *interoperability*, which means the ability of computer systems from a variety of vendors to participate in the network and to communicate with each other. Because Internet uses a well-known and widely used communications protocol, you can communicate via Internet with about any kind of computer hardware. Thus, to Internet, an IBM mainframe can talk to an Apple Macintosh which can talk to a DEC VAX, and they all are compatible with Intel-based PCs.

In addition, if your particular machine or network doesn't "talk" TCP/IP directly, you can still use the Internet to exchange data by wrapping information in TCP/IP packets, sending it to the remote location, and unwrapping it at the other end. For example, an Apple Macintosh at location A can send encapsulated data to an Apple Macintosh at location B, and to the two machines it appears as if they are using conventional AppleTalk.

File Transfer

Although you may transfer files of information as you work with mailing lists and other Internet entities, there also are designated file areas where information files, computer program files, graphics images, and other diverse data are stored and available for download across the Internet. (We showed one such repository on UUNET at the beginning of this chapter. If you haven't tried UUNET's 900-number archive, go back to the beginning of this chapter and try it now. That's the type of facility we're talking about here.)

There are two types of file areas that you are likely to access: anonymous and specific. The specific files are ones you are allowed access to because you have a logon account and password on the repository system (the one where the file was generated or where it is stored). The anonymous files are made available to a general Internet audience, whether or not they are members of the company or computing group that created the file.

As you might imagine there are thousands upon thousands of files available on the Internet at any given time. Luckily there are searching facilities that help you find and get what you need from the network. We'll discuss some of those in Chapter 4.

Shareable Software

Internet began with technically-oriented, computer-savvy people. And today, to access Internet you have to use a computer. So it should not be surprising that among the common and popular resources on Internet is a vast collection of shareable software. Distributed as shareware or *freeware*, Internet software offerings range from communications programs to routines that help you use Internet to games.

To use shareable software, you simply have to find what is available and where it is, then download it across the network to your own computer. We show you how to search for software and other information in Chapter 4, then in Chapter 6 we give you some specific examples to look for.

Sounds

It is not that widely used, yet, but sound and even photographs and motion video are becoming part of the Internet. As networking hardware gets faster and faster, and the facilities to attach to high speed networks become more widely distributed, look for sound and other "high end" information to become a part of Internet conferencing and electronic mail. Many corporations and universities already are doing it within their own dedicated networks, and you can find sound and picture files already on Internet. It is only a matter of time before these facilities will be a common and expected part of public networks such as Internet.

INTERNET TRAVELING COMPANIONS

The members of Internet are about as diverse as any community you could choose. The individuals who make up the Internet family are doctors, lawyers, Indian chiefs, engineers, corporate executives, college teachers and students, senior citizens, elementary students and kids of all ages.

But you also can categorize these companions into larger entities—groups that, because of their particular areas of interest or network usage, are segmented out for specific rate structures. In general these groups are:

◆ Educational

◆ Government

◆ Military

◆ Commercial

◆ Individual

Each of these groups receives a different rate structure, generally gravitates to different Internet facilities, and may operate under different guidelines.

For example, educational institutions are limited to providing access only to students and faculty, and they may not conduct commercial activities through their academic accounts. This restriction is made because educational institutions pay lower usage charges, and also because academic Internet traffic generally is routed over portions of the network that are subsidized by federal dollars earmarked for research and education.

If the site through which you access Internet has a commercial license, on the other hand, usage is less restrictive, but the charges are higher. There is no federal subsidy for commercial routes.

As an individual user, you will have to abide by whatever standards are established by the access provider you use and by the general rules of the road, which include an awareness of copyright laws (you can't upload a commercial software package and share it around, for example), international laws (you can't share certain technology such as computer encryption information with certain foreign countries), and common courtesy and politeness.

Although there are no "network police" monitoring your every conversation to make sure you comply with the rules, if you violate the rules and your license often enough you will get caught because enough people will become aware of it and you likely will be reported. That's one way the network works, through people looking out for each other and for the integrity of the network itself. Truly, Internet is a *community* of users, (mostly) all interested in the common good.

WHAT YOU LEARNED

There you have it, a general overview of the Internet. You have experienced some of Internet through our hands-on tutorial at the beginning of this chapter, we've shown you who and what are on Internet, and we've discussed some of the history of this interesting social and technical entity.

In addition, we discussed some of the types of information you can find on Internet and the different kinds of Internet clients, we provided a brief discussion of how you can access Internet yourself, and finally, we pointed out some of the "rules of the road" for traveling the Internet superhighway.

In the next chapter we'll show you how to arrange your own access to the Internet (if you don't already have it), and how to review what you're doing if you're already using Internet.

Chapter Two

MERGING ONTO THE INTERNET

Merging onto the Internet can present a complex array of choices. However, in this chapter we'll show you how to seek out the most economical and most functional Internet access method. And we'll give you more information about the Internet structure to make your travels easier.

We talked briefly in the last chapter about how you can become a part of the Internet. Depending on your present work or school situation, getting your own account for Internet access can be simple or a little difficult. The easy part is if your company or school is already an Internet player and the people who control such things are open to adding new users. In this case, you'll simply have to make a telephone request, or perhaps fill out a simple form, and you're on-line.

The difficult part comes if you don't work for anyone already on the Internet or you aren't in school, and you want to (or must!) minimize the cost of your Internet travels. In this case the process becomes more like solving a mystery or playing a game, but don't despair, just keep reading.

Here's a quick look at the major topics we'll cover in this chapter:

- What are the available Internet access points?
- How do you find Internet access for yourself?
- How can you get the most Internet "bang for your buck"?
- What software do you need to use Internet?
- What hardware do you need to use Internet?

As you move through this chapter, you will encounter some Internet terms and concepts that we may not explain right away. That's OK. If you don't know them, you'll pick them up in the next chapter. Or refer to the glossary at the end of the book.

Let's begin by discussing the various types of access points and how you might reach them yourself.

ACCESS POINTS: ROUTES TO THE NET

Throughout this book we have likened the Internet to a super-highway. Keep that concept in mind as we discuss access points to the Internet. An access point is like a highway interchange, a way to move from local streets and roads onto the interstate. Think about how you might use the interstate highway for a trip to the local shopping mall, for example:

- Get in the car.
- Drive out of the driveway onto your street.
- Follow the city street to a state highway.
- Take the state highway to an interstate interchange.
- Drive up the access ramp to the interstate.
- Follow the interstate to the proper exit for the shopping mall.
- Leave the interstate and follow a local road to the shopping mall.

Once at the mall you park your car and wander through the central areas and back hallways, looking for the right items at the right prices. You select your purchases, pay for them, then make your way back to the car and either drive the reverse route over the interstate to home, or get back on the interstate to connect you with other shopping areas before heading for home.

This interstate highway is a good analogy for the Internet. Your journey along the Internet to find files or discussions of interest is a lot like the trip along the interstate to the local mall we just described. And, like the interstate, you can take the Internet not only to local or regional locations, but to places anywhere in the country. In fact, this is where the analogy breaks down, because you can take the Internet almost anywhere in the world—you aren't confined to the borders of the United States or even to the continent.

To use any of the access methods we discuss, you'll need a way to connect your personal computer (IBM compatible, Macintosh, Commodore or UNIX workstation) to a computer that provides Internet access. You'll probably do this with a modem, communications software, and a dial-up telephone line. We'll discuss some of these hardware and software issues late in this chapter.

In computer parlance a node is a computer system that is attached directly to a network. In fact, a node can be a single computer, or it can be a network of computers through which you access another, broader network. Ultimately you leave the local area through a port attached to a single computer, but precisely how this works or which computer you are using may not be immediately obvious. It doesn't matter. A node is like the interstate entrance and exit ramps—it lets you move from a local or regional area toward some more distant place, using a general purpose access route.

As you might imagine, there are numerous, reasonably complicated hardware and software issues that surround attaching your computer or terminal to the Internet. As we explained in Chapter 1, you might connect through a dial-up connection to an Internet node, you might set up your computer as a node, you might be accessing the Internet through a local area network gateway, and so on. Luckily, we don't have to worry about these complex issues. What we are concerned with, however, is who builds and maintains these nodes, who is using them, and whether you can use them. You will learn more about nodes and gateways in our discussion of domains and addressing in Chapter 3.

That's the main concept. What we have to discuss here are the various routes you can use to "merge" onto the Internet, what you call them, and how to find them.

Academic and Freenet Access

For many Internet users, the academic route is the best, least expensive, and easiest road to follow to the Internet. That's because most educational institutions have some sort of Internet access for students and faculty. As a member of one of these groups at a college, university, technical school, or high school, you probably already have access rights to the Internet.

You're a member of the student body or a faculty member and you never heard anybody say "Internet"? That's not uncommon, but that doesn't mean you can't get on through your institution.

To learn more about access through an academic route, contact your local area network (LAN) administrator, local or regional MIS (Management of Information Systems) director, your supervisor, or coworkers. Somewhere along the line you'll find someone who knows the process for getting on Internet from an internal or dial-up node.

Procedures vary at each institution, of course, but frequently the only requirement is that you are a student with one or more classes or a member of the faculty. Many institutions offer one- or two-session training classes to show you the various options for using the school's computer facilities in general, and for getting on the Internet specifically.

Even if you are not now a student but you can't find another viable option for accessing the Internet, you might consider taking up public speaking, photography, SCUBA diving, computer science, or any class offered by a local school. Frequently the cost of tuition—which incidentally gets you the right to use the school's computer facilities for Internet access—is much lower than paying a commercial service.

You may have another low cost or no cost access option in your community in the form of a *freenet*. Free or nearly free access sometimes is provided through a local library or other institution. A freenet is a community supported operation that may provide e-mail services, on-line research, and Internet access. With some freenet services you may have to physically sit at the library or other institution that provides the service; with others you may be able to use dial-up access. Freenet access may require considerable research, so you shouldn't give up on freenet if your first pass at local facilities doesn't turn up anything. The number of institutions offering this type of Internet access is growing all the time. See the freenet list in Chapter 6 for more information.

Be aware that freenet access may provide a less than full-featured port to the Internet, depending on what institution is offering the service, how it is funded, and the like. But it can get you on when other avenues aren't available or are too costly.

Governmental Access

Accessing Internet through a governmental facility is like using a college or university. If you are a government employee or contractor, chances are there is Internet access somewhere within your facility. If you don't already know about it, you'll have to do some research. Simply start asking questions to learn where Internet is being used and how you can access it.

Accessing Internet through the government—especially a military or research facility—can be more complicated than from a university setting because of security issues. It is still possible, just ask lots of questions.

If yours is like most governmental facilities, there's probably a local network serving your department or workgroup, then a facility-wide or regional network tying some of these facilities together. If no one on your local network knows about or is using Internet, you'll just have to branch out, broaden your sphere, and find out who is.

Commercial Access

Guess what? Many large corporations also use the Internet regularly to conduct research, to use e-mail, or to transfer regular information from one division to another. If your company has more than one office and you know that your computers are part of the regular hardware in use at your firm, chances are pretty good that somewhere, someone in your company already is using Internet for something.

As with academic and governmental access, you'll simply have to find the right person who can tell you whether the Internet is being used and what you have to do to use existing facilities. At the very least you should be able to get e-mail services. But you might also arrange full-featured Internet access through your existing company link.

Third Party Access and UUCP

If you can't get to the Internet through academic, governmental, commercial, or freenet channels, you may settle for partial access through what we call "third party" channels (but see our discussion of commercial services—different from commercial access—that follows). Among these third party channels are the *CompuServe* network, *MCI Mail*, *America On-line*, BBS facilities such as FIDOnet, and a built-in facility of UNIX, *UUCP*. You can also find UUCP software for MS-DOS, Macintosh, Commodore, and other platforms.

With these methods of access you can do little more than exchange electronic mail and perhaps Internet News (see Chapter 3). With CompuServe, MCI Mail, and other commercial on-line services, you use Internet e-mail facilities from inside the basic service simply by providing an appropriate Internet mail address. In fact, you can use Internet to send messages to non-Internet addresses if both ends of the link have some way to attach to Internet.

MCI Mail is an on-line commercial service dedicated to e-mail while offering some research and other services. CompuServe is a commercial bulletin board, e-mail and on-line service that provides Internet-like services. America Online is similar to CompuServe. With any of these services, you arrange access by signing up and paying a fee. Then you use a modem and communications software to dial an access telephone number to log on.

CompuServe

For example, to send a mail message from CompuServe to one of the authors of this book, Tom Badgett at Operation Uplink on the Internet, you would use this address:

>**INTERNET: tbadgett@opup.org**

You would enter this address at the CompuServe **Send to (Name or User Id):** prompt. This command tells the CompuServe message handlers to send the created mail message to CompuServe's Internet node, and from there to the specified Internet address. Of course, as a CompuServe user you can receive e-mail via the Internet as well. See the next section for details.

NOTE

You are limited to a 50,000 character message when sending from CompuServe to the Internet, and you can't send binary or non-text files. You can transfer binary files into the mail system, but when you try to send the mail, CompuServe stops, telling you that you can't send non-text mail outside CompuServe.)

This does not really put you, the user, "on" the Internet, but it does let you use CompuServe facilities which you already have and are paying for to send mail to people or companies who are on the Internet but may not be on CompuServe.

You can send CompuServe users mail from the Internet as well. All you need to know is the recipient's CompuServe ID

Number. For example, Tom Badgett's CompuServe ID is 74365,1003. To send him a mail message from Internet, use this address:

74365.1003@CompuServe.Com

Notice that this address looks like the other Internet mail examples we have given. The difference is that instead of using the addressee's name you use the numerical CompuServe ID.

MCI Mail

Here's another example.

To send mail from MCI Mail to the Internet, use this address format. At the MCI **TO:** prompt, enter the name of the addressee followed by (**EMS**). So to send a message to Tom Badgett from MCI, use this at the **TO:** prompt: **TBadgett (EMS)**.

When you press **Enter** you will get an **EMS:** prompt. At this prompt, type **INTERNET**.

Next, you will see an **MBX:** prompt. At this prompt type the full Internet address, including the name of the addressee. Yes, you entered the name at the **TO:** prompt, but you must enter it again at the **MBX:** prompt. Here's a complete example of sending Internet Mail via MCI Mail:

TO: **TBadgett (EMS)**

EMS: **Internet**

MBX: **tbadgett@opup.org**

WARNING

Unlike CompuServe, MCI will accept a binary file for sending to an Internet mail account. However, when it is delivered on the other end, you'll find the file isn't what you sent. The file is transmitted as if it were a text file, so you lose the high bit data. Unfortunately, MCI Mail doesn't warn you about this.

You can send mail from the Internet to MCI Mail clients. Here's how. Access whatever mail system you're using on the Internet, create the text of the message, then send it to the addressee at mcimail.com:

TBadgett@mcimail.com

As we mentioned earlier, you can use the Internet as a pathway to carry mail between two non-Internet sites. Suppose you are using MCI Mail and want to send a message to someone on CompuServe. You can't do that directly, but you can use the Internet to carry the message for you, even though neither the source nor the destination address is on the Internet itself. Simply use the procedure we just described for addressing a message from MCI Mail to the Internet, but provide the CompuServe address in Internet style:

TO:	**TBadgett (EMS)**
EMS:	**Internet**
MBX:	**74365.1003@CompuServe.Com**

UUCP

To use UUCP facilities to send and receive mail via the Internet you need to make arrangements with a UNIX site that has access to the Internet. UUCP is a system built into most UNIX systems. (If it isn't included, you can get it as an option.) UUCP lets you transfer mail between your system and another automatically. You can also install UUCP functionality through software on non-UNIX systems. To get messages onto and off of the Internet, you want to UUCP to a system that is attached to the Internet. Again, you won't actually access the Internet directly, but you can send and receive messages. In addition, UUCP can dial out from a host system to another user to deliver mail directly.

With UUCP, Internet mail addressed to you arrives at the UUCP site you are using and waits there until you use UUCP on your system to dial up the remote site and download your messages. Likewise, you can send mail from your site via UUCP to the remote Internet node.

If UUCP turns out to be the best solution for you, you can get details on using it from the service provider or from the UUCP software vendor.

However, for most of us, UUCP is one of the last resort solutions. It doesn't give you full Internet access, for one thing, and for another, configuring your system for correct UUCP operation and finding a willing (and properly configured) site to work with can be a real problem.

SLIP and PPP

As we have said, the most complete Internet access is from a dedicated machine, probably a UNIX computer, attached directly to a high speed line on the Internet. There are solutions that are almost as good, though slower, and perhaps cheaper. What you ultimately pay for SLIP/PPP connections depends on the arrangements you make with an individual service provider. This method uses *SLIP* (Serial Line Internet Protocol) or *PPP* (Point to Point Protocol), versions of Internet software designed to operate over standard telephone lines at 9,600 bps or faster. (You probably could run slower than that, but you wouldn't want to). You can use dedicated telephone line access, or use dial-up lines to save the cost of dedicated lines.

As with Digital Equipment Corporation's dial-up DECnet and other similar options, SLIP and PPP are designed for personal computer or very small network access to Internet. With 9,600 bps or even v.32bis (14,400 bps) access, you don't have the bandwidth on the communications link to support very many users.

You still have to access the actual Internet through a service provider who can accept your call (or dedicated link) and put you on the network. Because you are handling most of the overhead including local data storage, addressing, and the like at your local computer, the cost of access may be a lot less than attaching through a dumb terminal (or a computer acting like a dumb terminal).

NOTE

A dumb terminal is a device that includes a keyboard, display screen and a communications port. It is used to communicate with a large, multiuser computer system, or as a modem-link to an on-line service. It contains no local storage or computing facilities.

As for the software, you probably can find SLIP or PPP software free for the asking if you can poke around the Internet or have someone do it for you. There is a lot of public domain software out there, some of it pretty good. One popular offering is KA9Q, a SLIP package that also supports packet radio (TCP/IP over a radio link). Another is PC-SLIP. PPP and SLIP offer comparable capabilities, with PPP perhaps being the newer protocol.

To use SLIP or PPP you would use communications software and a modem to log on to an Internet host, just as you would with any other access. Then you would start your SLIP software and the SLIP package on the host would establish communications with your local SLIP software. Once everything is working normally, your PC, Macintosh, or whatever computer you are using is tied into the Internet almost as if it were on a direct link. Your computer is set up with an IP address, so it functions like one of the "big boys."

You can issue Internet commands such as ftp and, with packages such as KA9Q, you can even receive incoming ftp and mail requests. Remote users can log in to your machine like an Internet host and issue commands just as you do when you log in to a remote Internet site from your PC.

If you don't already have some kind of gateway on your LAN, you can set up your own. By installing KA9Q or equivalent software, you can establish your own desktop machine as a gateway. This provides Internet access to authorized members of the network, including yourself from your own machine. There are many ways to get what you need. Just be willing to search out the solutions and be a little adventuresome. Learn the specifics of installing and using SLIP or PPP from the particular software vendor.

The only real advice we can offer in this regard is to call around and find out what your best options are. In the meantime, don't delay getting on Internet. You can always use the services of a company such as The Well (see the next discussion) to get on at a reasonable price, then check around to see if there is a better choice for you.

Commercial Services

If you haven't already figured out a way to get onto Internet through one of the other methods we have mentioned, you probably will have to turn to a commercial service. There are several companies offering pay-as-you-go Internet access. We'll discuss a few of them in this section.

The Well

The Well
27 Gate Five Road
Sausalito, CA 94965-1401
415-332-4335

We discussed The Well in Chapter 1 and showed you how to access The Well's guest account. The Well is a conferencing system that Internet users can access for research and sharing. And, as we told you then, you also can use The Well as a link to the Internet. You can't get to the Internet from The Well guest account, but once you sign up as a Well subscriber, you have Internet at your fingertips right at The Well **OK** prompt.

N O T E

If you have Internet access another way, you still may want to try The Well. It is an excellent resource for conversation, research, and exchanging ideas on everything from using the Internet to cooking old-time recipes. To get to The Well from anywhere on the Internet, use **telnet well.sf.ca.us**.

You don't have to do anything special to access Internet from The Well. As soon as you issue an Internet command—such as ftp, for example—you will be traveling the Internet. The first time you access the Internet from your Well account, you will be asked to read and agree to a 160-line document that spells out usage guidelines and restrictions on your Well Internet access.

Figure 2.1 shows you how the first part of this agreement looks.

Figure 2.1

The Well Internet Access Agreement

```
OK (type a command or type opt for Options): ftp
Hello, you have reached the WELL's Internet Access Agreement.

The following text contains the rules and standards to which WELL users
must agree to abide by in order to obtain access to the WELL's Internet
connection.

** Please read this agreement carefully.  Intentional or repeated violation
** of this agreement will result in prompt termination of the user's WELL
** account.

This document is roughly 160 lines long.  Please read the entire text.

The WELL has set up a public conference for discussion of the Internet, how
to use it, what is available on it etc.  To get there type:

        g Internet

at an OK prompt.  The WELL support staff does not provide technical
assistance in using the Internet, beyond the information we have made
available for the public Internet conference (which includes a very basic
cheat-sheet for telnet, rlogin, and ftp).

We hope you have great time exploring out there and that you bring back
– <b> backup. <space> continue. <q> quit – wonderful stories of your adventures.
```

In our opinion, The Well is one of the easiest to use and most reasonably priced of the commercial Internet options. As this book is written you can use The Well to get to the Internet for a $15.00 per month membership fee and $2.00 per hour of connect time. Compared to other commercial services that are designed primarily for business access, this is an extremely reasonable price.

NOTE

The above price is for basic access through The Well's local number in California. If you access The Well from an area that makes this a long distance phone call, you'll probably get a better rate by using the CompuServe Packet Network (CPN). This access will cost an additional $4.00 per hour. Still, compared to full commercial access that may run hundreds or even thousands of dollars a month, this sort of charge is quite reasonable. And, The Well's billing policy lets you pay only for what you use rather than trying to estimate a charge in advance or having you pay a minimal charge.

You can request information on The Well to be e-mailed to you by e-mailing a request through the Internet to **info@well.sf.ca.us**. You can send this message through other e-mail services such as CompuServe or MCI Mail. See our discussions of these services earlier in this chapter to find out how to address a message to The Well.

a2i Communications

a2i Communications
1211 Park Avenue #202
San Jose, CA 95126-2924

a2i Communications is billed as a national Internet provider, yet they presently offer only limited national access. It is expected that this service will grow, offering local access from a broader area.

As this book is written you have two options for reaching a2i: a 415 area code direct number (local call in Campbell, Los Altos, Los Gatos, Mountain View, San Jose, Santa Clara, Saratoga, and Sunnyvale) or by using an account on PC Pursuit, a service of U.S. Sprint (SprintNet).

The cost is a $30 one-time fee, then $30 per month membership. This entitles you to 30 hours of non-prime-time service (6 pm to 7 am local time Monday through Thursday, and 6 pm Friday to 7 am Monday). If you exceed the 30 hour non-prime-time allotment, you will be billed $3.00 per hour or increment. Prime-time access to PC Pursuit is $10.50 per hour.

PC Pursuit will give you access to Internet facilities through providers such as a2i, but it does not support e-mail. To get e-mail connections to Internet accounts, you must subscribe to another service, SprintMail. This involves an additional $15 initial sign-up fee and a minimum $20 per month usage charge. The usage charges break down this way:

Peak usage:	7 am–6 pm	
	0.23 per min.	
	plus 0.05 per 1000 characters.	
Off-peak usage:	6 pm–9 pm	
	0.12 per min.	
	plus 0.05 per 1000 characters.	
Night time usage:	9 pm–7 am,	
	0.07 per min.	
	plus 0.05 per 1000 characters.	

The SprintMail and PC Pursuit services are billed on a major credit card or through a direct electronic funds transfer from your bank. The system has access points in 44 cities. If you live in one of these and can save long distance charges to another system, then PC Pursuit alone or PC Pursuit to a2i or another Internet service may be a good choice. Otherwise, check for another local provider.

Note that you can use PC Pursuit to reach many of the providers we discuss in this chapter, including PSI and Panix. To find out more about using PC Pursuit or SprintMail, call U.S. Sprint in Reston, VA at 800-736-1130.

Figure 2.2 shows how a2i is described in an on-line document from a2i itself.

a2i offers benefits in addition to Internet access. There are on-line conferences and databases—the types of facilities offered by many Internet providers. You also get access to a Sun Unix environment for programming, running programs, data storage, and more. With systems of this type you have remote access to a full Unix system.

Figure 2.2

a2i on-line description

The a2i network is a professionally-run system based on a network of Sun machines. Our offerings include:

o Usenet news.
o Electronic mail.
o Internet access, including telnet and ftp. Our IP address is 192.160.13.1
o A SunOS (Unix) software development environment. All the standard tools are available.
o A command-line-oriented MS-DOS environment which may be invoked from within SunOS. In this environment, you can execute most archiving/dearchiving programs, virus scanning utilities, compilers, and assemblers.
o News feeds and electronic mail via UUCP, for UUCP subscribers.
o A permanent electronic mail address for you.
o Other services to be added.

The a2i network is directly connected to the Internet via a 56 kbps leased line. As a result, we can provide you with 'real-time' access to the Internet. For example, as an a2i subscriber, you can interactively converse with other users on the Internet via commands such as 'talk' and 'irc', or exchange electronic mail with them in a matter of seconds.

Two types of subscriptions are available through a2i: interactive subscriptions and UUCP subscriptions. (See our discussion of UUCP earlier in this chapter.)

An interactive subscription (or interactive account as it is sometimes called) is available through direct dial to a 415 area code number, as we mentioned earlier. Or, if you want some of the features of the a2i system such as conferencing, e-mail, and the like, you can telnet to the a2i network on Internet. (Telnet is an Internet command and software utility that lets you find specific Internet hosts and initiate the logon process with them). If your objective is to access the Internet, however, you'll have to use dial-up access, as just described.

Figure 2.3 shows the published a2i subscription rates for an interactive account.

There is no sign-up fee and no connect-time charge, just the specified monthly rate. With your subscription you get up to 5 megabytes of disk space as well. Not sure whether a2i is the link for you? The company offers a three- or six-month trial subscription. You pay the standard rate, but you can cancel at any time and get a proportional refund of the unused time. Note that there is a single rate structure for businesses and individuals. a2i states that each account is for the use of only one person. That means a business would need to arrange for a separate account for each user within the company.

Figure 2.3

a2i published interactive subscription rates

Prepayment term	Cost per month	Amount of payment
6 months	$12	$72
3 months	$15	$45
1 month	$20	$20

Another interesting service of a2i is the ability to establish your own domain name for sending and receiving e-mail. You would still use the facilities of a2i, but the people you correspond with would use your domain as if you had your own Internet connection. The current cost for setting up this type of addressing is $40 initially, then $5 per year for maintenance.

A UUCP account may be useful for companies that have local e-mail or USENET News accounts, or that want to offer public UUCP access. Remember that UUCP is a function of UNIX that, when properly configured, lets two systems communicate to share e-mail and USENET News. If you are an individual seeking Internet access, this is NOT the way to go. An individual account will let you send and receive e-mail and will give you access to USENET News, so you don't need the headache and heavy hardware requirements of UUCP.

There is a dual rate structure for UUCP accounts—standard and low volume. The standard account offers unlimited services, while the low volume account limits the user to a transfer of no more than 100 megabytes per month on the average. The UUCP account includes an interactive account and any required domain registration as well. The rate structure as published by a2i is shown in Figure 2.4.

Figure 2.4

a2i published UUCP
subscription rates

Prepayment term	Cost per month	Standard amount of payment	Cost per month	Low Volume amount of payment
6 months	$35	$210	$20	$120
3 months	$40	$120	$25	$75
1 month	$55	$55	$45	$45

To receive subscription information on a2i by e-mail send a request to **info@rahul.net**. You can send this message through other e-mail services such as CompuServe or MCI Mail. See our discussions of these services earlier in this chapter to find out how to address a message to a2i. Also, you can log on directly to the a2i network to browse through a lot of information about a2i. Simply telnet to **rahul.net** (if you can borrow a connection) or use the direct dial numbers (408-293-9010 for v.32bis/v.32, or 408-293-9020 for PEP) and log in as **Guest**. A menu-driven system will answer your questions and show you how to sign up for a2i.

N O T E

v.32bis and PEP are modem standards. v.32bis is the most common among high speed modems. PEP stands for Packetized Ensemble Protocol, a design promoted by Telebit Corp. as the only multicarrier modem (one that makes use of the entire telephone line bandwidth instead of just a few frequencies as most modems do) that also is compatible with v.32bis. The reason for separate dial-in lines with these two technologies is that while "compatibility" may be designed into a PEP product, there can be delays in getting a reliable link because of the increased overhead while the two modems negotiate over protocol and speed. In addition, there are times when PEP modems simply won't link properly with v.32bis units.

PSI

Performance Systems International (PSI)
510 Huntmar Park Drive
Herndon, VA 22070
703-904-7187

PSI is another provider of dial-up Internet access, but with many access points around the country. As this book was written there were at least 45 access points for PSI services through PSINet. In addition, you can access PSI's facilities through RAM Mobile Data's wireless messaging network using a GE Ericsson's Mobidem portable radio modem.

PSI offers a number of different services to address various access requirements. Contact PSI to find out how to fill your individual needs and to get current prices.

PSI's PSILink Global Messaging Service has two fundamental service options—lite and basic. Lite provides unlimited messaging and paging mailboxes. Basic adds anonymous ftp and USENET News facilities as well. This is a batch process supported through free PSILink software. You write e-mail or news postings off-line, then dial your selected PSINet node. The software takes over and checks your e-mail, downloading any new mail and uploading mail you are sending. Then the software checks your chosen newsgroups for new postings and posts anything you have to add.

You can't use telnet through PSILink (use PSI's Global Dialup Service—GDS—for this). However, PSINet can be accessed in over 175 North American cities and 40 foreign cities, and the list is growing all the time. Notice that while the PSILink service uses Internet for messaging, you may not have access to all the Internet services available from other providers.

On the other hand, you get free access software which makes the service extremely easy to use, and your charges are reasonable. As we prepared this book, prices for basic PSILink dial-up access were those shown in Figure 2.5.

Figure 2.5
Published PSILink
dialup rates

	2400 bps per Month	9600 bps per Month
PSILink Lite	$9	$19
PSILink Basic	$19	$29

You can download the latest PSILink software by using ftp over the Internet. ftp to **ftp.psi.com** and download **psilink.zip** from the PSILink directory (type **cd /psilink** at the ftp prompt). (For more information about using ftp, see Chapter 4.) This will give you an early look at the software you get as part of the PSI service. Of course, if you're not already on the Internet you'll have to borrow a connection or have someone download the software for you.

UUNET

UUNET
Suite 570
3110 Fairview Park Drive, Suite 570
Falls Church, VA 22042
703-204-8000
800-488-6383

Like PSI, UUNET offers access to its own networking and mail services through 2,500 connections, as well as offering Internet mail access. The AlterNet public TCP/IP service from UUNET is for businesses that need direct, continuous links among multiple offices. AlterNet provides a 10 Mbps (million bits per second) national backbone. Because AlterNet is a commercial service, some of the restrictions that may apply to Internet aren't applicable. Of course, you can send and receive mail from AlterNet to Internet.

Remember that AlterNet is designed for relatively high volume users—companies that want to link multiple sites with a high speed, national network. As this book was written, AlterNet prices were as shown in Figure 2.6.

Figure 2.6

AlterNet published prices

Link Type	Monthly Rate	Startup Charge
T1 (1.5 mbps)	$2,000	$5,000
T1-LV (Low Volume)	$1,000	$5,000
56K DDS	$1,000	$2,000
19.2K DDS	$500	$2,000
Async SLIP/PPP	$250	$1,500

You can have information on UUNET e-mailed to you by sending a request to **info@uunet.uu.net**. You can send this message through other e-mail services such as CompuServe or MCI Mail. See our discussions of these services earlier in this chapter to find out how to address a message to UUNET.

ANS

Advanced Network & Services, Inc. (ANS)
ANS CO+RE Systems, Inc.
2901 Hubbard
Ann Arbor, Michigan 48105-2437
313-663-7610

ANS offers national leased line and 800-dialup network services, including Internet access. The 800 service is called ANSRemote. Pricing for the various levels of this service are shown below.

✦ ANSRemote

  • Entry-level offering
  • Telnet/rlogin access to network
  • 1-800 access
  • $25/month + $8.50/hour
  • $25 one-time subscription fee

✦ ANSRemote/IP

  • Connects single PC or workstation as full network peer
  • SLIP/PPP
  • 1-800 access
  • $35/month + $8.50/hour
  • $25 one-time subscription fee

✦ ANSRemote/POP
  • Add on service to ANSRemote/IP
  • Provides e-mail post office box
  • Accessible via standard POP client (RFC 1225)
  • $10/month per box + ANSRemote/IP fees
  • $25 one-time subscription fee

ANS claims to be the only nationwide public data network that offers T3 (45 Mbps) connections. The company offers a broad range of services for companies, research and government institutions, and individuals.

Other Dial-up Connections

The service providers we have mentioned to this point are pretty much countrywide or worldwide providers. In addition, there are a number of so-called "regional" or "local" providers. Actually, once you get onto the Internet it doesn't really matter where your node is. The important consideration is the route you have to take to get to the node.

In other words, if you can access a node without paying long distance telephone charges but you have to pay more for the service, you may be ahead in the long run due to the savings on your communications costs. Likewise, if you can find a provider with a really low access fee, but you have to pay long distance fees to get there, you still may be better off if the long distance costs are reasonable and the access charges are competitive.

In this section we will list a few of these alternatives. If you live close by they are a good choice and, as we said, if you can use off-peak telephone times you may find these alternatives cost competitive over using CompuServe Packet Network, PC Pursuit, or other access methods to other nodes.

Panix

Panix is a public access Unix system in New York City that you can reach with a local call from anywhere in the city. You can also reach Panix through PC Pursuit. The cost for Panix dial-up Internet access is a one-time startup fee of $40, plus $19 per month. This provides unlimited access time to Internet.

Panix is expanding regularly. Soon (if not already) there will be local access numbers in the 516 and 914 area codes and New Jersey locations, as well as to the existing 212 New York City area code. In addition to Internet access, when you use Panix you get a single-keystroke menu system to help with such functions as e-mail and other Internet services. An optional learning mode helps you learn Unix, and Pine mail and Pico editing are available along with other easy-to-use applications. Experienced users can choose a Unix shell from several available.

Panix uses a fast T1 connection to the Internet, so once you get on-line things should go as rapidly as they can, given network traffic limitations that are built into any Internet access.

You can get more information by sending e-mail to **Info@panix.com,** or by calling 212-787-3100 with your modem.

The World

Software Tool & Die
1330 Beacon Street
Brookline, MA 02146
617-739-0202

Another low-cost regional access point is Software Tool & Die's The World in Boston (Brookline). As this book was written, the basic charges were $5.00 per month plus an additional $2.00 in connect time charges, or a flat fee of $20 per month for up to 20 hours of connect time. If you exceed your 20-hour allotment you will be charged $1.00 for each additional hour.

Call 617-739-0202 (voice) for information, or e-mail **office@world.std.com**. You can register or get more information by dialing 617-739-9753 and logging in as **new**.

MSEN

Msen, Inc.
628 Brooks Street
Ann Arbor, MI 48103
313-998-4562

MSEN, a southern Michigan company, is another provider that has been offering local and regional access, but which is expanding to national 800 access, PC Pursuit, the PSI dial-up network, and other methods. This provider offers a full range of Internet access services, plus some local BBS and data offerings you might find interesting.

This is a 56KBaud link, so Internet access speeds should be reasonably fast. For more information you can e-mail **inforequest@mail.Msen.COM**.

Netcom

Netcom On-line Communications Services
4000 Moorpark Avenue, Suite 209
San Jose, CA 95117
Voice   408-554-8649
Fax   408-241-9145
Access Numbers: 800-488-2558 (National on-line number list)

Netcom claims to be California's leading commercial Internet service provider. Indeed, Netcom gained a lot of attention during its first five years of operation, then really started to grow. This is a popular access point for Internet among California users as well as users from other parts of the country as Netcom gets access from other areas up and running.

Netcom Internet access is priced as low as $17.50 per month with no on-line charges, if you pay by credit card. If you want a monthly bill, the price is $19.50 per month. In addition, there is a one-time $20 registration fee. You can use a direct dial connection to Netcom, or you can establish SLIP access if you wish. There may be other access options. Call the company directly—dial 800-488-2558 to find out the nearest local access number for you. Dial that number and log in as **guest,** or telnet **netcom.com** and log in as **guest.** If the system asks for a password, use **guest** again.

NovaLink

NovaLink Information Service
A division of Inner Circle Technologies, Inc.
800-274-2814 (Voice)
800-825-8852 (On-line information and registration)

NovaLink offers an interesting set of Internet services at reasonable prices. As you can see, there is 800 number access for registration. Otherwise you access NovaLink through the CompuServe Packet Network (CPN). With CPN access and online charges, NovaLink is charging $6.00 per hour as this book is written, plus a $12.50 sign up fee. There are also discussion areas and the usual UNIX system services available once you get onto NovaLink. And, one of the main attractions (for some users, anyway) is NovaLink's intense role-playing fantasy game, Legends of Future Past.

At $6.00 per hour with CPN charges included, NovaLink is very reasonably priced. To get more information, dial the 800 number listed above with your modem and follow instructions on the screen.

We could go on. There are hundreds (at least) of local and regional providers, and new ones come on-line all the time. One way to find out about them is to get onto the Internet itself with your own account (or have someone conduct a search for you) and see what you can find. We'll show you, beginning in Chapter 4, how to browse the Internet for such information. Here's one source that supposedly is updated regularly and may have additional information for you. Send e-mail with the subject **Send PDIAL** to **info-deli-server@netcom.com.** You will receive the PDIAL (Public Dial-up Internet Access List) document which lists a lot of public access networks. Some of these may work for you.

The PDIAL document is available through Netcom, but it is not maintained or supported by Netcom. It is shared by users on the network. As with any information you obtain on Internet, use it skeptically and cross reference the information if possible.

VEHICLE CHECKPOINT: YOUR MODEM AND SOFTWARE

Whatever service or access method you use, in all likelihood you will need a modem and some communications software. The exception to this broad statement is if you are on a network that includes a communications server. In this case, you may be accessing the modem over the network and attaching to Internet (or a local host that gives you access to Internet) through this remote modem.

However, even if you are using a computer as part of a local area network, you may still have a local modem and your own communications phone line. In fact, in our experience, this is far more common than a network with a communications server or gateway.

So, assuming you will be using a modem and some communications software, we will give you some information in the next section to make getting connected a little easier.

Modems

A modem provides an important hardware component of on-line communications. The word *modem* stands for **mod**ulator/**dem**odulator, which describes the process of encrypting computer information for sending along a wire on one end (modulation) and decrypting it for receiving by the computer on the other end (demodulation).

Modulation is the process of superimposing one kind of signal on top of another. The signal that receives the modulated information is called the *carrier* because it "carries" the information. Radio transmitters and receivers work similarly to modems. A carrier wave—the powerful signal that lets you hear Fort Wayne's WOWO in Natchez, New York, or Knoxville—has superimposed on it an audio signal that consists of the words and music of the transmitted program. A receiver at the other end strips away the now unnecessary carrier wave, leaving the audio to send to the speaker.

A modem works in a similar way. A rising and falling audio tone is superimposed onto a carrier signal that transfers the information from the transmitting modem, along the telephone line, to the receiving modem. Although the actual process of generating and decoding this signal is complex, especially at the relatively high rates supported by modern modems, the basic theory of operation is fairly simple.

You probably remember from studies elsewhere that computers work by storing and manipulating information in binary form—a series of ones and zeros. The ones and zeros are represented by the presence or absence of voltage in specific memory locations. Well, that's how data is transmitted over a modem. A high frequency tone represents the presence of voltage (a logical one), while a lower frequency tone represents the absence of voltage (a logical zero).

The transmitting modem converts the voltage levels sent from the originating computer into this tone series; the receiving modem listens to the tones and converts them back to voltage levels that the receiving computer can understand. This is done logically a bit at a time, with a high tone representing a "set" or positive bit, and a low tone representing a "clear" or negative bit.

When we first started using modems with computers, modems weren't very fast. That's because of the inherent bandwidth limitations built into the telephone system. Because a relatively narrow frequency range is needed to carry voice data (about 300 Hz to 3000 Hz or cycles per second), there isn't much range on the line for very high speed data. As modem technology improved, however, engineers were able to cram more and more information into this bandwidth limit.

Whereas 110 bit per second (*bps*)—or *baud*—modems were the norm when we started using them (the authors of this book have been using computers a LONG time!), today 9,600 bps and 14,400 bps modems are very common and relatively inexpensive. (Wait just a little longer and we can expect to see regular communications links to 56K bps, 64K bps, or faster. Hardware and software systems get better and better!) Note that we used bps and baud to rate the speed of modems. You'll see both terms used today. While the two terms aren't precisely equal, usage convention has made them so.

Remember that it takes eight bits to represent a single character and, depending on the protocol you are using, there may be one or two bits for error correction and other uses. So as a general rule of thumb, you can assume that it takes ten bits to transmit a single character. Therefore, at the very least, the actual throughput of your modem may be one tenth of its rating in bits per second. A 9,600 bps modem, then, could transfer 960 characters a second over a good connection, and a 14,400 bps modem could send along about 1,440 characters per second.

This is a good rule of thumb, and on the average probably won't be that far off. However, there are other considerations that affect the actual throughput of a modem-to-modem link. For one thing, you may be talking over a less-than-perfect telephone line. If there is noise on the line or other interference that degrades the signal, the receiving modem may have to ask the transmitting modem to repeat some information. This takes time and reduces the overall throughput.

In fact, throughput can be reduced significantly if the sending modem has to repeat data frequently. This is because high speed modems don't send characters one at a time. They encapsulate data into packets or groups of characters, so the receiving modem doesn't ask for just the character or characters it missed; it must request a re-send of the entire packet of data in which there was missing information.

At the same time, this grouping of information—and the fact that most modems today also compress the data they send—can sometimes make up for the time lost in requesting re-sends on missed data. For this reason, you can still guess that data transfer is about one tenth of the modem's rated speed. In fact, with a good line and efficient software, you may see transfer speeds greater than one tenth the modem's rated speed. On a couple of the links we use regularly, we see fairly consistent data transfer between 1,600 and 1,700 bps with a pair of 14,400 bps error correcting modems.

What does this mean to you? At one level, not very much. It is doubtful that anyone reading this book is using a modem any slower than 2,400 bps, which has been the standard for general purpose communications for some time. And, when you are interacting with a menu system, entering commands at an Internet node, or chatting with another user across a communications link, 2,400 bps certainly is adequate. At 2,400 bps (about 240 characters per second, remember) the communications link will keep up with all but the fastest of typists, and screen updates (when the remote computer refreshes a menu or file list) will be fast enough.

Where you really notice the difference in speed is when you transfer files, either moving large amounts of information from your computer to an Internet host, or copying files from an Internet host to your machine. In this case, the faster the better. The faster modems—9,600 bps and above—not only transfer the files you want four to six times more quickly, they also reduce your on-line time, which is an important consideration if you are paying by the minute for your connection.

There is one additional consideration here: some packet switch networks and Internet gateways charge a premium for modem speeds of 9,600 bps or greater. For example, The Well, a conference system and Internet gateway, charges an extra $2.00 per hour when you switch to high speed. On the other hand, if you are paying long distance telephone charges or packet switch charges for this access, using the high speed probably is worth the premium price at the other end. You should compute the relative merits of high speed versus low speed, especially if you use the service a lot or if you will be on for a long block of time to transfer files or participate in a conference.

Communications Software

A modem is a very important part of your communications link, but it can't work alone. You also need software that connects the computer to the modem and handles a lot of other important and useful chores as well.

You may have received communications software with your modem. A number of modem manufacturers routinely include their own or a third party communications package with the hardware they sell. This will serve very nicely to get you started. You can learn your way around communications software and procedures, learn about your modem, and figure out whether this software fills all your needs or whether you need something more.

Communications packages can be rather Spartan, handling only the bare necessities, or they can include extensive features such as high end terminal emulation (more on that in a moment), configuration and system testing utilities, auto answer and bulletin board features, dialing directories, programming languages, and more. For getting on Internet, you just need the basics:

◆ Terminal emulation

◆ Serial port and modem communications support

◆ Information transfer protocol support

We'll offer a little more information on each of these communications software basics.

Terminal Emulation

When you communicate with a minicomputer or mainframe, that remote host expects you to be using a particular type of terminal that responds in a particular way to commands the computer sends. A terminal is a separate keyboard and screen that you use to talk to a large computer. The IBM PC and the early Apple machines were among the first computers to integrate the display electronics into the computer itself. Before that time, most computers were controlled through a serial line to a separate terminal.

The software in computers wants to be able to directly address the screen by placing characters and symbols at specific locations. The computer needs to be able to scroll the screen, clear the screen, and so on. Unfortunately, each manufacturer's terminal uses different codes. That's why your computer's communications software needs to know how to emulate, or act like, different kinds of terminals.

Fortunately, most on-line services today support a common terminal, the Digital Equipment Corporation VT100. If your software can emulate the VT100 or one of the later Digital terminals that includes the VT100 as a subset (VT200, VT320, and so on), then you'll have no problems navigating around the Internet. In fact, you can pretty much establish VT100 emulation as the default for your communications software, because almost anywhere you go on-line you'll find support for it.

Besides, most on-line services actually use the addressable screen and other features very little. You don't need heavy terminal support—just the basics.

Serial Port and Modem Communications Support

Early computers—and many of today's larger machines—use *serial ports* to communicate with the user through a remote terminal. Similarly, you communicate through a serial port on your computer with the modem, even if the modem is an internal device it is using a serial port assignment. A serial port is an electronic doorway that sends and receives information into and out of your computer. It is called a serial port because data is sent through it in serial fashion, one bit after another. A parallel port, on the other hand, transfers data eight bits or more at a time over parallel wires. Therefore, your communications software must know about serial port addressing, communications speed setting, and keyboard support.

That's pretty basic. In addition to being able to talk to the keyboard and the serial port, communications software has to know something about modems, or for most applications, about one type of modem. Unless you are going to issue commands manually from the keyboard, the software has to be able to configure the modem, set communications speed (baud rate), set and read modem registers (temporary storage locations), and the like.

The majority of modems today adhere to the so-called "AT" or Hayes command structure. This comes from a popular design from Hayes Communications, maker of the SmartCom series. Their command structure, an "AT" (for attention) followed by one or more numbers or letters, became a de facto industry standard that is followed by a majority of modem manufacturers.

Information Transfer Protocol Support

An important software consideration for Internet travelers is the ability to download files. Although some files you will want to download are in text format, most of them are likely to be in some binary form which you can't simply display on the screen and capture as they go by. For these files—program files or text files that have been compressed—you need a special communications protocol.

Remember we said that modems assemble data into blocks to transmit and receive over a telephone line? Well, a communications protocol takes this concept a step further. By assembling a data file or program into a series of packets and surrounding each packet with additional information about what is in the packet, data transfer programs can ship data around a network or across a telephone line with very little chance of making a mistake.

As you might imagine from this general description, there could be any number of ways to construct the actual error detection and correction part of this link. In fact, there are several methods, or protocols, that programmers use for error free data transfer. Each of these methods has a name. Among the common names are:

✦ XMODEM

✦ ZMODEM

✦ YMODEM

✦ KERMIT

In addition to these protocols, you should have some way to capture the text and graphic displays on your screen to disk. This allows you store conversations, system information, and other interesting things you come across.

Hardware Issues

In addition to communications software, you also need some kind of hardware to complete the Internet link. You can access the Internet through a variety of computer hardware, from an old dumb terminal (not a very practical solution, but possible), to a really low-end eight-bit microcomputer such as a Commodore 64, to a PC Compatible (any flavor) or an Apple Macintosh. With any of this hardware you only need two things—a modem and communications software. (In the case of a dumb terminal, you don't even need the software. You would just issue modem commands directly from the keyboard.)

Obviously, the type of traveling you will be doing on Internet affects your hardware requirements. If you intend to locate and download a lot of files or programs, then you'll need a reasonably powerful computer and a fair amount of disk storage. If you mainly want to send and receive short e-mail messages and perhaps talk interactively with the folk you meet, then the dumb terminal or eight-bit micro will do fine.

Whatever hardware you have, if you are interested enough in the prospects of getting on Internet to have read this far, don't wait. Find an access point and jump in. You'll learn more by doing than you can by reading and you also will discover quickly what kind of hardware upgrade you need, if any.

WHAT YOU LEARNED

This is a "nuts-and-bolts" chapter. You probably didn't need all of the information here, but you can come back and reference this material as you need it later.

We have shown you some of the many ways you can arrange Internet access for yourself, and have suggested which of these might be better for different situations. We have discussed communications software and modems, as well as the other hardware you need to use the Internet. Woven throughout this chapter are some obscure references to Internet locations and terms that may have you scratching your head right now. Don't worry. Work on getting yourself connected—you can pick up the additional knowledge you need through hands-on experience.

If you have worked through this chapter, following leads as we gave them, then you may have an Internet account by this time. You're ready to start poking around on the Internet. However, there's some additional information in Chapter 3 that will help you understand some of the things you encounter in your travels. Keep practicing with your Internet account (or keep working to get one if you don't already have it), but turn the page for some useful information for Internet travelers, including naming conventions, network information transfer protocols, electronic mail, conferences, and more.

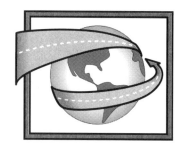

Chapter Three

TRAVELER'S AID: THE INTERNET BASICS

When traveling through cyberspace, it's important to keep your bearings no matter the duration or trajectory of your trip. A guide to the Internet's basic services helps you quickly orient yourself as you arrive at any destination. This chapter describes the practicalities of how the Internet and its resources are organized. Among the topics we'll cover are:

✦ The Domain name system

✦ The IP address system

✦ Using Internet Mail

✦ Conferences and News

✦ Transferring data files

We offer miscellaneous hints, tips, and shortcuts along the way to help you get the most out of your travels. Scan this chapter so you'll become familiar with the terms and procedures of visiting on the Internet.

NAMING CONVENTIONS AND PROTOCOLS

To get anywhere in life—the grocery store, a better job, or even peace of mind—you have to know where you are going and how to get there. The same is true of the Internet. As we discussed in Chapter 2, to get access to the Internet you have to know the name of an Internet host and you have to know how to access that host to begin your Internet travels.

The Domain Name System (DNS)

Luckily, the Internet is actually easier to travel from point A to point B than an interstate highway. When you travel an interstate highway you have to be aware not only of where you are going, but of which routes to take and where to exit. With the Internet, on the other hand, all you really need to know is where to start your journey and where to end it. The Internet hosts that you use along the way will take care of getting you from one place to another.

When you drive the interstate highway system you may go from Knoxville to Newark or from Philadelphia to Poughkeepsie. On the Internet you may go from **ns.opup.org**, for example, to **nnsc.nsf.net**, or from **martha.utcc.utk.edu** to **archie.unl.edu**.

We are familiar with Newark and Philadelphia, Washington or New York, so these names seem OK. **nnsc.nsf.net**, on the other hand, probably looks a little strange. But what if we said "get on Interstate 75 and go to Ooltewah"? Would that sound any less strange than "**nnsc.nsf.net**"? For folk used to traveling between Knoxville and Chattanooga in East Tennessee, Ooltewah is just as familiar as Washington or New York for the rest of us. So it is with Internet place names. Once you understand how names are constructed and get an idea of where places are, using Internet names won't be any more difficult than using the names of cities and towns to help you get from one place to another on vacation.

Let's look more closely at one of the Internet names we have mentioned: **archie.unl.edu**. Look at the last three characters in this Internet address: **edu**. This is the location's *domain*. In regular English, a domain is a person's field, an area of influence, or an area bound by defined limits. In Internet jargon, domain means about the same thing. An Internet domain specifies the type of organization or group that controls that specific Internet node.

You might guess correctly that the domain **.edu** is some kind of educational institution. Universities, colleges, secondary schools, and other educational institutions that provide Internet access and make information available to the network are identified with the **.edu** domain name.

Other types of organizations carry other domain designations. The common ones are shown in the following list:

com	Commercial	A company or other commercial interest.
edu	Education	A college, university, or other educational institution.
gov	Government	A federal, state, or local government site.
mil	Military	A military site such as the U.S. Army.
net	Network	Gateways or other hosts in a network.
org	Organization	A private organization such as a non-profit group, a foundation, or other association.

You may see some additional domains, sometimes called country codes, that signify the country of origin of the specified node or computer. These domains can be used alone or they may be used in addition to the ones listed above. This list is growing all the time, but here are some examples:

au	Australia
ca	Canada

de	Germany
fi	Finland
fr	France
jp	Japan
kr	Korea
il	Israel
nl	Netherlands
nz	New Zealand
se	Sweden
tw	Taiwan
uk	United Kingdom
us	United States

The domain designation doesn't tell you everything about the host, but it does help you understand the type of users that may be at that local site, what general types of data might be stored there and offered to the Internet, and what types of rules and restrictions you might encounter at the site.

There is other information in a host designation, including the name of the institution or company, perhaps, as well as the name of the local computer. We'll discuss the rest of the Internet host name in the next section.

Host Names

Let's look again at the sample name we discussed in the previous section: **archie.unl.edu**. This is a very simple and mostly obvious host designation. It doesn't have as many components as some names and it includes one part that is easily interpreted: Archie. We'll discuss Archie in Chapter 4, but for now suffice it to say that Archie is a more or less universal on-line searching tool for the Internet. From this host name, we know it is an Archie server located at an educational institution. All that remains to decipher is the **unl** part of the host name.

We know the type of facility it is—an Archie server—and we know the type of organization that sponsors it—educational. So we might guess that **unl** stands for the name of the educational institution. That is a logical and accurate guess. There's no way for you to know which educational institution, but the **u** might logically stand for "university."

In fact, this address comes from a list of available Archie servers that we'll show you how to find in Chapter 4. If we refer to this list we learn that this server is located at the University of Nebraska in Lincoln. Now the **unl** part of the host name makes a lot of sense, doesn't it?

Almost any facility on the Internet carries a similar naming scheme. Although this naming structure isn't as easy to interpret or remember (at least not at first) as that of a company or person, there is method to this madness. In addition to the domain name and a possible location, Internet node names typically include the name of the local computer or computer group, a project designation, and other information. An Internet address can be relatively simple—such as the Archie server address we just showed you—or fairly complicated.

Consider this example:

martha.utcc.utk.edu

This is one of the nodes the authors use for Internet access. As you can see from the **edu** domain name, it is an educational institution. The next part of the address to the left shows that this is from **utk**, the University of Tennessee at Knoxville.

The **utcc** part of the name stands for University of Tennessee Computing Center, and **martha** is the name of the computer on this node. In this case "martha" is a Sun workstation, but you have no way of knowing that without some behind-the-scenes information. Ultimately, it doesn't matter what the hardware is.

Interpreting any Internet address works the same way. You work backwards, right to left, and try to understand the address based on what you know about the location of the node, what type of information it contains, the domain type, and so on.

IP Address (Internet Protocol Address)

The Internet domain system helps users access Internet facilities. Although these names aren't all that easy to remember, they are a lot easier to use than the computer's way of looking at the same location.

The computers on the Internet use a number-based system to address and access Internet nodes. The name-based system discussed above is first translated into the number-based form the computer prefers before the specified system can be accessed. It is a little like storing phone numbers in a telephone memory system by company name. When you want to dial someone at a specific company, you look up the company name on your phone's LED readout and press dial. You don't know, and don't need to know, the actual number stored in that location. Once you identify the company, you can dial the phone number because you stored it there previously. You do have to remember the company name, but you don't need to know the telephone number that goes with it.

That's the way the *Internet Protocol* or IP address system works. You can use a series of numbers to access an Internet facility if you want to, but the name-based system is easier to remember.

Computer systems on the Internet store the name-to-number lookup system, then use the numbers to send information to the proper location. Remember that the Internet is composed of many different types of components: corporate networks, educational networks, regional networks, dedicated workstations. All of these components are connected by Ethernet backbones, T1 links, and dedicated and dial-up telephone lines. You can see that without a sophisticated system of identifications and addresses it would be impossible to pass information where you want it. This is managed by computerized *routers* that sit on the Internet monitoring traffic and studying the addresses of each *packet*.

The Internet Protocol sends data from point to point by grouping information into packets. A packet is an assembly of characters—usually less than 1,500 or so—that may have originated at multiple sources. The link that ties these various characters together is that they all are going to the same destination. In other words, they all have the same Internet address.

The packets are sent through a series of computers, in stair step fashion, until the ultimate destination is reached. Like a letter addressed for delivery by the post office. Internet data is addressed hierarchically. In this scheme the address consists of up to four numbers separated by periods. Each number is less than 256. For example, the Archie server example we used earlier (archie.unl.edu), has the IP address 129.93.1.14. If you were telling someone about this IP address, you would say "129 dot 93 dot 1 dot 14."

Some of the numbers in this address specify which network on the Internet should receive the packet. Once the proper network has received the packet, it is up to another router to send the packet along to the next stop, and so on until the specified computer gets the packet. From there, the packetized data is broken apart and stored in a file, displayed on a terminal, or sent to a user.

The Internet Protocol address moves from general to specific, left to right. The first two or three groups of numbers represent the destination's network address. This is the network that includes the ultimate computer destination. For example, many of the networked computers at the University of Tennessee in Knoxville belong to the network 128.169. The two remaining sets of numbers denote other facilities within the network.

As we said earlier, this number-based system is necessary for computers to talk to each other without duplicating addresses and without getting lost in a labyrinth of network wires. For us, however, the system of names both is easier to use and all we need to know about accessing Internet resources. It is good to understand the basics of IP addressing, however, so you know how information gets where it is going.

Another reason to know a little about IP numbers is that the machine that runs BIND, the Berkeley Internet Name Daemon, is sometimes down. BIND is what makes the Domain Name System tick. If the BIND on your local host were down, you might be deferred to another system in your network. If that alternate system were down too, then you would not have a nameserver, and the computer would not have a clue about names. In this case you would either have to wait for the name-server to come back on-line, or you would have to use the computer's number system.

Transmission Control Protocol (TCP)

The Internet Protocol handles sending prepackaged information around the network. However, that's only part of the story. Once the addressed packet is delivered, the data inside the packet has to be distributed properly. Remember that the packet may contain information from several sources. As the packets arrive, they have to be broken down and individual components need to be reassembled in the proper order.

This ability to share packets helps move data efficiently. Once the data gets where it is going, it is up to TCP software to open the packets and put the information together with data from previous packets in the proper order. Together the Internet Protocol and the Transmission Control Protocol form the familiar TCP/IP networking designation which you've probably seen many times as you have read about computer communications.

GETTING FROM HERE TO THERE: TELNET

How do you actually get from where you sit on a PC, Macintosh, or terminal out to somewhere else on the Internet? One way is to send and receive electronic mail. We'll show you more about that in the next section.

The most common way to attach to a specific host on the Internet is to use a communications command called **telnet**. This is software that automates the process of locating a specified host and initiating the log on process. Once you know the name of a remote host and you are logged on to a computer that has an Internet link, you can attach to that host with telnet:

telnet ns.opup.org

or

telnet 128.169.92.86

NOTE

Interestingly, the **ns.opup.org** address is, itself, an alias for **mamaclaus.opup.org**. This sort of lookup is done frequently to simplify addresses.

You can also attach to a remote host with ftp (file transfer protocol) and with other utilities, which we will discuss in Chapter 4. ftp is another software utility that lets you locate a specified host and initiate a file transfer session with it automatically. ftp works like a specialized telnet command.

ELECTRONIC MAIL

We've talked about how information moves along the Internet from computer to computer, but how do individual users get information? That's all part of the Internet addressing scheme. By simply adding another level of address you can identify a particular individual, organization, or group to receive electronic mail, or *e-mail*.

Electronic mail is one of the main uses for any network such as the Internet. Because the wires and computers are in place at locations all over the world, it is natural to want the ability to send messages to companies and individuals over this network. Most Internet users find e-mail to be a useful and interesting part of the technology.

You can send simple notes and messages or large files by simply providing the proper Internet address for the person or company you want to receive the information. You'll need a mail program, but once you know a person's Internet address you can swap electronic messages at will.

Electronic mail addresses look like the network addresses we discussed earlier, except that there is a person's name or the name of a company or organization at the front of the address. This part of the address is separated from the rest of the network address by a commercial "at" sign (@).

For example, Tom Badgett's current address is:

tbadgett@opup.org

You can read this easily enough, from left to right: "tbadgett at opup dot org." The **tbadgett**, of course, is the name. You can tell that not only because you knew the name before you started, but because it is set off from the rest of the address with the "at" sign.

The **opup** part of the address stands for Operation Uplink, an Internet group, and **org** shows that this Internet entity is an organization. Pretty simple, if you know what this group is. You would have no way of knowing what **opup** stands for unless you found that information somewhere or knew someone from that organization.

Other e-mail addresses can get a little more complicated. For instance, if Tom Badgett were using another node within the University of Tennessee at Knoxville network, the address might be something like this:

tbadgett@martha.utcc.utk.edu

Even if you don't know anything about where this computer is located, you know two things as soon as you look at the address. You know that the addressee is tbadgett at some network on some computer system, and that this is an educational institution. (If you don't see this much of the address immediately, reread the section on domains earlier in this chapter.) We described part of this address earlier. **martha** is the name of a Sun workstation that is part of the **utcc** or University of Tennessee Computing Center, located at the University of Tennessee at Knoxville (**utk**).

Obviously it isn't necessary for you to know this level of detail about every address you use on the Internet. It is enough that you know the correct sequence of names and abbreviations. However, the more you use the Internet, you will find yourself interpreting each address—breaking it down so that it has an additional level of meaning for you. This makes Internet travel more fun, and helps you to remember the addresses you use frequently.

As with any Internet information, e-mail is not passed directly from your machine to the destination machine. There may be one or several additional computers or networks that handle the message along the way. The message you send is given an address that includes the person or company name and the other routing information needed to get it to the proper computer. How it gets there depends on the source and destination systems and how they reach the Internet. There may be several stops along the way, and the time between sending the message and the message arriving at its destination may be several minutes or several hours.

Now let's discuss in more detail how you go about sending and receiving electronic mail over the Internet.

Sending Mail

For many users, electronic mail, or e-mail, is one of the most important reasons for being on the Internet in the first place. The concept of being able to type a few lines, a page, or even thousands of words and then send them off to someone in Atlanta, Alaska, or Almost Anywhere at the speed of light is impressive.

We've already discussed e-mail addressing. Remember that to send someone an e-mail message, you have to know their user ID or logon name, and the name of the system where their home account is located. The best way to get this information is to ask the person you want to write. You can also send an e-mail message to Postmaster@Domain if you know the person's Domain address. Or, try **fingername@Domain** to discover what logon name the person uses. You could try the first initial and last name, for example, the first name and last initial, etc. until you come across the person you are trying to reach. Once you have an address where you want to send mail, actually sending it is fairly easy.

Depending on the Internet node you use, there may be one or several ways to send mail. We will discuss two of the most common here. You should ask your service provider for specifics on other systems.

UNIX Mail

Since the majority of the Internet nodes you are likely to access are UNIX-based, there is a very good bet that the UNIX *Mail* command is available. To access this facility, simply type **mail <recipient>** at the system prompt. The <recipient> part of the mail command is the Internet address of the person or persons you want to receive the mail message. So, to compose a message to one of the authors of this book, Tom Badgett, you could type:

> **mail tbadgett@opup.org**

The mail system will respond by clearing the prompt and then waiting for you to type the text of the message you want to send to the recipient specified on the command line. Depending on how your local system is configured, you may also be asked for a subject at this time. If you are, enter the subject of the message, then press **Enter** or **Return** at the end of the line. Now simply enter the text of the message, placing a carriage return at the end of each line. This is a simple text editor—not as sophisticated as the word processor you're probably using, but enough to let you enter the text of a message.

Notice, that the mail system—if it is configured in the conventional way—is also monitoring the keyboard input for commands while it is in this mode.

While typing your message, you may be able to enter commands that let you do additional things. Standard mail uses a "tilde escape" sequence to issue commands to **mail**. For example, if you type ~e on a line by itself while entering a mail message, you invoke an editor for the current message. Likewise, ~C lets you specify a carbon copy address, ~S lets you specify the subject, and ~H prompts you for additional header information.

If these commands don't work as we've described, it means you have a different version of mail or that your mail system has been configured differently. There are two things to try. At the main system prompt, enter this command:

> **man mail**

This is a UNIX command that says look up the on-line manual for the mail command and display it on the screen. Press the **Space bar** as each screen of data is presented to bring up the next screen. Turn on screen capture or a log file in your communications software so you can have a local copy of the document to help you with later mail activity.

If the commands and procedures described in the manual don't work, you should send a message to the local system administrator or Internet service provider to find out how the mail system is configured.

There is a third thing to try when you are having problems with this or any other activity while using an Internet node: try using the UNIX **talk** command to discuss the situation with someone else on-line with you. To do this, first type **who** or **w** at the system prompt. The system will respond with a list of current users. (If you use **w** instead of **who**, the system will also tell you what each user is doing. This can help you decide who to talk with.) If you know one of the users, choose that name. Otherwise, pick a name at random and issue the **talk** command:

talk username

If you want to talk to someone who is not logged on to your local host, use **talk username@host**. The host name is not necessary to talk to someone on the machine you are using.

The specified user will see a message on the screen indicating that you want to talk. If this user responds, you will see a split screen—half yours and half the other user's. You can type on the keyboard in your half of the screen and the text will appear at the other user's end. When the other user types, the text appears in the other half of your screen.

Of course, the user you select may be busy doing something else and may not respond. If that happens, simply choose another user. First type **Ctrl-C**, then reissue the **talk** command with a new user ID. Once a connection is established, just ask your question and wait for an answer. This is a handy way of getting the information you need and of meeting other people as well.

After you have typed the message you want to send with mail, press **Ctrl-D** as the first character on a new line, or enter a **period** on a new line by itself and press **Enter**. The message will be sent to the user you specified on the command line when you started the mail application.

Pine

If you are comfortable with a command-line interface, the **mail** command is all you need to send and receive messages to anyone on the Internet. However, most of us appreciate a user interface that is easy to understand and that anyone can use. There are several such interfaces on Internet systems, but one of the most common is Pine. To access this mail system, simply type **pine** at your local node's prompt. If Pine is on your system, you will see a screen similar to the one in Figure 3.1.

Figure 3.1

Sample Pine
e-mail screen

```
    PINE 3.07        MAIN MENU        Folder:inbox  14 Messages


    ?   HELP         - Get help using Pine

    C   COMPOSE      - Compose and send a message

    I   MAIL INDEX   - Read mail in current folder

    F   FOLDERS      - Open a different mail folder

    A   ADDRESSES    - Update your address book

    O   OTHER        - Use other functions

    Q   QUIT         - Exit the Pine mail program

  Note: In Pine 3.0 we are encouraging folks to use the MAIL INDEX to read
        mail instead of VIEW MAIL, so it is no longer on the main menu. Once
        in the mail index, it is available as usual as the "V" command.

  [ * * This is a new version of Pine. To use old Pine run "pine.old". * * ]
? Help      Q Quit       F Folders      O Other
C Compose     I Mail Index A Addresses
ALT-Z FOR HELP | VT100  | FDX | 57600 N81 | LOG CLOSED | PRINT OFF | ON-LINE
```

As you can see, Pine—or any similar menu-oriented mail system—is much easier to use than the command-line mail system from inside UNIX. We won't spend a lot of time on using Pine here because everything is presented in the menu and with on-screen prompts. Besides, Pine frequently is modified at a local site, so it may not be exactly like our version. But don't be afraid to use it, even if nothing in the provider's literature or on-line help mentions Pine. It probably is out there somewhere. Just type **pine** and find out.

With a system such as Pine, you can compose messages in the editor and also attach files that reside on your local system to send with the letter. This might be useful if you want to send someone a PKZIP file (which is in binary format, so you can just mail it), a program file, or a graphics image.

If you select **C** for Compose from the main menu, Pine clears the screen and presents a screen similar to the one shown in Figure 3.2.

Figure 3.2

Pine Compose Message screen

```
        PINE 3.07         COMPOSE MESSAGE        Folder:inbox  73 Messages

To      :
Cc      :
Attchmnt:
Subject :
----- Message Text -----




















^G Get Help  ^C Cancel    ^R Rich Hdr              ^K Del Line ^O Postpone
^X Send      ^D Del Char ^J Attach                 ^U UnDel Lin^T To AddrBk
  ALT-A FOR HELP | VT100  | FDX | 57600 N81 | LOG CLOSED | PRINT OFF | ON-LINE
```

At this screen, enter the **To:** address and specify another address for the carbon copy on the next line, if you wish. Move the cursor to the **Attchmnt:** line, press **Ctrl-J**, and enter the name of a file stored on your local system. Provide the complete path if the file is not in your local home directory.

Type a subject on the **Subject:** line, then press **Enter** or **Tab** to place the insertion point or cursor inside the editor area. Now you can type your message.

When the text of the message is complete, simply press **Ctrl-X** to close the editor screen and send the message to the addressee(s). If there was a file attached to the message, the recipient will be told and will be able to download the message using a file transfer protocol.

Receiving Mail

When you get on the Internet and start poking around, you doubtless will start corresponding with other Internet users. You may leave your e-mail address for someone to send you information, or you may send someone a message that will generate a response. After you have participated in a conference, someone may find your address and want to ask a question or follow up on the topic. Whatever the reason, you will start getting mail of your own if you make your presence known on the Internet.

The good news is that receiving mail on the Internet is even easier than sending it. Let's look at the same two systems we discussed in the last section, UNIX Mail and Pine.

UNIX Mail

Usually when you log on to a system and you have mail waiting, you will get a message that says something like:

You have new mail

or

Mail waiting

When you see this message, simply type **mail** at the system prompt to see any unread mail messages. The system will fill the screen, then wait for you to press the **Space bar** before presenting another screen of information. When the first message is completed, you will see the second one, and so on. If you want to capture these messages and read them or print them later off-line, turn on a log file or a text capture utility inside your communications software before typing the **mail** command.

NOTE

If you type **mail** without specifying an addressee for a new message and you don't have any new mail, you will get a message like:

No new mail for TBadgett

and the mail software will terminate.

After you have read all of your new mail messages, you will be presented with the mail command prompt. This prompt may be a question mark (?), an ampersand (&), or whatever else the system administrator has specified. From this mail command prompt, you can issue certain mail commands, including the ones shown in Figure 3.3.

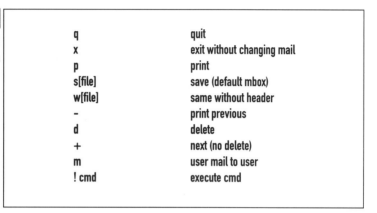

Figure 3.3

Typical UNIX Mail commands

q	quit
x	exit without changing mail
p	print
s[file]	save (default mbox)
w[file]	same without header
-	print previous
d	delete
+	next (no delete)
m	user mail to user
! cmd	execute cmd

To exit the command mode, simply press **Enter** or type **Q**, for quit. You will be returned to the main system prompt for the system you are using. Turn off screen capture or file logging at this point and your mail is saved.

If a message is a simple one and you are sure you don't need it again, or if you have captured it to your local computer as it was being read, issue the **d** (delete) command after the message is displayed. This frees up disk space, and it keeps you from having to step through old messages each time you enter the mail system. On the other hand, it doesn't hurt to leave a few messages out there for reading later. Each message is presented in reverse order, so the newest messages are displayed first. When you have read the most recent ones you can exit mail and go back to the system prompt, leaving previously read messages on the system.

When you receive mail over the Internet, the heading can appear a little complicated, but it really isn't. Figure 3.4 shows what is in a typical heading. Note that the heading shows the date and time of the message, who and where it is from, who it is to, and a message ID. Depending on the mail system, there may be other information there as well. Keep the heading when you save a message, because it helps you remember who it was from, and it makes it easier to respond later if you wish.

Figure 3.4

Sample mail header

```
From tbadgett Tue Aug 24 16:50:38 1993
Return-Path: <tbadgett>
Received: by MamaClaus.OPUP.ORG (4.1/SMI-4.1)
id AA05265; Tue, 24 Aug 93 16:50:37 EDT
Date: Tue, 24 Aug 1993 16:50:07 -0400 (EDT)
From: Tom  Badgett <tbadgett@OpUp.ORG>
Subject: Mail Header Sample
To: tbadgett@OpUp.ORG
Message-Id: <Pine.3.05.9308241607.A5261-6100000@MamaClaus.OPUP.ORG>
Mime-Version: 1.0
Content-Type: TEXT/PLAIN; charset=US-ASCII
Status: RO
```

You can see that this message came from within Pine and that it was addressed to and from the same person.

Addressing a mail message to yourself is a good way to create reminders. Anytime you are on-line and you think of something that you need to remember later, simply send yourself a mail message. The next time you log on, you'll get that message.

You can configure the Mail program to display different header information, so the version in use on your system may not produce messages that look exactly like the ones in this example. With some systems the heading may be a lot simpler. All that really matters is the name and address of the person who sent you the message. The rest of the header information usually isn't that important.

Pine

When you log on to a system and are told there is mail waiting, you can read the mail when it is convenient for you (you don't have to do it right away). Type **pine** to display the main screen shown in the previous section (or something close to it).

From the main screen, choose the menu item that displays your mail. It may be **I** for Index, as it is in our example, or it may be something else. Read the menu carefully and pick the one you need. Pine displays a screen similar to the one shown in Figure 3.5.

Pine Index (Read Mail) screen

```
     PINE 3.07       MAIL INDEX       Folder:inbox  Message 73 of 73

     58   Sep 16  Niels Jonker         (870)  News Sentinel online.
     59   Sep 16  ...dreamer...      (1.467)  Re: News Sentinel online.
     60   Sep 16  The Spectre        (1.194)  Re: News Sentinel online.
     61   Sep 16  Bob Wilson          (188K)  Mountain crest street map
     62   Sep 16  Niels Jonker       (1.810)  Re: News Sentinel online.
     63   Sep 16  Niels Jonker       (1.314)  Re: your mail
     64   Sep 17  Da Gorf            (1.431)  Re: News Sentinel online.
     65   Sep 17  jack lail        (19.792)   CC List (fwd)
     66   Sep 19  Niels Jonker       (3.409)  Internet Access in East Tennessee.
     67   Sep 21  Niels Jonker        (620)  The book? How're ya doing?
     68   Sep 21  Niels Jonker       (1.304)  Data needed.
     69   Sep 22  jack lail          (3.812)  Fw: Netter's Abbreviations (fwd)
     70   Sep 23  Bob Wilson         (5.383)  ASC chichi rept
     71   Sep 24  Clay I. Spinuzzi   (1.735)  Re: EMOTICON.TXT
     72   Sep 24  Holly H. Towne      (927)  Re: Internet Video
     73   Sep 24  Holly H. Towne     (3.491)  Re: Internet Video




   ? Help        M Main Menu  P Prev Msg     - Prev Page  F Forward     D Delete
   O OTHER CMDS V View Mail  N Next Msg SPACE Next Page  R Reply        S Save
     ALT-Z FOR HELP | VT100 | FDX | 57600 N81 | LOG CLOSED | PRINT OFF | ON-LINE
```

You can use the up and down arrow keys to select the message you want to read, then press **Enter** or **Return**. The message will be displayed one screen at a time. Pine will wait for you to press the **Space bar** to view any subsequent screens.

There's a menu at the bottom of the screen to show you how to delete files, save files, and perform other functions. Pine, or whatever menu system your provider supplies, should make reading and managing mail a lot easier than with UNIX Mail.

ON-LINE COMMUNITIES

Downloading files and exchanging e-mail are interesting and vital parts of the Internet experience. But once you've mastered these skills, you'll want something more, something to give you more direct contact with other users. That's when you'll want to experiment with conferences, news and real-time conversations.

We talked about conferences when we discussed The Well in Chapter 1. But you can find conferences on many Internet nodes, groups of people who come and go, reading each other's comments, offering an interesting or off-the-wall opinion of their own, returning later to see what else has transpired.

A news group—or simply news or Internet news or network news—is a variation of a conference. Like a conference, a news group discusses varied topics in a store-and-forward manner. You check into to a group, read previous comments about a topic, add some of your own if you wish, and move on somewhere else. Later, you may come back to find out if anybody responded to your statement or question.

The main difference between conferences and news is that news is somewhat more organized, with a network-wide organization and software tools designed to help you find specific topics and comments. News topics are organized under broad subject headings and the discussions are pretty much network wide rather than confined to a single node or private system.

Conversations, on the other hand, provide one-on-one or group discussions in real time about anything you can imagine. Whereas conferences and news use store-and-forward procedures, conversations or chats as they are sometimes called, are exchanges among Internet users while they are on-line.

We will introduce you to each of these interesting Internet features in this section. In later chapters we will offer some hands-on hints on how to find and download information you need.

WARNING

With any interactive exchange, anything can happen. Sometimes you may see a series of angry, rude, or profane responses to what appears to be a simple request. What you don't see is the exchange that took place between these individuals on another conference or in person. Be aware that such behavior sometimes comes at you unannounced.

Conferences

Many Internet providers have active conferences or forums, and as you saw with The Well, the topics cover a broad range of subjects. Usually if you want to join a conference you can issue a command (which, unfortunately, varies with the system you are using) to find out what conferences are available. The partial list in Figure 3.6 gives you an idea of how this exchange might take place. This sample is from The Well.

Figure 3.6

Sample conference list–The Well

```
OK (type a command or type opt for Options): browse

Topic - Number of responses - Header
100  87 Introductions — Me and the Net
104  23 What is the Internet (topic 4) Discussion
105 119 Acceptable Use of the Internet (topic 5) Discussion
106   0 Netiquette (topic 6) Discussion
107 131 About Telnet (topic 7) Discussion
108 162 About FTP (topic 8) Discussion
109  43 Tools for Finding Info on the Net (topic 9) Discussion
110  81 Libraries and Collections of Info (topic 10) Discussion
111 104 Frequently Asked Questions (topic 11) Discussion
112 247 Best Books & Articles on Internet (topic 12) Discussion
113  13 LISTSERVs (topic 13) Discussion
114  33 Zen and Articles on the Net Readable on the WELL (topic 14) Discussion
116  38 What Are Muds and Muses? (topic 16) Discussion
200  63 anonymous FTP into the WELL
   <topic is frozen>
201   4 topics to look at for linking here
202 157 Internet Access for the Masses
```

Notice these topics and the number of responses. Some have dozens of responses, and some have none. These conferences are started by someone who has a topic of interest they want to discuss. Sometimes the conferences are temporary—not designed to last very long once the question of the day is answered. Others are long-term topics.

Different systems have different types of conferences and topics. For most systems, an interactive session within something called a conference is conducted by selecting the conference you want to join, then viewing a series of messages. You will see where a user has asked a question about something he or she is interested in. Then you will see one or more answers to the query from other participants in the conference. All of this may, or may not, happen in real time. Usually a conference takes place over hours or days.

We can't show you actual conversations from a conference because the information placed on Internet systems is owned by the person who typed it or placed it there. However, the exchange in Figure 3.7 is typical of conference exchanges you will see on The Well and other Internet systems.

Figure 3.7

Sample conference interchange from The Well

Topic 202: Internet Access for the Masses
By: Likado Tango (LTango) on Wed, Jul 29, '92
    157 responses so far

A place to report on Internet access for the masses. Looking for
a way to telnet to The WELL on the cheap? Maybe you'll find it
here.

157 responses total.
Topic 202: Internet Access for the Masses
2: Ben Franklyn (BeFrank)   Thu, Jul 30, '92 (04:21)   4 lines

You could try lobbying universities in your area that have Internet access.
Ask them for a dial-in login. My local university let me in after I showed them
I am working for a non-profit organization. Different schools have different
rules and regs. Doesn't hurt to ask!

Topic 202: Internet Access for the Masses
1: Likado Tango (LTango) Wed, Jul 29, '92 (18:23)   123 lines

I just learned about a new system in Podunk. They are offering 800 number
access at a reasonable price. Call (voice) at 800-555-1212 for information.
I understand there's a guest account for info, but I don't have the number (yet).
Topic 202: Internet Access for the Masses
3: Tillie Chutcha (TC)   Wed, Jul 29, '92 (19:24)   2 lines

 Thanks, LTango. That was just the lead I needed. Looks like it'll work here. BTW, the
modem access number is 800-555-2121. Enjoy!

Topic 202: Internet Access for the Masses
4: Olive Branch (OBranch)   Thu, Jul 30, '92 (04:21)   2 lines
Maybe. But their price of $12 per connect hour is a little much for me. I'd like to find
something R E A L L Y cheap. Let's keep looking.

This sample is a sequence of responses to the primary question or statement, "A place to report on Internet access for the masses." This is a well-defined topic that generated a lot of response. With other topics it is more difficult to see the boundaries, and the conversation flows in a less-organized manner. Also, there may be a statement followed by two or three responses, then someone else may ask a question or make a statement. The next responses are in answer to the second query. Then someone new logs in to the conference, reads the first statement and makes a response to that one, way down in the file.

This may sound a little confusing—and sometimes it is—but it also is fascinating to log in to such a conference days or weeks after the fact and read through the progression of responses. The hindsight offered by a distance of time can put the discussion into a new light, offering perspective that is educational and/or interesting.

News

Network news is a variation of conferencing. Whereas a conference is usually designed and controlled by a single local system, news is of a more global nature. Internet nodes share information about news topics with each other, so when you log on to your service provider's computer you have news topics and location information at your fingertips.

As you might imagine, keeping track of topical discussions across a network as large as the Internet can be somewhat complicated. Luckily, programs called "news readers" take care of your part of this management. When you access a news reader, it seeks out a pre-determined news server, an Internet node that stores the news item exchanges. The server you use depends on the news reader and how the reader is configured.

News servers collect news items from a variety of sources, including USENET (where the majority of news items originates), local news sources, e-mail and other places. Mail files are stored on the server for a pre-determined period, then discarded. Many of them are updated by later versions; some go away forever once they become outdated.

As we mentioned, USENET is the source of a large amount of available news files on the Internet. USENET is not really a separate entity, rather it is a set of rules or agreements for sharing news across the network. A group of volunteers work under these guidelines to present news items (files that contain comments and discussions, really) to the various news servers on the Internet.

In addition, there are agreed major topics for news sessions, and all exchanges on news take place within these agreed topic areas. Table 3.1 shows the seven main newsgroup topics.

Topic	Description
comp	Computer topics
news	News and news software
rec	Recreation
sci	Science
soc	Social
talk	General discussions
misc	Everything else

Table 3.1

The seven main newsgroup topics

In addition to these standard topics, you will find many additional topics. (How many topics depends on the system you're using and how much they adhere to guidelines.) There are a dozen or so recognized alternative topics, but you'll find additional topic types as well. For example, in browsing around The Well, a California-based conferencing system, you will find newsgroups with the ba. type (for Bay Area). These can be very specific topics, from where to eat to houses offered for sale. The news system is well-designed and managed under guidelines that came from USENET, which again is a loose organization of users that agree on voluntary usage guidelines. However, you are bound to see local topics and usage conventions that don't follow the guidelines precisely.

Figure 3.8 is a sample listing of news within the news reader software **nn** from one Internet node. This illustration shows only a very small portion of available topics. As you can see on the second line, there were 1,021,121 articles when we captured this screen, 2,230 of which were new articles.

Figure 3.8

Sample news topics

```
Newsgroup: news.announce.newusers
Articles: 21 of 1021121/2230 NEW
a David C Lawrenc 667  List of Active Newsgroups, Part I
b David C Lawrenc 667  >List of Active Newsgroups, Part II
c David C Lawrenc 915  Alternative Newsgroup Hierarchies, Part I
d David C Lawrenc 735  >Alternative Newsgroup Hierarchies, Part II
e David C Lawrenc 834  List of Moderators for Usenet
f David C Lawrenc 152  How to Create a New Usenet Newsgroup
g Stephanie Silv 1476  >Publicly Accessible Mailing Lists, Part 5/5
h Jonathan Kamens 784  How to become a USENET site
i Jonathan Kamens 284  Introduction to the *.answers newsgroups
j Jonathan Kamen 1371  List of Periodic Informational Postings, Part 1/6
k Jonathan Kamen 1354  >List of Periodic Informational Postings, Part 2/6
l Jonathan Kamen 1096  Changes to List of Periodic Informational Postings
m Jonathan Kamen 1264  >List of Periodic Informational Postings, Part 3/6
n Jonathan Kamen 1239  >List of Periodic Informational Postings, Part 4/6
o Jonathan Kamen 1451  >List of Periodic Informational Postings, Part 5/6
p Jonathan Kamen 1443  >List of Periodic Informational Postings, Part 6/6
q Ron Dippold    715  Usenet Newsgroup Creation Companion
r Stephanie Silv 1024  Publicly Accessible Mailing Lists, Part 1/5
s Stephanie Silv 1395  >Publicly Accessible Mailing Lists, Part 2/5
```

This was just one of many screens we stepped through that day to find interesting topics. Once we found an area that looked promising, we selected the topic by moving the cursor to it and pressing **Period**, or by pressing the letter displayed to the left of the entry. (Depending on your terminal configuration you may not be able to cursor to the entry.) Notice that the letters beside the entries are lower case letters. Upper case letters are used for the program's commands.

A topic area is displayed in Figure 3.9. We have reformatted this entry a little to make it easier to see, and we have changed the origin information to something nonexistent (or we think so!). But this gives you an idea of the kind of entry you can find within a news topic. The information you find in News is always varied, ranging from business hints to hobby discussions to household and education information. Consider another entry, shown in Figure 3.10. Again, information has been changed, but this certainly is the type of entry you'll find throughout Network News.

Forsale:
486DX/33 w/64k cache
4MB Ram (60ns)
130 MB HD
101-key Maxiswitch keyboard
3-button mouse
Teac 1.44 disk drive
Teac 1.2 disk drive
1 meg SVGA video card
Non-Interlaced 14" SVGA Color Monitor
Medium Tower Case w/230 watt PS
9600/2400 baud fax/modem
Comes complete with all manuals and packaging.
$1295 and I'll pay for shipping costs. E-mail me if interested!

* Origin: ClipBoard BBS (415) 239-0454–
Andy Sellers - via FidoNet node 1:125/1 UUCP:
...!uunet!shelter!415!Andy.Sellers
INTERNET: Andy.Sellers@f415.n125.z1.FIDONET.ORG

– 09:08 –.market.computers– 1 MORE –help:?–Top 66%–

From: UCISRCY@CIS.Unocal.Com
Organization: Unocal Corporation
Date: Wed, 25 Aug 1993 19:56:56 GMT
Newsgroups: sci.environment,sci.energy,ca.environment,rec.autos.tech,
sci.answers,rec.answers,news.answers
Subject: Electric Vehicles FAQ Part 1/3

Here is a *partial* listing of electric vehicle clubs and alternative
energy publications last updated 24-AUG-1993. If you have any additions
or corrections to this list, send them to me and I'll add them. This list will
be published monthly. This file is available for FTP from HMCVAX.CLAREMONT.EDU
in the directory INFO-EV-ARCHIVE as RESOURCES.PARTn
(There are 3 parts right now). I try veryhard to keep this list up to
date, but since I've gleaned this information from a number of sources,
no guarantee is made for correctness. (If you find anyerrors *PLEASE*
let me know and I'll fix it! :-))

Electric Vehicle discussions have occurred in the following usenet
newsgroups: Sci.Environment Sci.Energy CA.Environment Rec.Autos.Tech

Contents:
    1) Common questions and answers
    2) Electronic Lists
    3) Publications
    4) Books
    5) Governmental Agencies
    6) EV Associations

Internet News is somewhat of a strange animal, as computer facilities go. It has been around since before Internet became as popular as it is today, and it continues to grow. As you can see from the sample topics, you can find something on News that fills about any need. But it is hard for any book to describe adequately for you what News is and how to use it. The best learning experience is getting on the Internet, finding a service provider that has the **nn** program, and giving it a try. With the help of this news front end, you will learn your way around quickly and begin to find news items for yourself.

You probably have one of these reader programs right on your local host system. At the system prompt, type **nn**, for example, to see if the program is available. You can try **tin** or **rn** as well. One of these should be available.

Next, you should turn to your local system administrator if you don't already have a version of one of these readers available. Find out if there is another command to use, or if there are plans to install a reader soon.

Finally, you can search Internet using Archie or another tool to find reader software for your own system. If you use Archie, use the command **set search exact** to specify an exact search match, then use the command **prog tin** or **prog nn** or **prog rn** (we prefer **tin**). You should get a list that shows several systems that include a directory with the name you searched for. Use ftp to download the program file, then go back to your system administrator for help in getting it installed.

News Management Software

One of the advantages that a news conversation has over many conferences is the management software that helps you navigate through a topic. As with everything else on the Internet, **nn** is just one of several possibilities available for helping you learn about news and how to use it. Ask your service provider or system administrator for options on your particular system.

Among the more common options is **rn**, an older utility that is quite popular but which lacks some of the features of **nn**. Both

rn and **nn** are generally part of the UNIX system you're using. A popular "third party" option is **tin,** a program closer to **nn** than **rn,** and one that offers a number of desirable features. If none of these is available on the system you are using, try **trn,** a full-featured reader package similar to **tin.**

We'll discuss some of the main points of **tin** and **nn** in this section and leave you on your own for more information on **rn** and **trn.** With any of these systems, you can get a lot more information with the **man** command. Simply type **man** followed by the name of the program you want to study.

We've already shown you some sample output from the **nn** program and discussed how it works. Let's look next at **tin.** It is similar to **nn,** but, we think, has a better user interface. It is easier to see the levels of information you are viewing within **tin.** Figure 3.11 is a display of available newsgroups on The Well during one session. Obviously, with over 3,000 groups available, this screen is only a small portion of the list. When you use **tin,** you can first look at the list of groups or topics, then display a summary of responses within any topic.

Figure 3.11

tin newsgroup topic list

```
      Group Selection (3039)                    h=help

    1    407  news.announce.conferences           Calls for paper
    2         news.announce.important             General announc
    3    132  news.announce.newgroups             Calls for newgr
    4     70  alt.3d                              Discussions of
    5   1052  alt.activism                        Activities for
    6     75  alt.activism.d                      A place to disc
    7      5  alt.aeffle.und.pferdle              German TV carto
    8   1601  alt.alien.visitors                  Space creatures
    9   1150  alt.angst                           Anxiety in the
   10    354  alt.aquaria                         The aquarium &
   11     95  alt.archery                         Discussion of a
   12     35  alt.artcom                          Artistic Commun
   13   1014  alt.astrology                       Twinkle, twinkl
   14   3240  alt.atheism                         Discussions of
   15     66  alt.autos.antique                   Discussion of a
   16      6  alt.bacchus                         A newsgroup for

    <n>=set current to n, TAB=next unread, /=search pattern, c)atchup,
  g)oto, j=line down, k=line up, h)elp, m)ove, q)uit, r=toggle all/unread,
    s)ubscribe, S)ub pattern, u)nsubscribe, U)nsub pattern, y)ank in/out

ALT-Z FOR HELP | VT100 | FDX | 57600 N81 | LOG CLOSED | PRINT OFF | ON-LINE
```

Figure 3.12

Display of responses
within topic

```
    alt.alien.visitors (144T 405A 0K 0H R)                      h=help

    1  +     FactComm 1                                    Michael Parks Swai
    2  + 29  Strange Black Helicopters...                  Robert Dinse
    3  + 2   UFO Abduction Research PLEASE REAC            Center for Psychol
    4  + 26  First the Canals, now the Face...             Jason Haines
    5  +     Ufo sighting in AZ                            Searchnet Zec
    6  + 8   Mothman Prophecies                            Paul Milsom
    7  + 2   ***************  WEIRDOS  ****************     Ralph 'Hairy' Moon
    8  + 4   Jacques Vallee and Common Sense               Evan M Corcoran
    9  +     Vallee email?                                 Evan M Corcoran
   10  + 12  X-Files 9/17/93 (#2)                          Don Nellesen
   11  +     Answer                                        John_-_Winston@cup
   12  + 3   Why I have great difficulty believing i       Marc Milanini
   13  +     * SpaceNews 20-Sep-93 *                       Robert Rouse
   14  + 3   This morning's JOHN SPRINGER show             Superuser
   15  + 4   Jesus Christ coming back on a UFO             alpha
   16  +     testit                                        Operator

    <n>=set current to n, TAB=next unread, /=search pattern, ^K)ill/select,
   a)uthor search, c)atchup, j=line down, k=line up, K=mark read, l)ist thread,
   |=pipe, m)ail, o=print, q)uit, r=toggle all/unread, s)ave, t)ag, w=post


ALT-Z FOR HELP | VT100  | FDX | 57600 N81 | LOG CLOSED | PRINT OFF | ON-LINE
```

Figure 3.12 is a display of responses within a selected topic. You first select a topic from the list in Figure 3.11, then browse through the list of what people have to say about it in Figure 3.12. When you select a topic shown in the list in Figure 3.12, you can read a paragraph or several paragraphs of comments by that person about the selected topic.

As you can see, there's a lot of information on these screens, including the menu prompt. We find **tin** extremely easy to use. Just type **tin** at your system prompt and see what you find.

Let's look a little more closely at these screens. Figure 3.11 shows some available newsgroups. At the left side of the display is the newsgroup number, followed by the number of unread messages in that group. The third column is the name of the newsgroup, which is followed by a brief description. You can select a newsgroup by moving the highlight up and down the screen and pressing **Enter** or **Return** when the one you want is highlighted.

Notice the names of these groups. They all begin with an abbreviation. In our illustration you see two kinds of newsgroups, **news** and **alt**. The **news** type is one of the seven main groups we discussed earlier, and the **alt** group is one of the alternative newsgroups.

For more information on how **tin** works, use the **man tin** command at the system prompt. Note that **tin** and other news-readers can be configured to display different information on the screen, so your **tin** screen may not look exactly like these examples. Don't worry about these differences; whatever the format, it should be obvious and relatively easy to use.

DATA TRANSFER

We've shown you a glimpse of what you may find on the Internet once you start traveling on your own. But how do you grab the information you find, and how do you share information of your own with other travelers? We'll talk about these concepts in this section.

Sending Files

We've demonstrated one way to send files over the Internet: the mail system. Especially if you are using Pine or another menu-driven mail utility, it is relatively easy to send text or program files along with a mail message. This is probably the most direct and easiest of all file sharing methods for when you have a specific file that you want to send to one or more specific Internet travelers.

Why would you want to do this? Suppose you get into a discussion with someone about water quality problems in Tennessee Valley Authority lakes and streams. You happen to be an environmental expert who has conducted a recent study of the problem for TVA. Rather than try to reconstruct the information you have gathered painstakingly over weeks or months, you simply send the other traveler an e-mail message and attach a spreadsheet or word processor file to it. Because these files are in the format created by the spreadsheet or word processor applications, not

ASCII or text format, the user on the other end of the link can load them up and see fully-formatted documents.

You also might want to share a graphics image with someone else, ship a shareware program over the wire, or send someone a mailing list or other database file. Whatever the reason, you surely will want to send files across the Internet occasionally. You will also want to receive files, either from another Internet user or by *downloading* information from a remote host. Downloading is the process of copying a file from a remote system down to your system. When you send a file from your machine to a remote computer, you are *uploading* a file, copying it up from your machine to the Internet.

Addressing Files

The simplest method for addressing files is to use a mail facility that will let you attach a file. Note that some mail programs will insert or attach a text file, but won't handle binary information. A binary file is one that uses all eight data bits and that is saved in a format other than text. Program files are like this, as are spreadsheet files, database files, most word processor files, and anything you have compressed with PKZIP, COMPRESS, or other compression routines.

If you can't send a file via mail, then you'll have to upload it to some system available to the Internet, then send the recipient a mail message describing where the file is and how to get it. For example, you might upload a file to your local host into a public directory such as **incoming**. If you can't access a public directory directly, use ftp to attach to your host at a point that should provide public access. Change to one of the public directories, probably **/pub/incoming** or something similar, then upload the file using whatever protocol is available on your host. (See the discussion of file transfer protocols in the next section.)

Here's a sample dialog with the local host to show you how to get the file into a public area. Change **ftp.opup.org** to the name of the system you want to use.

ftp **ftp.opup.org**
login as **anonymous (or ftp)**
cd **/pub/incoming**
type **bin**
type **put <filename>**

Then send the recipient mail telling them where the file is located. To get the file, enter this sequence:

ftp.opup.org
cd /pub/incoming
get <filename>

The file transfer protocol utility, or ftp, lets you download files from remote systems to your own. We will describe it fully in the next chapter.

You could also send a file by establishing a link to the machine the recipient calls home, then uploading the file into his or her directory where it will be available for downloading to that user's local computer. The precise process you use depends on a number of factors, including the size of the file, what rights you have on your own system, what rights you have on the remote system, personal preference, and so on. Having *rights* means you are authorized to copy files over to a specific system—you have "write" rights, in other words.

Receiving Files

You receive files in the same way that you send them—just reverse the process. Supply the other person with your mailing address and have them send you a mail message with a file attached. When you get the mail, the mail system will indicate that a file was sent with the text message. Note, however, that some older mail systems limit the size of the file you can transfer in this way to 64 kilobytes. In some cases you can download the file right from the mail system by selecting a download option from the menu. You will then be prompted to select a protocol and prepare your own system to receive the file. With other systems you save the attached file onto your Internet machine, and from there download it outside of the mail system to your local computer.

Protocols

Whether sending or receiving files, you probably will need some form of file transfer protocol to get bytes from point A to point B. This is because you need error correction, for one thing. If you simply send a text file to a remote system as if it were being typed by a very fast typist, there are bound to be errors. There's a lot of traffic on the Internet, and data collides, telephone lines drop out, noise of one kind or another develops. You can't achieve reliable file transfer in this manner. Besides, as we mentioned earlier, much of the file data you want to transfer will be in the form of binary data: compressed files, program files, data files. A text-based link won't understand these files, so you couldn't get reliable data transfer anyway.

Enter file transfer *protocols*—program utilities that package data in specific ways, surrounding it with new information that helps the receiving computer know whether or not everything got transferred properly. As these packets of data arrive at their destination, the software on the other end checks what was received against what was sent. If there is lost data, the receiving machine tells the originating computer to send that packet again. This send, check, resend process can go on until the packet arrives as it was sent.

There are dozens of these protocols, but the ones you are most likely to encounter on the Internet are ZMODEM, XMODEM, and Kermit. ZMODEM is among the most popular, newer protocols. XMODEM is an older protocol that is still used by many hosts and communications programs. Kermit is a universal protocol that should be on any machine you try. In its latest versions, Kermit is very fast and very reliable, and can handle file transfer situations that choke the other protocols. Older versions of Kermit, however, are slower and maybe even less reliable than ZMODEM.

rotocol transmission of file data requires a sending and a
ing component. If you are using a PC or a Macintosh with
unications software, chances are that you have the ability
d and receive files with several protocols. The other half of
k is on the remote host with which you are communicating. Whether this remote host is a Sun workstation or other
UNIX machine, an IBM Mainframe, a Hewlett-Packard minicomputer, or a Digital Equipment Corporation VAX, there
should be file transfer protocol software available.

With most systems on the Internet, the file transfer protocol
software is started with the same set of commands:

sz	Send a file via ZMODEM.
rz	Receive a file via ZMODEM.
sx	Send a file via XMODEM.
rx	Receive a file via XMODEM.
Kermit	Launch the Kermit application from which you can send or receive files.

To use protocols to send and receive data, simply enter the command at the host prompt. If you are sending files, specify the file
name on the command line, like this:

sz int01.zip

Note that when we say "send" a file, we mean that you want to
send it FROM the host to which you are attached TO your own
computer. This is how you download data to your machine.

To use receive, simply type **rz** or **rx** at the remote system
prompt. You will be told to start the file transfer. When you use
receive on a remote system, you are uploading data from your
machine to the remote machine. Receive tells the remote computer to get ready to receive data.

Kermit is a little different. To use Kermit to send or receive
files, simply type **kermit** at the command line. The prompt will
change and the Kermit utility will wait for further commands. To
send (download) a file, type **send** and the name of the file on the
command line. Then start up Kermit on your local machine and
the transfer will be initiated automatically. To upload a file (send

a file from your computer to the remote computer), type **receive** at the Kermit prompt, then start Kermit at your machine.

Note that on some systems you can enter any of these program commands (except Kermit), but you may get the default utility for which that system is configured. Also, if you use the **man** command to display information about protocol utilities, you may get information on all of these utilities—not just the one you asked for.

Be aware that transferring files with a protocol utility can become tricky at times. Remember that you are transferring program or other data that uses all eight bits to define a word. That's one reason you need the protocol in the first place. However, some hosts, especially when you go through more than one computer to actually get to the Internet link, are configured to strip off certain control codes. This means that if you try sending information over a 7-bit link (one that requires you to set your modem for 7 data bits), there is a chance that the protocol software on either end of the connection won't link up, or if it does, you may not get reliable data transfer.

An example of this problem is when you use the CompuServe Packet Network (CPN) to talk to The Well. CPN uses a communications setting of E71 (Even parity, 7 data bits, one stop bit), but The Well likes to see N81 (No parity, 8 data bits, and one stop bit). CPN talks to your machine with E71 and talks to The Well over the Internet, so during file transfers you may lose some information.

If you initiate a data transfer and the system starts to transfer data but then hangs, you may have to hang up the modem and re-dial the connection. If you try this a couple of times with more than one protocol and still have trouble, then you probably have a problem somewhere in the route to your destination machine. As a last resort try Kermit, because it will work when some of the others won't. But if you can't even transfer data with Kermit, give up and try another way.

Here's what we do in those circumstances. We first look for a direct dial-up link into the destination system. That's the quickest and surest way of getting reliable data transfer. It probably means you'll have to pay for a long distance phone call, but if the destination machine is within the same country or even the same continent, the cost won't be prohibitive if you are using 9600 bps or above.

The next thing to try is to get on another Internet link, transfer the data up to that machine, then use ftp to get it over the Internet to the computer where you want it. You also can use a mail system from the second host to send the file to yourself at your service provider or to send it directly to the ultimate recipient if you wish.

We'll talk more about using protocols and transferring data as we discuss some of the resources you will find on the Internet. This section at least gets you started. We'll bring up specific issues as you need to know about them. Use the index to locate a particular topic if you need more information now.

WHAT YOU LEARNED

We've covered a lot of information in this chapter, from how Internet machines and the people who use them are named to how you transfer files across the Internet. We showed you how to use electronic mail, we discussed file transfer protocols, and we talked about conferences and newsgroups.

With this chapter you have gained a fairly solid background of information about some of the tools and facilities of the Internet. In the next chapter we will continue discussing Internet features, but ones that are more fun and directly useful. The information in this chapter is baseline and practical. In the next and following chapters we start doing some hands-on searching for places to go and people to see.

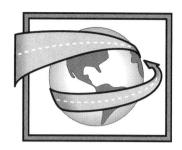

Chapter Four

NAVIGATIONAL TOOLS

We've spent a good deal of space in this book so far telling you about the Internet and how you can join this fascinating world of international travel and investigation. In the Introduction and the first three chapters, we covered everything you need to know about getting attached to the Internet.

If you investigated the leads we suggested and you're still not using the Internet, go back to Chapter 1 and try your hand at The Well. As long as you can afford the fee, *anyone* can use The Well to get on the Internet and meet a lot of knowledgeable people. Use The Well to get started; from there you can learn about alternatives if you find you need some.

In this chapter, we'll show you where to find and how to use the following on-line tools that will help you find people and information on the Internet:

- ✦ Archie
- ✦ File Transfer Protocol (ftp)
- ✦ Gopher
- ✦ WAIS
- ✦ WHOIS, Finger, and listserv
- ✦ World Wide Web (WWW)

Early users of the Internet were at a distinct disadvantage compared to those of us using the Internet today. For one thing, there weren't as many people or computers on the network, and there wasn't nearly as much useful information out there for them to access. But there was another disadvantage that continued even as the Internet grew—there weren't many tools to help them find who and what *was* out there.

In fact, probably the only reason so much useful work got done with the Internet in those days is that there was relatively less to look through to find what was needed. Today, with millions of users and an untold amount of information and other facilities, it would be extremely difficult to use more than a small percentage of the available information without tools to help.

Think about it. How do you know which road to take off of the interstate highway to drive to a small town, and then how do you get around from town to town once off of the interstate? You use maps, with varying levels of detail, drawn by people who have studied the system.

How do you find out what is in a book if you want to look for a specific topic? You use the index and table of contents and perhaps a list of illustrations. These tools help you narrow down your search for something specific from all of the data the author put into the book.

What about a computerized database? You may have thousands upon thousands of names and addresses or inventory records stored on a disk. How do you find a specific one out of the thousands of records? You use a database search utility that lets you specify certain criteria about the record or records you want, and the software handles the searching for you.

Without some kind of software help you'd never be able to find even a portion of the resources available on the Internet, at least not within any reasonable time. In this chapter we will talk about several of the most common searching tools that you can use to find an almost unbelievable array of Internet information.

ARCHIE (ON-LINE FILE-FINDING UTILITY)

The utility *Archie* is one way to find program or data files on the Internet. Archie is a database of directory listings from Internet computers willing to register their available files for general access. The list is updated automatically about once a month. When you want to find information on a particular topic, you run the searching component of Archie and ask it to find files that contain certain groups of words or letters. Archie displays a list of files—sometimes more than you really want to see—that seem to be about the topic you specified.

Accessing Archie

Before we discuss any specifics of how Archie works, lets talk about how you access it. As with many things on the Internet, the precise answer to this depends a little on which Internet server you are using. If your system administrator has set up a command file to attach you to an Archie server, all you need to do is type **archie** at the system prompt. Some systems have another command you use to attach automatically to one of the available Archie servers. Check with your service provider for the proper command for you.

NOTE

Not every Internet node or service provider maintains the Archie program and database. You have to attach to the proper node and log on to Archie there before you can use it.

If there is a command file set up for you, it simply issues the proper command to attach to a specific Archie server where you can log on and go to work. If you type **archie** at your service provider prompt and nothing happens or you discover there is no Archie command file, then you can use telnet to attach to an Archie server. To get the latest list of Archie servers, type **site** at the Archie prompt. You should get the list shown in Figure 4.1, or one that resembles it. Remember that like everything else on the Internet, the list of Archie sites is changing all the time.

Figure 4.1

Archie server list

archie.ans.net	147.225.1.10	(ANS server, NY (USA))
archie.au	139.130.4.6	(Austrailian Server)
archie.doc.ic.ac.uk	146.169.11.3	(United Kingdom Server)
archie.edvz.uni-linz.ac.at	140.78.3.8	(Austrian Server)
archie.funet.fi	128.214.6.102	(Finnish Server)
archie.internic.net	198.49.45.10	(AT&T server, NY (USA))
archie.kr	128.134.1.1	(Korean Server)
archie.kuis.kyoto-u.ac.jp	130.54.20.1	(Japanese Server)
archie.luth.se	130.240.18.4	(Swedish Server)
archie.ncu.edu.tw	140.115.19.24	(Taiwanese server)
archie.nz	130.195.9.4	(New Zeland server)
archie.rediris.es	130.206.1.2	(Spanish Server)
archie.rutgers.edu	128.6.18.15	(Rutgers University (USA))
archie.sogang.ac.kr	163.239.1.11	(Korean Server)
archie.sura.net	128.167.254.195	(SURAnet server MD (USA))
archie.sura.net(1526)	128.167.254.195	(SURAnet alt. MD (USA))
archie.switch.ch	130.59.1.40	(Swiss Server)
archie.th-darmstadt.de	130.83.22.60	(German Server)
archie.unipi.it	131.114.21.10	(Italian Server)
archie.univie.ac.at	131.130.1.23	(Austrian Server)
archie.unl.edu	129.93.1.14	(U. of Nebraska,Lincoln (USA))
archie.uqam.ca	132.208.250.10	(Canadian Server)
archie.cs.huji.ac.il	132.65.6.15	(Israel server)
archie.wide.ad.jp	133.4.3.6	(Japanese Server)

If you issue the command

telnet archie.unl.edu

at the system prompt, you should see this response:

Trying 129.93.1.14 ...

Connected to crcnis2.unl.edu.

Escape character is '^]'.

SunOS UNIX (crcnis2)

login:

At the **login:** prompt, type **archie** and press **Enter,** and the system will respond with the screen shown in Figure 4.2.

As the prompt suggests, you can type **help** at the command line to find out more about this particular Archie server and the commands you can use. If you type **help** at the **unl-archie>** prompt, you will see the display in Figure 4.3.

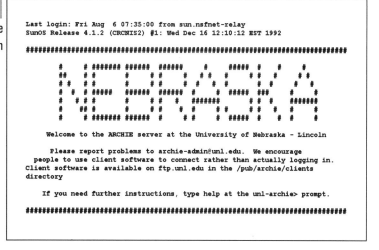

Figure 4.2

Typical Archie
login screen

```
Last login: Fri Aug  6 07:35:00 from sun.nsfnet-relay
SunOS Release 4.1.2 (CRCNIS2) #1: Wed Dec 16 12:10:12 EST 1992

#############################################################################

     #   # ###### ##### #####   #    #### #   #
    ##  # #    # #   # #   #   # #   # #  # #   #
    # # # #    # #   # #   #  #   #  # #  # #  #
    #  #### ###### ##### #   ##### ### #  #
    #   # #    #   # #   # ######   # #   # ######
    #   ## #    #   # # #   # #   #  # #   #    #
    #    # ###### ##### #   # #   #  ##### #    #

        Welcome to the ARCHIE server at the University of Nebraska - Lincoln

          Please report problems to archie-admin@unl.edu.  We encourage
     people to use client software to connect rather than actually logging in.
     Client software is available on ftp.unl.edu in the /pub/archie/clients
     directory

          If you need further instructions, type help at the unl-archie> prompt.

#############################################################################
```

Figure 4.3

unl-archie help topics

```
Currently, the available help topics are:

    about    - a blurb about archie
    bugs     - known bugs and undesirable features
    bye      - same as "quit"
    email    - how to contact the archie email interface
    exit     - same as "quit"
    help     - this message
    list     - list the sites in the archie database
    mail     - mail output to a user
    nopager  - *** use 'unset pager' instead
    pager    - *** use 'set pager' instead
    prog     - search the database for a file
    quit     - exit archie
    set      - set a variable
    show     - display the value of a variable
    site     - list the files at an archive site
    term     - *** use 'set term ...' instead
    unset    - unset a variable
    whatis   - search for keyword in the software description database

For information on one of these topics type:

    help <topic>
```

The precise topics available under help depend to some degree on the Archie server you are using.

One other thing about accessing Archie is worth mentioning. Archie, as you might imagine, is an extremely popular service. Without Archie, or something like it, your ability to find files on the Internet would be severely limited. Archie is so popular, in fact, that you frequently see a message like the one in Figure 4.4.

Figure 4.4

Rutgers Archie
busy message

```
> telnet archie.rutgers.edu
Trying 128.6.18.15 ...
Connected to dorm.Rutgers.EDU.
Escape character is ']'.


SunOS UNIX (dorm.rutgers.edu) (ttyqa)

login: archie
Last login: Thu Aug 5 16:18:04 from gwusun.seas.gwu.
SunOS Release 4.1.3 (TDSERVER-SUN4C) #2: Mon Jul 19 18:37:02 EDT 1993
     Sorry, but there are too many concurrent archie users on this
machine right now. At this point, you have several options. First of
all, the most preferable alternative would be to use an archie client
such as xarchie (cs.rochester.edu:/pub) or the "archie" command line
client (ftp.std.com:/src/util). These clients reduce the load on the
server, as well as often providing additional functionality.  Another
alternative would be to contact one of the other archie servers. ( a
list of alternate servers is appended to this message ) If you aren't
in a rush, you could submit your request by email. Just send a message
to archie@archie.rutgers.edu with the subject line "HELP" to get
detailed instructions. Oh, and the final option is to try here again
later :)
                              - Archie Mgt
                        (archie-admin@archie.rutgers.edu)
```

The list of available Archie sites mentioned in this message is similar to the one shown in Figure 4.1. Simply use telnet as we showed you earlier and try a different site. If you get an "Archie busy" message from one site, simply try another. Or you can do as the Rutgers Archie message suggested, and use an Archie client to conduct your search.

What is an Archie client? It is simply a local software package that handles some or all of the local user input/output and sends formatted requests to Archie. Using a client reduces the direct load on the Archie database software, because the client only attaches to Archie when it is ready to send or receive information. Use a client when you can. In fact, if you have an **Archie** or **QArchie** or **XArchie** command on your local system or on your service provider, it probably is a client package of some kind.

Some clients offer a command line interface similar to Archie itself. Other clients are better, providing menu-driven access, and some clients force you to enter a command line that is complex and difficult to understand. Normally you can type **help** at the Archie or Archie client prompt and find out what commands are available.

Using Archie

Once you gain access to Archie, directly or through a client, you are ready to search for specific information.

To understand how this works, consider the directory listing from a local PC for a moment. The listing of one directory might look something like the one in Figure 4.5. If you are using a Macintosh or other desktop machine, you have some kind of directory facility that is similar to this one.

Figure 4.5

Typical PC directory listing

```
      Volume in drive C is GATEWAY2000
      Volume Serial Number is 2950-15EB
      Directory of C:\WP\WINWORD\BOOKS\INTERNET

      .              <DIR>      07-03-93   11:49a
      ..             <DIR>      07-03-93   11:49a
      00INTNET DOC     138897  08-05-93    2:46p
      01INTNET DOC     170876  08-05-93    2:26p
      02INTNET DOC     417028  08-24-93    6:11p
      03INTNET DOC    1599060  08-26-93    9:01p
      04INTNET DOC       8804  08-30-93   10:49a
      0GINTNET DOC       3211  08-30-93   10:44a
      A2I      NTE      10416  08-22-93    8:00p
      A2I_1    LOG      70370  08-22-93    8:01p
      ARCHIE   LOG     128118  08-17-93    1:16p
      CPN      LOG     157358  08-09-93   10:08a
      DIRLIST  TXT          0  08-30-93   10:56a
      IMA      LOG       5314  08-18-93   12:04p
      INETLOG  802     262358  08-02-93    6:30p
      INTENET  NT1       3012  08-02-93    4:09p
      INTERNET MCI       4360  07-03-93   10:26a
      INTERNET CI1        977  07-03-93    9:53p
      INTERNET CIS      10722  07-03-93    1:40p
      INTERNET INF      31101  07-03-93    3:05p
      INTERNET CI2       4873  07-07-93    9:42a
      INTERNET COR       4712  07-05-93    1:36p
      INTERNET NTE      71394  07-16-93    2:59p
      INTERNET NT1      16070  07-22-93   11:30a
      INTERNET OUT      14682  08-02-93   11:31p
      INTERNET LOG     251637  08-02-93    6:09p
      IWELL    LOG      12470  08-21-93   10:00p
      MAIL     LOG     171378  08-21-93    5:38p
      MAIL_MAN DOC      53847  08-17-93    3:54p
      MARTHA   LOG      10047  08-17-93    1:43p
```

This list of files looks a little different from what you might find on an Internet UNIX system. The names of the files under MS-DOS usually must be shorter, for one thing. Under UNIX you usually can have much longer file names. This helps you to understand what might be in the file, but only if the person naming the file is creative and descriptive in their file-naming conventions. Figure 4.6 shows a file list from one UNIX system on the Internet. Some of the names are longer, and you could search a database of those names to come up with some topics, but they still don't tell the full story.

Figure 4.6

Typical UNIX system directory

```
ls -l
total 41
drwxrwxr-x   5 jayr    pubdom     3072 Aug 28 23:39 amiga
drwxrwxr-x   4 root    pubdom      512 Jun 16  1988 appleII
drwxrwxr-x   3 jayr    pubdom      512 Mar 30  1990 atariST
drwxrwxr-x   2 root    pubdom     1024 Oct 10  1991 bmugsig
drwxrwxr-x   4 root    host        512 Mar 24  1988 c64
drwxrwxr-x   3 root    pubdom     1024 Dec 13  1991 cpsr
drwxrwxr-x   3 root    pubdom      512 Jul 18  1991 dtp
drwxrwxr-x   3 jayr    pubdom     1536 May 19 01:16 forth
drwxrwxr-x   3 jayr    pubdom     3072 May 24 19:49 hypercard
drwxrwxr-x   3 root    pubdom     4608 Aug 21 03:07 ibmpc
drwxrwxr-x   3 root    pubdom      512 Feb  5  1991 jewish
drwxrwxr-x   2 root    pubdom      512 Oct 15  1989 kermit
drwxrwxr-x   3 root    pubdom      512 Nov  6  1990 lan
drwxrwxr-x   3 root    pubdom     1024 Mar 30 08:55 mac7
drwxrwxr-x   3 jayr    pubdom     9728 Aug 27 08:18 macintosh
drwxrwxr-x   3 root    pubdom     2048 Dec 28  1992 midi
drwxrwxr-x   3 jayr    pubdom      512 Sep 27  1989 music
drwxrwxr-x   3 root    pubdom      512 Sep  9  1991 naplps
drwxrwxr-x   3 root    pubdom      512 Feb 15  1992 next
drwxrwxr-x   3 root    pubdom      512 Feb  4  1993 os2
drwxrwxr-x   3 root    pubdom      512 Aug 14  1990 wholeearth
drwxrwxr-x   2 root    pubdom      512 Oct 18  1991 windows
```

Most of the information stored in the Archie database is in the form of a series of directory names. The database stores information from roughly 1,000 sites—sometimes more, sometimes less—and you can search the files through Archie to find out where they are. Do this with the **prog** command, the **find** command, or whatever command your particular Archie server uses.

N O T E

prog should be universal, but some servers implement additional commands to do the same thing, just to make things easier. After all, **find** is more intuitive than **prog** to look for information, right?

Figure 4.7 shows one search in Archie using the **prog** command, along with the results.

Figure 4.7

prog search in Archie

```
>prog pine
Processing Case Insensitive Substring Search for 'pine'

Host esel.cosy.sbg.ac.at

    Location: /pub/mirror/guitar/NEW.THIS.WEEK/m
       DIRECTORY drwxr-xr-x        512  Jul 13 00:50  Tony.MacAlpine
    Location: /pub/mirror/guitar/m
       DIRECTORY drwxr-xr-x        512  Jul 13 00:52  Tony.MacAlpine
    Location: /pub/mirror/guitar/w/Lucinda.Williams
            FILE -rw-r--r--       2133  May 20 14:01  Pineola.crd

Host knot.queensu.ca

    Location: /wuarchive/systems/linux/binaries/usr.bin
            FILE -r--r--r--     398604  Apr  6 04:43  pine3.05.1.bin.tar.z

Host hpcsos.col.hp.com

    Location: /mirrors/.hpib0/linux/binaries/usr.bin
            FILE -r--r--r--     398604  Apr  6 03:43  pine3.05.1.bin.tar.z

Host world.std.com

    Location: /obi/obi2/DARPA/drafts
    (?%)        FILE -r--r--r--        111  Dec 28 1992  happiness-for-all-01.txt%.Z
            FILE -r--r--r--        111  Dec 28 1992  happiness-for-all-01.txt.Z
```

Notice that on the Archie command line we had entered the command **prog pine** which told Archie to search the directory listing for any filename that includes the string **pine**. We were looking for information on the Pine mail system that we mentioned in Chapter 3. Notice what Archie found for us. (This is only a small part of the total list that this command produced. We cut it down so we could show you in general how such a search works.)

The first *hit* in this search doesn't have anything to do with the subject we hoped to find, but the directories listed do include the string "pine." The next two listings show the file **pine3.05.1.bin.tar.z**. This is more like it. Apparently this is version 3.05 of the Pine program, stored in a combined (*tar*) and compressed (*Z*) format. The final entry in this sample is not what we wanted. The file name includes the word "happiness," which does include the string "pine," which is what we told Archie to find. Still, we got two correct hits, and a lot more information on Pine that we didn't show you in this figure. The search worked by locating the search text we specified within the filename database maintained through Archie.

We can then use ftp (see information on using ftp later in this chapter) to download the files located in this Archie search that seem to be what we need.

If the list that **prog** (or **find**) generates about a specific topic is too long, you can narrow down the search by changing the search parameters. You can't use boolean searches with AND and OR, but you can specify as much information as you know about the topic.

N O T E

A boolean or logical search uses special words to expand or to narrow a search. You might want to find "dogs AND cats" in the same reference, or look for any article that included either "dogs OR cats." Suppose you wanted articles that mentioned "dogs AND NOT cats." Boolean logic can construct complex searching criteria, but you are limited to more simple searches with Archie.

For example, if I knew enough about my Pine search to know that I wanted information on version 3.0 and higher, I could use the search command:

prog pine3

This would eliminate all of the file names that include the word pine as an incidental part of the name. As you conduct searches with Archie, try to be creative and use search parameters that will produce as specific results as possible.

You can narrow the search by adding additional parameters to the search line. For example:

prog ^text	locates **text** only when text is at the beginning of word.
prog text$	locates **text** only when text is at the end of the word
prog ^text$	locates **text** only when it is an exact match

Notice that Archie is capable of several kinds of search. The default is "case insensitive substring", but you can use the command **set search <type>** to change to one of these search types:

✦ regexp (regular expression)

✦ substring (the default)

✦ casesub (Case sensitive substring)

✦ exact (Exact match)

Use **help set** at the Archie prompt to get more information on these options.

Also, note that the information you find with Archie may be in one of several formats. It may be plain text, it may be a program binary for UNIX, MS DOS, Macintosh, and so on, and it could be a compressed text or program file. Compressed files are identified with a .z or .Z or .gz (among others) at the end of the file name. When you see a capital Z, it means the file was prepared using Compress. The lower case z or the gz means the file was prepared with gzip. You need Uncompress for UNIX systems or a compatible utility for MS DOS or other operating system to restore a file that ends in Z and you need Gunzip to restore a file that ends in z or gz.

Suppose you issue a **prog** command and get nothing back? Archie may say something like "Nothing Appropriate," or "No Matches." Or, you may conduct a search that results in several files, but none of them is what you really wanted.

When this happens, you can use another Archie command that accesses another database. Try **whatis** followed by the information you want to find. This searches the file description database, an auxiliary file that contains descriptions of many of the files tracked by Archie. This data file may not be as complete as the main Archie filename database, however, because it is maintained by volunteers and the information is submitted and updated on a voluntary basis by the people who create the files.

When information is submitted to the file description database, however, it can help you find what you want more easily. Here's an example. Suppose you wanted to search for files that reference SCUBA or diving. You conduct the search but don't find what you want. Try using **whatis**:

whatis scuba

With this search you may find scuba mentioned in files that are named after good diving sites or travel locations. In short, you can try **prog** or **find** first, then try **whatis** to locate information that is not as easily spotted from the names of the files.

Again, if you have problems using your particular Archie server or Archie client, you should be able to type **help** at the prompt to get more information on available commands.

Finally, here's a command that will show you just who participates in maintaining the Archie database. At the Archie prompt, type **list**. You should see a screen similar to the one in Figure 4.8. This figure shows only a small portion of the display generated by this command. As you can see, when this listing was prepared, 952 sites were offering information about their

Figure 4.8

Typical Archie list command

```
unl-archie> list

952 sites are stored in the database

a.cs.uiuc.edu                   128.174.252.1    12:25 28 Jun 1993
abdallah.cd.chalmers.se         129.16.79.20     13:21  7 May 1993
accuvax.nwu.edu                 129.105.49.1     05:20 23 Mar 1993
acm.acm.rpi.edu                 128.213.5.10     21:30  1 Oct 1992
acsc.com                        143.127.0.2      04:48 18 Jan 1993
aelred-3.ie.org                 192.48.115.36    00:06 23 Jul 1993
aeneas.mit.edu                  18.71.0.38       01:07 23 Jul 1993
agate.berkeley.edu              128.32.155.1     01:32 23 Jul 1993
ahkcus.org                      192.55.187.25    01:11  9 Feb 1993
aisun1.ai.uga.edu               128.192.12.9     01:41 23 Jul 1993
aix.rpi.edu                     128.113.26.11    01:47 23 Jul 1993
aix1.segi.ulg.ac.be             139.165.32.13    01:53 23 Jul 1993
ajk.tele.fi                     131.177.5.20     02:17 23 Jul 1993
ajpo.sei.cmu.edu                128.237.2.253    02:23 23 Jul 1993
akiu.gw.tohoku.ac.jp            130.34.8.9       02:35 23 Jul 1993
alf.uib.no                      129.177.30.3     02:44 23 Jul 1993
alfred.ccs.carleton.ca          134.117.1.1      02:50 23 Jul 1993
```

directories and files that can be downloaded via ftp. Sometimes there are more sites—1,200 or so—and sometimes fewer.

When you have finished an Archie or Archie client session, type **quit** at the prompt to be returned to your local or service provider prompt.

FILE TRANSFER PROTOCOL (FTP)

Once you've found information files on the Internet that you want to move to your own machine, how do you do it? We described in the last chapter how you can use file transfer protocols such as XMODEM and ZMODEM to move data files from one machine to another. If the ultimate destination is your desktop computer, which you are using in terminal emulation mode to access an Internet service provider, then a protocol transfer may be the best choice.

However, there are probably lots of files out there on the Internet that reside on systems for which you have no access rights. Even if you know the domain name of the machine that has a file you want, when you telnet to that machine it will ask you to log on. If you don't have an account on that machine with a valid password, you are going nowhere. You need the ftp facility to get you into the foreign host and to transfer the file for you.

In addition, you may be getting a file that is in compressed format, and you will need to use UNCOMPRESS, for example, on the host before you try to use it. The files may be bundled into tar packages and you will need the tar program (a tape archive utility that is part of UNIX) first, or you simply may have more available storage on your provider machine than you do on your own.

Besides, you may be attaching to the Internet through a direct connection or a low-cost or no-cost local dial-up machine. In this case, you may prefer to conduct the protocol transfer from your local service provider host to your desktop computer rather than across the network. This is particularly true if you are accessing a remote file on a system that charges for connect time, such as The Well.

It is just such conditions that ftp is designed to address. The ftp utility has two ends—the one at your Internet node, and the one at the remote host where the file you want to download resides. ftp works like an Archie client, accepting a command for an ftp connection at your local host, and sending the appropriate commands to the remote host, and initiating the connection dialog.

Suppose, for example, you want to download to your Internet host the file **bicycles-faq** which is located in the **/pub/usenet-by-group/news.answers** directory on host **charon.mit.edu**. This is a remote host and you don't have an account on this machine. (By the way, faq with a file like this means "Frequently Asked Questions".)

If this host supports something called "anonymous ftp," then you can get the file quite easily. Remember, normally when you log on to a computer system you have to have a user account and a password to get in. With some facilities, however, service providers agree that they will let anybody in to conduct certain procedures. Among these common, anybody-can-do-it procedures is getting public archive files through ftp. Here's what you need to do. Type the following:

ftp charon.mit.edu (or other host name you want to access)

You will see a screen similar to the one in Figure 4.9.

Figure 4.9	

Sample ftp login screen	`ftp charon.mit.edu`
	`Connected to charon.mit.edu.`
	`220 charon FTP server (Version 6.6 Wed Apr 14 21:00:27 EDT 1993) ready.`
	`Name (charon.mit.edu:tbadgett) :`

At the **Name** prompt, type **anonymous** or **ftp**. You will be asked for a password. Enter your e-mail address (e.g. **tbadgett@opup. org**). Then you will be at an ftp prompt something like **ftp>** .

ftp.microsoft.com

If you are sure where the file you want is stored, simply issue a **get** command with the full path and file name of the file you want. In this example you would type:

ftp> **cd /pub/usenet-by-group/news.answers**

That will make the directory that contains the **bicycles-faq** file the current directory. Now you can copy it to your system with the **get** command, like this:

ftp> **get bicycles-faq**

Since this is a frequently asked questions file we assume it is a text file. ftp file transfers usually default to text format. If you want to transfer a program or other binary file (such as a compressed file, for example), you should issue the **binary** command prior to initiating the transfer. Simply type **binary** at the **ftp>** prompt. If you have specified binary, then want to transfer a text file, issue the **ascii** command prior to initiating the transfer.

The ftp software will automatically transfer the specified file from the resident system to your system. From there you can use the list files command (**ls**) to see if it arrived in your home directory. You can use another protocol (ZMODEM, XMODEM, etc.) to download the file to your desktop machine, or you can manipulate it with a resident editor or viewing program on your local host.

Notice that the file name and directory information for this sample came from an Archie search conducted earlier. However, when we attempted to download the file, we got an error message: **Not a plain file**. If this happens it may mean that you have typed the path or file name incorrectly. Remember that UNIX commands and file names are case sensitive. If the name shows up as all lower case, it must be entered that way. On the other hand, if there is even one upper case letter in the name, you must include it or the system won't be able to find it.

If the name and path are entered as you found them in Archie, it probably means that someone has changed the file name or moved the files since the Archie listing was updated.

Check out the directory with the **ls** command to find out what files are in that directory. If you get a very long list (which you probably will, since this is a public archive directory), you can narrow down the directory list by including the file name you found in Archie. In our example, you would issue the command like this:

ls bicycle-faq

When we tried that, we got a listing that looked like this:

bicycle-faq/part1
bicycle-faq/part2
bicycle-faq/part3
bicycle-faq/part4
bicycle-faq/part5

Now there are five files, part1 through part5, all stored in the bicycles-faq subdirectory. The five files we got in our list are actually stored in a subdirectory called **bicycle-faq** that is located within the **/pub/usenet-by-group/news.answers** directory we started with.

Now we can get the files with the following command sequence:

cd bicycles-faq
get part1

If you want all five files, then issue the **get** command four more times with part2, part3, part4, and part5 arguments.

When downloading multiple files in a directory, use **mget** instead of **get**. This tells ftp to "message" you on each file, asking if you want it. Answer **y** or press **Enter** to get the listed file. Answer **n** or anything else to skip it.

When you have transferred the files you want, type **quit** at the **ftp>** prompt to be returned to your home system.

That's anonymous ftp. Many systems support it, and it is an excellent way to get copies of files from other systems that you ordinarily couldn't access. You can also use ftp to move files very rapidly across the network between systems you do have an account on. If you log on to a system and use your logon name and password at the ftp prompt, you will be placed in your home directory. From there you have whatever access rights you normally have on that system.

If you can't access ftp from your local host, you can use e-mail to retrieve public files from ftp sites. To get more information on how to do that, send an e-mail message to **mailserver@rtfm.mit.edu** with "send usenet/news.answers/finding-sources" in the body of the message.

You can also use ftp to upload information to a remote host. Employ a similar process for getting a file, but instead of using **get,** use the **put** command. **Get** copies a file or files from the remote system to your home system; **put** copies a file or files from your home system to the remote system.

There are a number of other ftp commands. You can get a list on screen by typing **help** at the ftp prompt. A typical help screen for ftp is shown in Figure 4.10.

Here are some additional useful things to know about using ftp. When in ftp you can list the files in your local directory by preceding the **ls** command with an exclamation. ls shows files in the remote ftp directory; **!ls** shows the file in your current directory on your local host.

You can upload information to make it available to ftp on your own and perhaps other machines. Look for the **incoming** directory and place files you want to share there. You could send an e-mail message to other persons telling them what you made available.

Figure 4.10

Typical ftp
help screen

```
ftp> help
Commands may be abbreviated.   Commands are:

  !              cr           macdef       proxy        send
  $              delete       mdelete      sendport     status
  account        debug        mdir         put          struct
  append         dir          mget         pwd          sunique
  ascii          disconnect   mkdir        quit         tenex
  bell           form         mls          quote        trace
  binary         get          mode         recv         type
  bye            glob         mput         remotehelp   user
  case           hash         nmap         rename       verbose
  cd             help         ntrans       reset        ?
  cdup           lcd          open         rmdir
  close          ls           prompt       runique
```

Remember—you can't share anything you don't own, so don't upload copyrighted material unless you own the copyright.

When listing files in a directory you can format the display so it is easier to read with **ls -C** (provides columnar output instead of scrolling output). Use **ls -l** for additional detail about the files (such as size). And you can probably use **dir** instead of ls -l.

Most ftp commands can be issued with only three letters. So to change the file format to binary instead of ASCII, you need only say **bin** instead of **binary** at the ftp prompt, or use **mge** instead of mget. Most other commands work with three letters as well.

After downloading a file in ftp you can view the contents of text files in your current local host directory with the cat command: **!cat filename**. The exclamation point sends the command back to your local host so you don't have to exit fdtp to use the command. If the file is binary you'll see meaningless garbage on the screen and may even break your link with the remote system because of some code that scrolls across your screen.

GOPHER (FILE BROWSER)

Archie is not the only useful tool you'll discover on Internet to help you find the information you want. Gopher is another one.

Gopher does some of the same things as Archie, but in a different way. (The name Gopher, by the way, comes from a description of its function—it goes for things. Someone who serves a low level function in a company or on a project is sometimes called a "go fer" or "go for," so the name Gopher stuck.)

Instead of looking for specific information like Archie, Gopher lets you browse through Internet resources using a menu system. As with the Archie **whatis** command, your success in using Gopher depends to a fairly large degree on how information was catalogued or tagged when it was put into the Gopher database. Sometimes it is pretty creative and complete. Then again, you will find information about the same topic stored under different headings, depending on who made the decision. Overall, however, you'll find Gopher a useful and interesting tool to help you find your way around the Internet.

To use Gopher you need client software installed on your local machine or at your Internet service provider. To use this client—a software package that automatically connects to one Gopher server over the Internet then provides you a menu—simply type **gopher** at the service provider prompt. As with Archie, there are other implementations of the Gopher client, including **xgopher**. Which one you use depends on your site. If the **gopher** command doesn't work, check with your service provider to find out how to access Gopher.

Once the local client software logs on to the previously-specified Gopher host (this specification is part of the client software—in all likelihood you don't have any control over where you attach to Gopher), you should see a screen similar to the one in Figure 4.11. The screen you see depends on the type of Gopher server you are using. There are versions that have graphical user interfaces that support a mouse. The one we are showing here is a very common text-based client and was accessed from The Well. There are other clients on other Internet servers. Just type **gopher** at the system prompt and see what you get.

As you see, you can learn about Gopher by stepping through the menu. For example, select number 1 from the menu for "Information About Gopher."

Figure 4.11

Typical gopher
menu screen

```
   --> 1.  Information About Gopher/
       2.  Computer Information/
       3.  Discussion Groups/
       4.  Fun & Games/
       5.  Internet file server (ftp) sites/
       6.  Libraries/
       7.  News/
       8.  Other Gopher and Information Servers/
       9.  Phone Books/
      10.  Search Gopher Titles at the University of Minnesota <?>
      11.  Search lots of places at the University of Minnesota<?>
      12.  University of Minnesota Campus Information/

      Press ? for Help, q to Quit, u to go up a menuPage:
```

After that, you can narrow down your search by selecting one of the general topic areas, such as Discussion Groups, Fun & Games, Libraries, or Phone Books.

With a menu system such as this, the best way to learn about it is to put your hands on it. Type **gopher** at your service provider or local prompt. When you have the main Gopher menu up, select the first item to learn more about Gopher. You will then see a screen like the one in Figure 4.12.

Figure 4.12

Gopher information
screen from
main menu

```
   --> 1.  About Gopher.
       2.  Search Gopher News <?>
       3.  Gopher News Archive/
       4.  comp.infosystems.gopher (USENET newsgroup)/
       5.  Gopher Software Distribution/
       6.  Gopher Protocol Information/
       7.  University of Minnesota Gopher software licensing policy.
       8.  Frequently Asked Questions about Gopher.
       9.  Gopher+ example server/
      10.  How to get your information into Gopher.
      11.  New Stuff in Gopher.
      12.  Reporting Problems or Feedback.
      13.  big Ann Arbor gopher conference picture.gif <Picture>

   Press ? for Help, q to Quit, u to go up a menuPage:
```

Just step through the menu selections on this screen until you have learned all you want for the moment, then return to the main screen by pressing **u** on the keyboard.

It might be a good idea to turn on screen capture or file logging within your communications package when you use this menu system. Save the information to a GOPHER.LOG file—then you can refer to it at any time without retrieving it on-line again.

As we said, the client software is really an interface between your local machine or another Internet host and the Gopher application itself. You step through menus, make selections, and set up searches within the client, and the client goes to Gopher to find the data. In fact, the menu itself is sent from the Gopher application to the Gopher client for display on your local screen. In the end you really don't need to know how it works—just use it.

For example, suppose you select **Phone Books/** from the main Gopher menu shown previously. You will see a screen like the one shown in Figure 4.13.

Figure 4.13	
| Phone Books/ selection in Gopher | ```
Internet Gopher Information Client v1.11      Phone Books

  --> 1.   University of Minnesota <CSO>
      2.   About changing information in the U of M directory.
      3.   Phone books at other institutions/
      4.   Internet-wide e-mail address searches/
      5.   X.500 Gateway/
      6.   WHOIS Searches/
  Press ? for Help, q to Quit, u to go up a menuPage: 1/1
``` |

From this screen you can choose **Internet-wide e-mail address searches/** to present the display shown in Figure 4.14.

And so on. You simply step through the levels of the menu until you locate the resource you want. Note that you are prompted at the bottom of each menu screen to press **?** for Help, **q** to Quit, or **u** to go up one menu level.

Menu entries that end with a forward slash (/) will show another menu or a file. If the menu entry ends in a question mark (?), that item is searchable, which means it contains an index of key words which you can search for specific entries. When you select an indexed item, you will see a search input screen similar to the one shown in Figure 4.15.
```

Figure 4.14

Internet-wide e-mail
address searches in
Gopher

```
Internet Gopher Information Client v1.11
Internet-wide e-mail address searches

 --> 1.  Gopher to Netfind Gateway/
     2.  Netfind search for Internet e-mail addresses overview.
     3.  Netfind server at AARNet (Melbourne, Australia) <TEL>
     4.  Netfind server at Catholic University, Santiago, Chile <TEL>
     5.  Netfind server at OpenConnect Systems, Dallas, Texas <TEL>
     6.  Netfind server at Slovak Academy of Sciences, Czech and Slova..<TEL>
     7.  Netfind server at University of Alabama, Birmingham <TEL>
     8.  Netfind server at the University of Colorado, Boulder <TEL>
     9.  USENET contributor e-mail addresses <?>
     10. USENET contributor e-mail addresses overview.
     11. X.500 directory <TEL>12. X.500 directory overview.

     Press ? for Help, q to Quit, u to go up a menuPage:      1/1
```

Figure 4.15

Gopher "Words to
search for" screen

```
                 Internet Gopher Information Client v1.11

                                   Movies

 --> 1.  Search Movie Archive <?>
     2.  Current USENET Movie Reviews/
     3.  1987/
     4.  1988/
     +----------------------------Search Movie Archive----------------------+
     !                                                                       !
     ! Words to search for   lucas                                          !
     !                                                                       !
     !                                 [Cancel ^G] [Accept - Enter]         !
     !                                                                       !
     +-----------------------------------------------------------------------+




     Press ? for Help, q to Quit, u to go up a menu               Page: 1/1
     Alt-Z FOR HELP| VT100 |   FDX | 57600 E71 | LOG CLOSED | PRINT OFF | ON-LINE
```

For example, suppose we wanted to see a list of movie-related
files that contain the word Lucas (for the director). Select **Fun &
Games/** from the main Gopher menu (on the University of
Minnesota server we used), then choose **Movies/** from the Fun &
Games list. Finally, choose **Search Movie Archive <?>** to display
the search screen. Enter **Lucas** in the search field. The result we
got from this search was as you see in Figure 4.16.

Figure 4.16

Gopher menu search
for Lucas

```
Internet Gopher Information Client v1.11
Search Movie Archive: lucas

--> 1.  fun/Movies/1987/Jun/KOYAANISQATSI : From: cracraft@ccicpg.UUCP (St.
    2.  fun/Movies/1987/Jun/RETROSPECTIVE: STAR WARS : From: leeper@mtgzz..
    3.  fun/Movies/1987/Jun/THE UNTOUCHABLES-2 : From: moriarty@tc.fluke.C.
    4.  fun/Movies/1987/Jul/RETROSPECTIVE: LABYRINTH : From: reid@decwrl.d.
    5.  fun/Movies/1988/May/LADY IN WHITE : From: leeper@mtgzz.att.com (Ma.
    6.  fun/Movies/1988/May/WILLOW : From: jfreund@dasys1.UUCP (Jim Freund.
    7.  fun/Movies/1988/Jun/MISC: 12th Annual SF Lesbian & Gay Film Festi .
    8.  fun/Movies/1988/Jul/OUT COLD : From: moriarty@tc.fluke.com (Jeff M.
    9.  fun/Movies/1988/Aug/SOMEONE TO LOVE : From: thakur@eddie.MIT.EDU (.
    10. fun/Movies/1988/Sep/PUpcoming Films : From: leeper@mtgzz.att.com (.
    11. fun/Movies/1989/May/INDIANA JONES AND THE LAST CRUSADE : From: mor.
    12. fun/Movies/1989/May/INDIANA JONES AND THE LAST CRUSADE-1 : From: l.
    13. fun/Movies/1989/Aug/THE ABYSS-1 : From: leeper@mtgzx.att.com (Mark.
    14. fun/Movies/1990/Jan/SPY SMASHER RETURNS : From: teb@stat.Berkeley..
    15. fun/Movies/1990/Jan/MISC: TOP TEN of 1989 : From: ecl@mtgzy.att.co.
    16. fun/Movies/1990/Mar/HENRY: PORTRAIT OF A SERIAL KILLER : From: bau.
    17. fun/Movies/1990/Apr/DERSU UZALA : From: watson@ames.arc.nasa.gov (.
    18. fun/Movies/1990/May/LONGTIME COMPANION : From: Hoffman.es@XEROX.CO.
    19. fun/Movies/1990/Jun/LONGTIME COMPANION : From: leeper@mtgzx.att.co.
    20. fun/Movies/1991/May/BACKDRAFT : From: butterworth@a1.mscf.upenn.ed.
    21. fun/Movies/1991/Aug/DEAD AGAIN : From: leeper@mtgzy.att.com (Mark .
    22. fun/Movies/1991/Oct/RAMBLING ROSE : From: leeper@mtgzy.att.com (Ma.
    23. fun/Movies/1992/Jan/HEARTS OF DARKNESS : From: eugene@nas.nasa.gov.
    24. fun/Movies/1992/Apr/MISCELLANEOUS: Academy Award Winners (1992) .
    25. fun/Movies/1992/May/K2 : From: eugene@nas.nasa.gov (Eugene N. Miya.
    26. fun/Movies/1992/Jul/PRELUDE TO A KISS : From: leeper@mtgzy.att.com.
    27. fun/Movies/1992/Jul/MISC: Siskel & Ebert Ten Best Lists (1979-199 .
    28. fun/Movies/1992/Jul/PRELUDE TO A KISS-1 : From: frankm@microsoft.c.
    29. fun/Movies/1992/Aug/COOL WORLD : From: lon@edsi.plexus.COM (Lon Po.
```

As with most Gopher searches, you take pot luck; you may or may not get precisely what you had in mind. Suppose we select the third entry in the movie list: The Untouchables. This was not a George Lucas film, of course, but Gopher found Lucas in the index. When the file is displayed, we see that the reviewer mentions George Lucas films by way of introducing the review, but this is not an article about a George Lucas film.

If any of the entries from a Gopher search seem strange, you can display the associated files and find out why the file was selected. The server will highlight the key word you were searching for inside the file. Simply display screen after screen until the key word you specified appears. It may or may not relate to the topic you wanted to find. If you entered more than one word on the Search For line, try entering only the main word you're really interested in. This will drop the files that have the modifier word you specified, for example, leaving only the files with the main entry.

It will take a little practice to learn to get the most out of Gopher searches, but that is one of the fun aspects of the Internet. Get on and go for a ride!

WIDE AREA INFORMATION SERVERS

The Internet Wide Area Information Servers, or WAIS, is another information locating tool. WAIS (pronounced "ways") doesn't replace Archie or Gopher, but is used in conjunction with them.

WAIS is an indexed database of Internet information. This is significant because, when you conduct a WAIS search, you aren't looking at the source files. You are searching an index file that points to the information in the database. That database information can be text files, program files, graphics, or anything else you can store on a computer. We've shown a crude representation of an index and its related data in Figure 4.17.

Figure 4.17

Drawing of index and related data

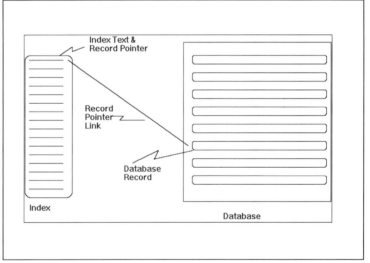

The difference between Gopher and WAIS is that WAIS includes a searching tool, so that instead of stepping through menus and lists until you come across something you want, you can specify what you're looking for and WAIS finds it.

WAIS is a *distributed application*, which means that both data and the software that searches the data are stored in multiple locations. When you submit a search to WAIS, the program steps through a series of checks, decides where the search should be conducted, and then hands off the search criteria to the host that contains the database you need to search.

This distributed search scheme is pretty sophisticated, but the actual searching you can do with WAIS isn't much different from Archie and Gopher. You can't conduct boolean searches or narrow searches with any of these tools. The best you can expect is to get into the right ball park; locating the correct section of bleachers and then a particular person is a little more difficult.

NOTE

Arriving on the scene are WAIS clients that have some expanded search capabilities. Investigate the boolean WAIS—a booleanized version of WAIS from **ftp.bio.indiana.edu**—or get the new free WAIS.

Accessing WAIS

To conduct a WAIS search you first have to get access to a WAIS client, just as you do with Archie and Gopher. Where do you find a WAIS client? It's a little like walking on water: you have to know where the stumps are.

To find the stumps (WAIS clients), you could use Archie and conduct a prog search for WAIS. That will show you where there are files on the Internet with WAIS in the name. In fact, we tried that and got the results shown in Figure 4.18. (Only a part of the search is shown.)

From this partial list (a search for WAIS produces a LONG listing) you can see that there are several sites that seem to have WAIS access. We arbitrarily selected **sunsite.unc.edu** and used telnet to access this host. The result is shown in Figure 4.19.

This site—as many sites do—tells you how to log on to WAIS. (At this site you use the SWAIS client.) Once in WAIS, you get the screen shown in Figure 4.20.

Figure 4.18

Archie search for WAIS

```
Host syr.edu

    Location: /novell
        DIRECTORY drwxrwxr-x          512  May 13 1992  wais

Host uceng.uc.edu

    Location: /pub/wuarchive/systems/mac/info-mac/card
        FILE -r--r--r--     261026  Mar  9 10:13  hyper-wais-14.hqx

Host ruby.ils.unc.edu

    Location: /pub/internet_software
        FILE -rw-r--r--     162526  Apr 13 15:28  wais

Host sunsite.unc.edu

    Location: /pub/.cap
        FILE -rw-r--r--         71  Jul  6 23:28  wais
    Location: /pub/Z39.50/Standards_documents
        FILE -rw-r--r--      37911  Nov  7 1992  wais
    Location: /pub
        DIRECTORY drwxr-xr-x       1024  Aug 17 15:21  wais

Host cac.washington.edu

    Location: /msdos/lwp
        DIRECTORY drwxr-xr-x        512  Aug 20 12:45  wais

Host nic.wisc.edu

    Location: /userinfo
        DIRECTORY drwxrwxr-x        512  May 14 1992  wais
    Location: /
        DIRECTORY drwxr-xr-x        512  May 18 20:16  wais
```

Figure 4.19

Sunsite.unc.edu WAIS
telnet access

```
telnet sunsite.unc.edu
Trying 152.2.22.81 ...
Connected to sunsite.unc.edu.
Escape character is '^]'.
***************** Welcome to SunSITE.unc.edu *****************
SunSITE offers several public services via login. These include:

For a simple gopher client,                    login as gopher
For a simple WAIS client (over 500 databases), login as swais
For WAIS search of political databases,        login as politics
For WAIS search of LINUX databases,            login as linux

For a FTP session, ftp to sunsite.unc.edu. Then login as anonymous

For more information about SunSITE, send mail to info@sunsite.unc.edu


SunOS UNIX (calypso)


    login:
```

Figure 4.20

First WAIS screen with topic list

```
login: swais
Last login: Tue Aug 31 07:54:48 from AULA.RZ.Uni-Augs
SunOS Release 4.1.3 (SHOOP) #5: Tue Jun 29 15:56:38 EDT 1993

University of North Carolina Office For Information Technology

You could be running this code on your own machine.
You'll find it and other WAIS stuff available via anonymous ftp
from SunSITE.unc.edu in the pub/wais directory.

These databases are also available via gopher.
Just point your gopher client to sunsite.unc.edu 70
and enjoy using these databases from your gopher interface.

you're probably a vt100 or should be
TERM = (unknown) vt100
It takes a minute to load all the database information
SWAISSource Selection        Sources: 540
#Server      Source                                    Cost
001:  [     archie.au]         aarnet-resource-guide    Free
002:  [weeds.mgh.harvard.ed]   AAtDB                    Free
003:  [munin.ub2.lu.se]        academic_email_conf      Free
004:  [wraith.cs.uow.edu.au]   acronymsFree
005:  [    archive.orst.edu]   aeronautics              Free
006:  [ bloat.media.mit.edu]   Aesop-Fables             Free
007:  [ bloat.media.mit.edu]   aesopFree
008:  [ ftp.cs.colorado.edu]   aftp-cs-colorado-edu     Free
009:  [nostromo.oes.orst.ed]   agricultural-market-news Free
010:  [sunsite.unc.edu]        alt-sys-sun              Free
011:  [    archive.orst.edu]   alt.drugs                Free
012:  [    wais.oit.unc.edu]   alt.gopher               Free
013:  [sun-wais.oit.unc.edu]   alt.sys.sun              Free
014:  [    wais.oit.unc.edu]   alt.wais                 Free
015:  [alfred.ccs.carleton.]   amiga-slip               Free
016:  [munin.ub2.lu.se]        amiga fish contents      Free
```

We wanted to search the Internet for information about young people and amateur radio. From this list of topics (you can't see all of it in Figure 4.20) we chose two indexes: **kidsnet** and **k-12-software**. You select topics by moving the highlight down the screen to a topic then pressing the **Space bar**. An asterisk appears beside the ones you have selected. Then you enter the key words you want to search for—in this case **ham radio**. As you can see in Figure 4.21, we got 21 hits on the topic Ham Radio from these two databases.

Notice that some of these references obviously have to do with amateur radio and, since they were found on indexes that were targeted at kids, are probably a good match. Others don't seem to have titles that show a relationship between kids and ham radio. They may or may not be appropriate, but Figure 4.21 gives you a clue.

Figure 4.21

Ham Radio search
for kids

```
SWAIS              Search Results                          Items: 21

  #      Score              Source      Title                               Lines
001:    [1000] (           kidsnet)    Scott Loft Re: KIDSNET & Ham Radio      22
002:    [ 940] (           kidsnet)    Mark Halla Re: RE: KIDSNET & Ham Radio  10
003:    [ 910] (           kidsnet)    VO76GZHB@U Re: RE: KIDSNET & Ham Radio   11
004:    [ 728] (           kidsnet)    Scott Loft Re: More on Amateur Packet Ra 32
005:    [ 576] (           kidsnet)    phil@bts.c Re: Nixpub Posting (Long)    978
006:    [ 546] (           kidsnet)    aftp-list@ Re: Anonymous FTP List - Site 2788
007:    [ 455] (           kidsnet)    Mark Halla Re: RE: More on Amateur Packe  6
008:    [ 455] (           kidsnet)    Scott Loft Re: RE: More on Amateur Packe 14
009:    [ 455] (           kidsnet)    Mark Halla Re: More on Amateur Packe      7
010:    [ 424] (           kidsnet)    LVRON@SATU Re: An article I got from a N 166
011:    [ 394] (           kidsnet)    opresno@ex Re: kids-93 newsletter #3    422
012:    [ 364] (           kidsnet)    mjkll@po.C Re: School Shuttle simulation 137
013:    [ 364] (           kidsnet)    yanoff@csd Re: Internet Services List     47
014:    [ 364] (           kidsnet)    yanoff@csd Re: UPDATED Internet Services  61
015:    [ 364] (           kidsnet)    Tom Grundn Re: Ammunition for K-12 Netwo 268
016:    [ 364] (           kidsnet)    yanoff@csd Re: Updated Internet Services 113
017:    [ 364] (           kidsnet)    yanoff@csd Re: Internet Services Listing 164
018:    [ 364] (           kidsnet)    yanoff@CSD Re: Updated Internet Services 201
019:    [ 364] (           kidsnet)    yanoff@csd Re: Updated Internet Services
        238
020     [ 364] (           kidsnet)    Rhonda ChInternet Resources for Sc      494
021     [   0] (      k-12-software)   Search produced no result. Here's the Ca 4204
```

Notice the numbers in brackets just to the right of the entry numbers. These are the result of calculations performed during the WAIS search to show how close to your specified search criteria each article appears to be. A 1000 means that file matched better than any of the others. Any file with less than 1000 didn't match as well. This points you in the right direction, at least, toward finding the information you were looking for.

The only way to know for sure is to use the cursor movement keys to highlight the articles you want to view and then press the **Space bar**. You are prompted at the bottom of the screen to press **w** for a key word search or **s** for sources.

As with the other resources we have discussed in this chapter, WAIS software is mostly self-instructing. You read instructions on the screen and do what they say. The best way to learn about WAIS is to put your hands on it and try it out.

OTHER NETWORK TOOLS & TECHNIQUES

We couldn't possibly tell you about every Internet utility. We've mentioned the major ones earlier in this chapter. In this section we will briefly introduce you to a few more tools you can use to help you in your Internet travels.

whois Information Tool

whois is another Internet database, and is also an application that helps you to search this database. This file stores a list of Internet users compiled and maintained by the DDN Network Information Center (NIC) at **nic.ddn.mil**—that's where the data is located. The client software that lets you access the information usually is stored on your local machine or on your Internet service provider's machine.

So when you type a command such as:

whois Tango

you access the client program whois on your local machine and tell it to send a request for information about users with the last name Tango to the **nic.ddn.mil** server. If your machine has the proper whois software client, you will get a screen display like the one in Figure 4.22. (We have substituted made-up information in this example.)

Figure 4.22

Typical whois search results (Tango)

```
Whois: Tango
Tango, Likado A. (LAT28)ltango@PICA.ARMY.MIL
   Army Armament Research Development
   and Engineering Center, Armament Munitions and Chemical Command
   Attn: SMCAR-ISE, Tango B/5031
   Picatinny Arsenal, NJ 07806-5001
   (201) 555-1212/6054 (DSN) 880-1212/6054
```

Note that you may get an error message instead of the answer you expect when you try to use whois. That's because some local sites have not updated the whois client software since the site where the information is stored was changed. This change occurred when the ARPAnet was retired. If your whois client software still tries to connect to the old ARPAnet host, you get an error message similar to the one in Figure 4.23.

If this occurs, you may not be able to use your local whois client software (you may be able to enter a command line option to point the client to the proper location—contact your service provider), but you can still use whois by using telnet to get to the database site. Use this command from your service provider prompt:

telnet rs.internic.net

Figure 4.23

whois wrong host error message

```
> whois tango

Putt's Law:
Technology is dominated by two types of people:
Those who understand what they do not manage.
Those who manage what they do not understand.
-----------------------------------------------------
Hi!  You have attempted to contact a whois server at SRI-NIC.ARPA.
Your WHOIS client program is either extremely old or your software
vendor is really out of it.  Please complain to them.
To contact the current DDN NIC WHOIS server, it will be
necessary to either:

a) Use a command-line option to tell your WHOIS client
   to connect to a different host (NIC.DDN.MIL),

b) Or, recompile WHOIS with the CORRECT name for the DDN NIC,
   NIC.DDN.MIL, in place of the ancient SRI-NIC.ARPA.

For further information about the DDN NIC, please contact the new
contractor, GSI, at 1-800-365-3642.  Thank You.
-----------------------------------------------------
[caw 91/09/24]
```

You should see a screen similar to the one in Figure 4.24.

Figure 4.24

nic.ddn.mil whois log in prompt

```
> telnet rs.internic.net
Trying 198.41.0.5 ...
Connected to rs.internic.net.
Escape character is '^]'.


SunOS UNIX (rs) (ttyp4)


**********************************************************************
* -- InterNIC Registration Services Center  --
*
* For gopher, type:                   GOPHER <return>
* For wais, type:                     WAIS <search string> <return>
* For the *original* whois type:      WHOIS [search string] <return>
* For the X.500 whois DUA, type:      X500WHOIS <return>
* For registration status:           STATUS <ticket number> <return>
*
* For user assistance call  (800)444-4345|(619)455-4600 or  (703)742-4777
* Please report system problems to ACTION@rs.internic.net
**********************************************************************
Please be advised that the InterNIC Registration host contains INTERNET
Domains, IP Network Numbers, ASNs, and Points of Contacts ONLY. Please
refer to rfc1400.txt for details (available via anonymous ftp at
either nic.ddn.mil [/rfc/rfc1400.txt] or ftp.rs.internic.net
[/policy/rfc1400.txt]).
Cmdinter Ver 1.3 Tue Aug 31 02:12:50 1993 EST
      [vt100] InterNIC >
```

Type **whois** at the prompt, and you will be connected to a whois client at the remote host with the prompt **whois:**. From there you can enter names of Internet users to get more information about them.

NOTE

The whois database doesn't track every Internet user. It only has about 70,000 to 100,000 entries for people who work on the Internet, maintaining it and configuring it. You may also find there the names of people conducting research about networking through Internet resources.

If you don't have access to telnet and your local whois command isn't working properly, you can submit your request via e-mail. To do this, send an e-mail message to **mail service@ nic.ddn.mil** and enter your **whois** command in the **Subject** field of the message header. If you were looking for someone named Tango, for example, you would enter **whois Tango** in the **Subject:** field of your mail software. You won't get an immediate response this way, of course, but after the mail process has had time to work, you will receive an e-mail message with the results of your query.

There are a couple more whois concepts worth mentioning. First of all, we have shown query examples that have only one result. You ask for a name and you get a single response with information about that individual. There may be times when you enter a name and get a list of several names with only minimal information. When this happens, issue a new query and enter the last name, a comma, and the first name from the list to get detailed information about a specific individual.

Also, there is information in the whois database besides just the name data we have demonstrated. You can search the whois files for information about networks or domains on the Internet. The process for finding this information is the same as when you are searching for a name, except that you enter the network entity you want to find. Also, you have to telnet to a different location.

Suppose we wanted to know more about ORNL, which stands for the Oak Ridge National Laboratory, a government research and manufacturing facility at Oak Ridge, TN. We would enter a whois query such as:

whois Oak Ridge National Lab

The whois server returns a list like the one in Figure 4.25.

Figure 4.25

whois search for ORNL

```
Whois: Oak Ridge National Lab
Oak Ridge National Lab (NET-ORNL-NETB2)
    Oak Ridge, TN 37831

    Netname: ORNL-NETB2
    Netnumber: 134.167.0.0

    Coordinator:
       Maxwell, Don  (DM257)  MII@ORNL.GOV
       (615) 576-4182

    Domain System inverse mapping provided by:

    DNS-EAST.ES.NET               134.55.6.130
    MSR.EPM.ORNL.GOV              128.219.8.1
    NS1.LANL.GOV                  128.165.4.4

    Record last updated on 30-Jun-93.
```

You could try conducting a search for ORNL (or whatever abbreviation you know that the target entity uses) and you may or may not get a response. We entered **whois ORNL** and didn't find anything, so we tried **Oak Ridge National Lab** and got better results. Sometimes you get different results. We tried a **whois University of Tennessee** search and got about 70 networks listed in several cities across Tennessee.

Remember to turn on capture or logging software when you start searching with whois or any other tool. That way, when the information scrolls up the screen, you are capturing it in a file that you can review later with a text editor.

Here's an interesting search to try: **whois Whitehouse**. Try that and see what you get.

Finger

Finger is another information facility that is probably on your local system. It is used to display user information similar to whois, except that you have to know who is on a specific system for it to work. If you issue the **finger** command at your service provider prompt and follow it with the name of a user, you will get information displayed about that user.

For example, try using the finger command with your own login ID, like this:

finger tbadgett

You should get a display similar to the one in Figure 4.26.

Figure 4.26

Sample finger display

```
> finger tbadgett
Login name: tbadgett  In real life: Tom  Badgett
Directory: /home/tbadgett        Shell: /usr/local/bin/tcsh
On since Aug 26 00:10:54 on ttyp0 from MARTHA.UTCC.UTK.
Mail last read Thu Aug 26 00:15:01 1993
No Plan.
```

If you issue the **finger** command without an argument, you will see a list of users currently on the system. However, you can use finger with users who are not currently logged on. If you want to see who has been using the system, try this command:

last -25

That will show you the login names and addresses of the last 25 logins. From that list you can pick a name and use finger to get more information. Finger should work with either the login name, first name, or last name of the person you're interested in. In fact, you can enter just about any information from the person's record and get a full display.

In addition, you can use finger across the network to get information about users on other systems, assuming you know enough about them for finger to locate the record. Simply include the destination system as part of the **finger** command:

finger tbadgett@well.sf.ca.us

This may not always work, however, because individual systems may disable finger for security reasons. If you use the command we just showed you to finger a user at The Well, for example, you will see a message such as:

Due to security and privacy considerations, the WELL currently does not honor incoming finger requests.

Other systems may say simply, **Connection refused**.

If it works, finger can provide an additional level of detailed information about the users with whom you interact on the Internet.

listserv

listserv is one more of the many tools available to help you obtain specific information across the Internet. It isn't universally available, but it is a software system that maintains mailing lists. A mailing list is a named list of Internet addresses that acts like a single entity. Once the list is created, mail can be sent to everyone on the list by addressing a message to the list name.

Usually, where **listserv** is supported, it can be accessed via mail just like another user. For example, if you want to receive a file from a listserv site, you can send an e-mail message addressed to **listserv@Domain**. The body of the message should read:

get filename filetype

The filename component of this message is obvious. The filetype is a designation used on the host. You have to know the name of the file and its type to get it with this method.

You can also use listserv to subscribe to a mailing list at a specified site, if you know the domain name of the site and the name of the mailing list. Simply send a mail message to **list-serv@Domain** with the message:

subscribe filename

The listserv software handles the request and adds your mail address to the list. If at some later time you want to remove your name from the list, send a message to the listserv site with the message:

signoff filename

World Wide Webb (WWW)

Internet users, designers and programmers are never satisfied, and thank goodness they aren't. That's how we have established all the tools and utilities that make using the Internet so much easier. One of these tools, still not too widely used (compared to things like Archie, for example) but growing and changing all the time, is the World-Wide Webb, or WWW. Like Gopher and WAIS, WWW is an Internet searching tool based on indexes and text searches. In fact, WWW moves Internet toward the next generation of computer tools with a feature called *hypermedia*.

What is hypermedia? It means slightly different things on different systems and with different searching software, but in general hypermedia is a text-based database that includes links among documents. These links are based on key words found inside each document.

For example, if you are reading a document about exotic animals and see a reference to Sabre Toothed Tiger, you can select Sabre Toothed Tiger and open a document specific to that topic. While you are reading about Sabre Toothed Tigers, you see a reference to Pleistocene Epoch. By selecting that topic, you open a document dedicated to it, and so on. Depending on how the particular text groupings are organized, you may be able to continue this process indefinitely, getting deeper and deeper into a topic, or jumping across topics as new ones present themselves.

The concept of hypermedia is an important one for computer-based research and education. As we learn to code files and build more sophisticated search tools, look for hypermedia to become a natural part of most database front ends, word processors, and other search and data management tools.

In WWW, hypermedia is read and accessed with a software tool called a *browser*. A browser is simply a utility that lets you read text and select additional references based on that text. A browser may include a menu system that points you toward the general topics you want to study. Then you can access additional information in two ways, with a graphics browser and with a text-based browser. In our example with saber toothed tigers, a text-based browser might show that this is a linked term by placing a number in brackets beside it:

In addition, saber toothed tigers [22] were common during very early periods, when...

By entering **22** and pressing **Enter** at the bottom of the page that includes this reference, you can open a separate document about saber toothed tigers. If you are using a graphics-based browser, on the other hand, the words or phrases that represent links to other documents will be shown highlighted in some way. You can use the cursor keys or a mouse to select the highlighted text and jump to the second document.

Where do you get browsers? Several are in use or under development. You can access a text browser via telnet (we'll show you how in a moment), and you can download graphics-based browsers for MS-DOS, Macintosh, X-Window and other implementations by browsing around inside WWW documents. As this book is written, the WWW project is very much under development, so be willing to experiment and do some of your own searching. It is a fascinating project and fun to play with. Let's look at some examples.

To access a basic WWW text-based browser, enter this command at your Internet service provider prompt:

telnet info.cern.ch

This connects you to a WWW server at European Particle Physics Laboratory, where WWW was primarily developed. This is a good place to start with WWW—the "head shed," so to speak. The first screen you see will look similar to the one in Figure 4.27.

Figure 4.27

Initial WWW
screen @ cern host

```
Overview of the Web
                              GENERAL OVERVIEW

    There is no "top" to the World-Wide Web. You can look at it from many points of view. If
you have no other bias, here are some places to start:

    by Subject[1]          A classification by subject of interest. Incomplete but easiest to
                           use.

    by Type[2]             Looking by type of service (access protocol, etc) may allow to find
                           things if you know what you are looking for.

    About WWW[3]           About the World-Wide Web global information sharing project

Starting somewhere else

    To use a different default page, perhaps one representing your field of interest, see
"customizing your home page"[4].

What happened to CERN?

1-6, Up, <RETURN> for more, Quit, or Help:
ALT-Z FOR HELP | VT100 | FDX | 57600 N81 | LOG CLOSED | PRINT OFF | ON-LINE
```

Notice that the screen in Figure 4.27 is a hypermedia browser. The numbers after certain words and phrases show that you can get additional information on these topics by entering the proper number at the end-of-screen prompt. The prompt tells you there are six possible choices on this screen. For example, if you enter **1** at the prompt, you get the **classification by subject** of interest screen shown in Figure 4.28.

This is as good a way as any to get a feel for hypermedia and its implementation in WWW. Simply telnet to the cern site and poke around for a few minutes. You can do this with a computer and simple terminal emulator, or even a dumb terminal. That's one of the benefits of a text-based system.

```
                    The World-Wide Web Virtual Library: Subject Catalogue
                                    WWW VIRTUAL LIBRARY

        This is the subject catalogue. See also arrangement  by  service type[1]. Mail www-
    request@info.cern.ch to add pointers to this list, or if you are prepared to take over
    administration of a subject area.

    Aeronautics      Mailing list archive index[2] . See also NASA LaRC[3]

    Agriculture[4]  Separate list, see also Almanac mail servers[5] .

    Astronomy and Astrophysics
             Abstract Indexes[6] at NASA,    Astrophysics work at
             FNAL[7] , Princeton's[8] Sloane Digital Sky Survey,
             the STELAR project, Space Telescope Electronic
             Information System[9] , the Southampton University
             Astronomy Group[10] , the National Solar
             Observatory[11] , Astrophysics work at the AHPCRC[12].
             See also: space[13] .

    Bio Sciences[14]          Separate list .

    Computing[15]             Separate list.
    1-83, Back, Up, <RETURN> for more, Quit, or Help:
    ALT-Z FOR HELP|VT100|FDX|57600 N81|LOG OPEN|PRINT OFF|ON-LINE
```

Text-based systems are the norm on Internet, for now, but graphics interfaces—Microsoft Windows, Apple Macintosh, X-Window Systems—are on the rise. For example, you can download software to provide a graphics interface to WWW. You'll need different software for different platforms.

One place to look for this software is the host **fatty.law.cornell.edu** in the directory **/pub/LII/Cello**. Use ftp to attach to this site, read the notices there, and download what you need. For example you can download the **cello.zip** file to get a Microsoft Windows front end to WWW. You can see in Figure 4.29 a sample of how this graphics browser might look—we say "might" because this software, like much WWW stuff, is under development and subject to change.

At this point you probably can't look at WWW as your primary searching engine on Internet, but keep tabs on it. WWW, or something like it, is destined to become an easy-to-use window into the vast array of information on Internet.

Figure 4.29

Sample Cello Graphics
WWW Browser

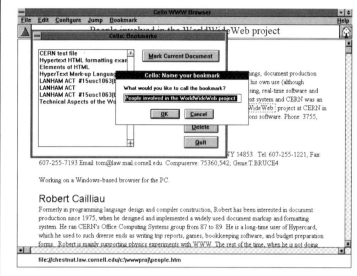

QUICK UNIX REFERENCE

Throughout your travels on the Internet you will encounter some UNIX command lines. UNIX is a rich operating system that handles the housekeeping chores on many of the hosts you use on the Internet. We give you an annotated reference to UNIX commands (not all of them, just a select few) in Appendix A. Here's a table (Table 4.1) that shows you the basic commands and what they do. They'll help you with a lot of what you need to navigate on Internet. For more information on these commands, turn to Appendix A. In this table, items in angle brackets represent arguments that are added to the basic command.

Table 4.1

UNIX Command
Summary

Command	Function
Bye	Logoff or cancel connection
cat <filename>	catenate file (display file)
cd <directoryname>	change directory to directory-name
cp <file1> <file2>	copy file1 file2
Ctrl-C	cancel process
Ctrl-D	terminate input
Ctrl-Z	suspend process
date	display current system date
ed <filename>	edit specified file
kill <project id>	kill specified process
Logout	terminate connection
ls	list files
mail address	send or read UNIX mail
man command	display command description
mkdir <directoryname>	make directory directoryname
ps	process status
pwd	working directory name
rm <file>	remove file
rx	receive XMODEM
rz	receive ZMODEM
sx	send XMODEM
sz	send ZMODEM
send <address>	send text to address
tar <-cf file.tar> <directory>	tape archive. Combine directory into single file.tar
w	(w)ho. Display user id and current activity
whereis <filename>	show location of filename
who	display user id and info

WHAT YOU LEARNED

The tools and utilities we have talked about in this chapter aren't the only ones that are available on the Internet, but they're enough for you to start finding your way around. As you travel, follow your fingertips, keep your eyes open, and make use of what else you find. Remember, we have touched on Archie, Gopher, and WAIS—software tools that help you locate other information on the Internet. We have shown you how to locate these facilities and how to use them to find what you need.

In the next chapter we'll use some of these tools to find specific information that will give you a taste of what's out there. And, we'll start building a resource list of interesting and useful things. Additionally, we'll show you how to use some useful Internet tools to talk interactively with other travelers. We'll discuss talk and send, UNIX-based commands that let you converse in real time, plus we'll introduce you to IRC (Internet Relay Chat), a fascinating, interactive discussion tool that lets you share ideas and comments with others. Finally, we'll offer some suggestions on Internet etiquette ("netiquette") and provide a brief profile of who you are likely to find on the Internet.

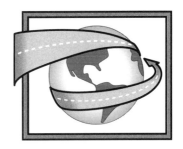

TRAVELER'S TALES: TALKING AND LISTENING

The excitement of an electronic journey often sparks from encounters with fellow travelers. Talking, sharing, arguing, and playing games are common community bonds on the Internet. In this chapter you learn how to talk more directly across the Internet. You don't have to send someone an e-mail message then wait for them to check a mailbox before they respond. You can use commands such as talk and send to exchanges messages right now. Also, an Internet-wide feature called Internet Relay Chat lets you start or join discussion groups with an unlimited number of other Internet users. We'll show you how to use these commands and more in this chapter. Among the topics we'll cover are:

+ Using Talk and Send
+ Using IRC (Internet Relay Chat)
+ Internet etiquette
+ Showing emotions
+ Exploring games

Talking on the Internet

Most of what we have talked about so far in terms of getting information across the Internet involves locating and downloading files, and using store and forward electronic mail. When you use electronic mail, you type a letter and send it to someone to read whenever they get around to checking their mailbox. There are ways to converse in real time with the people you find on the Internet. We'll talk about two of those methods, talk and IRC, in this section.

Using Talk and Send

One of the quickest and simplest ways of conveying information to someone who is on-line with you at a local or remote host is with the **talk** command. If you know that someone you want to talk with is logged on, simply issue the command:

talk username

To find out who is on the system, use the **who** command or simply **w**. These two commands display a list of current users. The **w** command adds information about what each user is doing, such as using mail, using IRC, and so on. Figure 5.1 shows results for a typical **who** command, and Figure 5.2 shows results for the **w** command on the same system. Remember, you can use **who** to display more detailed information about a specific user if you need to:

who tbadgett

Once you have determined that the person you want to contact is on the system, use talk to display a split screen like the one in Figure 5.3.

Figure 5.1

Typical who command

```
pollard   ttypc    Sep  2 13:05    (PERSIL.SLIP.UTK.)
leon      ttype    Sep  2 13:00    (DCA2.UTK.EDU)
operator  ttypf    Aug 30 16:15    (OPLOCAL3.UTCC.UT)
harp      ttyq0    Sep  1 10:35    (MAGIC.UTCC.UTK.E)
jepeway   ttyq1    Sep  2 09:05    (lemon.cs:0.0)
sunil     ttyq2    Sep  2 09:37    (polysun.engr.utk)
mkovarik  ttyq3    Sep  2 10:55    (SLEEMAN.UTCC.UTK)
kovarik   ttyq4    Sep  2 10:42    (SLEEMAN.UTCC.UTK)
rell      ttyq5    Sep  2 13:06    (DCA2.UTK.EDU)
hamed     ttyq6    Sep  2 10:19    (VISION9.ENGR.UTK)
snyder    ttyq9    Aug 30 09:21    (voodoo.utcc.utk.)
snyder    ttyqa    Aug 30 10:42    (voodoo.utcc.utk.)
springer  ttyqc    Sep  2 11:26    (ENTROPY.UTCC.UTK)
bagri     ttyqe    Sep  2 09:36    (MIRAGE.UTCC.UTK.)
bagri     ttyqf    Sep  2 09:36    (MIRAGE.UTCC.UTK.)
bagri     ttyr0    Sep  2 09:36    (MIRAGE.UTCC.UTK.)
mcconnel  ttyr1    Sep  2 11:16    (MACSTAT2.UTCC.UT)
eljazzar  ttyr8    Sep  2 11:03    (saturn.utcc.utk.)
bill      ttyr9    Sep  2 11:48    (UX.UTCC.UTK.EDU)
root      ttyra    Aug 31 12:05    (r1w2.pub:0.0)
harp      ttyrd    Sep  2 12:07    (MAGIC.UTCC.UTK.E)
root      ttyre    Aug 31 12:05    (r1w2.pub:0.0)
ximing    ttys8    Sep  1 12:15    (UTKVX1.UTK.EDU)
```

Figure 5.2

Typical w command

```
chung     ttypc    1:07pm                         -csh
leon      ttype    1:00pm                         vi .mailrc
operator  ttypf    Mon 4pm 3days                  -csh
harp      ttyq0    Wed10am 23:45        6         vi .twmrc
jepeway   ttyq1    9:05am   4:02        9     9   xterm -T
Uther -name Uther -e lo
sunil     ttyq2    9:37am      6        8     2   -sh
mkovarik  ttyq3    10:55am    12       39         -csh
kovarik   ttyq4    10:42am     5        4         -csh
rell      ttyq5    1:06pm                         w
hamed     ttyq6    10:19am  1:31                  -csh
snyder    ttyq9    Mon 9am    33                  -sh
snyder    ttyqa    Mon10am    34       36         -sh
springer  ttyqc    11:26am     4        6         rn
bagri     ttyqe    9:36am   3:31                  -sh
bagri     ttyqf    9:36am     51                  -sh
bagri     ttyr0    9:36am   1:49                  telnet utkvx3
mcconnel  ttyr1    11:16am              7     6   rn
eljazzar  ttyr8    11:03am    40                  -sh
bill      ttyr9    11:48am  1:06       12         -csh
root      ttyra    Tue12pm 2days                  -sh
harp      ttyrd    12:07pm  1:00                  -sh
root      ttyre    Tue12pm 2days                  -sh
ximing    ttys8    Wed12pm 22:19        2         -csh
```

Figure 5.3

Split talk screen

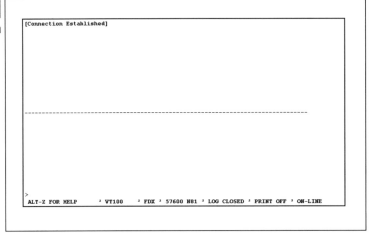

When the connection is established, anything you type appears at the top of the split screen, and whatever the other person types appears at the bottom of the screen. This is a two-way link, so you both can type at the same time. It is a useful way to share a quick bit of information with someone else on-line with you, or to ask someone a quick question.

A similar command is **send**. This is a one-way link that lets you send a sentence to a specific user. To use **send**, type the following at the system prompt:

send username

The cursor moves down one line and waits for you to type the text. You can enter one or more lines, pressing **Enter** at the end of each line. When you have entered the last line, enter a **period** (.) by itself at the beginning of the last line, and the text will be sent to the specified user.

Using IRC (Internet Relay Chat)

When you want to go beyond talking briefly with a single user, you might want to try *IRC*, the *Internet Relay Chat*. This is a varied real-time conference system that lets you talk with as many people as you like, grouped together on *channels* by topic. Many users liken IRC to on-line CB, and that's not a bad analogy.

Accessing IRC is a little like getting to Archie or Gopher. You probably have a local command file that will attach you to a pre-selected IRC server when you type the command **irc** at your service provider system prompt. Or, the following command sequence may work on your system:

irc nickname server

Contact your service provider for the precise procedure for getting access to IRC.

Once on IRC, you will be presented with a split screen. There is only one line and a status bar at the bottom of the screen, and the top part of the screen is blank (see Figure 5.4).

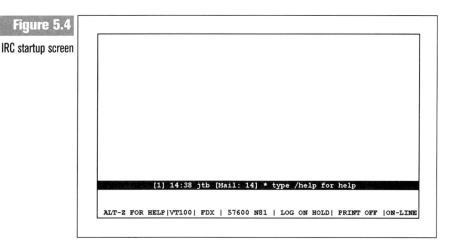

Figure 5.4

IRC startup screen

```
[1] 14:38 jtb [Mail: 14] * type /help for help

ALT-Z FOR HELP|VT100| FDX | 57600 N81 | LOG ON HOLD| PRINT OFF |ON-LINE
```

From this screen you can join a channel in progress or start your own conversation.

To find out what commands are available (and they vary slightly from server to server), type a forward slash and help: **/help**. You should see a screen similar to the one in Figure 5.5.

Figure 5.5

Sample IRC help
screen

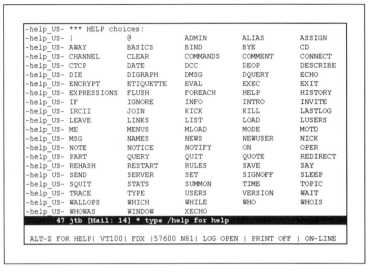

```
-help_US- *** HELP choices:
-help_US- !              @              ADMIN       ALIAS      ASSIGN
-help_US- AWAY           BASICS         BIND        BYE        CD
-help_US- CHANNEL        CLEAR          COMMANDS    COMMENT    CONNECT
-help_US- CTCP           DATE           DCC         DEOP       DESCRIBE
-help_US- DIE            DIGRAPH        DMSG        DQUERY     ECHO
-help_US- ENCRYPT        ETIQUETTE      EVAL        EXEC       EXIT
-help_US- EXPRESSIONS    FLUSH          FOREACH     HELP       HISTORY
-help_US- IF             IGNORE         INFO        INTRO      INVITE
-help_US- IRCII          JOIN           KICK        KILL       LASTLOG
-help_US- LEAVE          LINKS          LIST        LOAD       LUSERS
-help_US- ME             MENUS          MLOAD       MODE       MOTD
-help_US- MSG            NAMES          NEWS        NEWUSER    NICK
-help_US- NOTE           NOTICE         NOTIFY      ON         OPER
-help_US- PART           QUERY          QUIT        QUOTE      REDIRECT
-help_US- REHASH         RESTART        RULES       SAVE       SAY
-help_US- SEND           SERVER         SET         SIGNOFF    SLEEP
-help_US- SQUIT          STATS          SUMMON      TIME       TOPIC
-help_US- TRACE          TYPE           USERS       VERSION    WAIT
-help_US- WALLOPS        WHICH          WHILE       WHO        WHOIS
-help_US- WHOWAS         WINDOW         XECHO
         47 jtb [Mail: 14] * type /help for help

ALT-Z FOR HELP| VT100| FDX |57600 N81| LOG OPEN | PRINT OFF | ON-LINE
```

From here the best way to find out about using IRC is to use the available help topics. Try **/help etiquette**, for example, to view a file that tells you some of the conventions of using IRC. Try **/help newuser** or **/help basics** for more information on getting started.

You can find out what topics are currently being discussed and how many users are working on each topic with the **list** command:

/list

This will produce a list similar to the one in Figure 5.6, except that it will be much longer. Be aware that some of the conversations that take place on IRC are strictly adult.

When you identify a conversation you'd like to join from the list, you can type the following:

/join channelname

Your name is then added to those on that channel. Note that channels usually carry alphabetic names, such as #vine, #hamradio, or #bicycles. The pound sign (#) must be the first character in the name, but other than that requirement, a session can be named almost any way.

Figure 5.6

Partial IRC channel list

```
*** Channel    Users  Topic
    *** #pulse      4       Hey Ladies....I'm HERE!!!!!!
    *** #zircon     1
    *** #queen2     2
    *** #malacca    1
    *** #Randomnes  1       OD on BCNU -- September 6!!!
    *** #singapore  2
    *** #gbm        1       GAY_BLACK_MEN
    *** #buaya      2
    *** #omni       3
    *** #ffi        1
    *** #jen]       2
    *** #Roma       1       yes folks....that's Italian for Rome
    *** Prv         1
    *** #sexx       2
    *** Prv         2
    *** #desdemona  1
    *** #Talk      15       Stop messing with the channel!
    *** #wolvesden  1
    *** #mod        1
    *** #BoyScout   1
    *** #Sauna      1       Huh, heat ..
    *** Prv         2
    *** #Higgins    1
```

If you don't see a channel name that appeals to you, create your own by using **/join** and a name that does not already exist. Just be sure to place the pound sign at the beginning of the name. Before you create your own channel, try the **list** command. (Use **Ctrl-S** to stop the screen and **Ctrl-Q** to start it again.) Notice that some channels have a description or comment beside them. After you create your own channel, you can add comments with the **/topic** command:

/topic   <—-Wherein we discuss the weather

Then when anyone uses **/list**, your channel is displayed with this topic beside it:

#Wx   <—-Wherein we discuss the weather

When you use the **/join** command, the others on the channel will see a message:

Tom has joined Channel #Bicycle

This lets everyone on the channel know you're there. Depending on who else is in the group, you may get a series of hellos from people welcoming you, or you may feel invisible. If no one talks to you for several minutes, you might try saying something to one of the other participants.

Pick a nickname and type a message that begins with the name:

Curly: I'm really interested in the trip you mentioned. Tell me more.

Without knowing who this person is, it is impossible to predict the response. You may get something like:

Who are you?

At that point, respond with your nickname and perhaps your city. Each participant's nickname is displayed at the beginning of the line, but unless someone goes out of the way to find out more, that's all anyone knows.

If no one responds to you at this point you can figure you have just joined a tightly closed clique. You might as well use **/leave channel** (where **channel** is the name of the channel you just joined) to back out of that conversation and move on somewhere else. In the unlikely event that you get an abusive message when you log on (**Get out of here! Who do you think you are?**), simply type **/leave channel** and don't go back. You gain nothing in arguing with boorish, inconsiderate people. When you're ready to leave IRC entirely, use **/quit** on the command line to return to your local host.

What about using some of the IRC commands after you get linked up with someone on a channel? Maybe you'd like to find out if there is anyone on IRC from Canada. Use the **/who** command with some additional information:

/who *.ca

You'll get a list of users currently logged on to any channel with **.ca** as the last entry in their user ID. This is the international abbreviation for Canada.

To find out who is on your channel, use **/who** with the channel name:

/who #tea

You'll get a display that shows you the real names, host names, and other information about everyone currently logged on to the channel **#Tea**.

Suppose you suspect that someone you know is on IRC somewhere, but you don't know where. You can use **/who** to find out. Just join a channel (some **/who** features don't work if you're not on a channel), then use **/who** with the name of the person you're looking for. The display will show you that person's name and which channel he or she is currently on.

When you join an IRC channel, you are identified by the nickname you used to log on to IRC. You can change this with the **/nick** command:

/nick tomtom

IRC displays a message like: **Tom is now known as tomtom.**

Learning your way around IRC is a lot like learning another language, finding your way around a new town, or playing blindman's buff. But there's also nothing like it. Get on, browse around, use **/help** as often as you need, and ask questions of those you meet. Soon you'll be a veteran traveler, one whose IRC passport is full of stamps and whose memories are sharp and fresh. Enjoy!

INTERNET CULTURE

Whenever any group gathers, whether you realize it consciously or not, there is an underlying culture that most people observe—a set of rules or guidelines of language, behavior, and common history. As you move from one group to another—from family to work to school and so on—the culture changes. You have a different relationship with members of your family during breakfast than you do with your coworkers at the office. There's also a difference between the relationship among you and your coworkers and between you and the boss.

The same is true as you travel the Internet. In general, you should approach the people and groups you meet on the Internet as you would coworkers in your office. The relationship will be semi-formal and generally relaxed. As you spend more time on conferences and talking within groups, you will find a few individuals or groups with whom you are more comfortable.

It has been said many times, but we'll say it again here: don't get lulled into a false sense of detachment as you exchange electronic mail or live conversations. We see a lot of messages cross the Internet in conferences and other public places where it is obvious that a couple of individuals have a history of disagreement. Their written tone is inappropriate, their language harsh. It is impolite to impose this kind of personal conflict on the others who share the conference.

Also, even as you get to know one or more individuals better than others, maintain a sense of restraint and propriety. Until you know who you really are talking with, there's no way to know who is on the other end of the wire.

Who is Internet?

The Internet is composed of companies, groups, and individuals from virtually all walks of life. The sameness of the text-based screen strips away the size of the office, the cut of the suit, the glitter of the diamonds, and the shape of the bike. We've talked to company presidents, government officials, college students, teachers, housewives, and elementary school kids.

What comes through is the knowledge each individual brings to the keyboard, a sense of helpfulness, a willingness to share, a tolerance for and acceptance of those who know less or whose lifestyle may be different.

The point is, don't ever assume anything about another Internet user. Just as you would when meeting someone in person for the first time, maintain a courteous, open demeanor as you get to know each other.

Internet Etiquette (Netiquette)

Etiquette in any social situation is a varied and personal call. What is appropriate for one group or pair of individuals may be unsuitable for someone else. Our best advice is to try to match your language and tone to that of the others with whom you relate on the Internet. And, trite as it may seem, the golden rule—treat others like you want to be treated—is hard to beat as a general operating principal.

Language

We've mentioned earlier in this book that there are occasions on the Internet when language becomes raw. It depends on your background and orientation, of course, but we don't believe it is necessary or appropriate to sprinkle your Internet conversation with four letter words, personal or racial slurs, or any other language that might be offensive to the person you are talking with or to anyone else who may view the message.

You will see some of this on the Internet, unfortunately. When it occurs it is best ignored. Calling attention to someone else's inappropriate behavior won't usually gain you anything and may in fact cause another inappropriate barrage.

Such comments on the Internet are called *flames* and the person who acts this way is sometimes called a *flamer*.

Joining Conversations

Conferences and IRC conversations are generally open so that anyone can wander through the electronic room where they are taking place and listen in or comment. Just as you would slowly approach two people standing together talking, you should develop the habit of making yourself known if you want to join a discussion, and then wait to be recognized.

In addition, make sure you are up to speed on what is being discussed and who is taking part in the conversation before you jump in. As we've said, it is sometimes easy to let the electronic medium isolate you from the people on the other end of the link to the point that normal social conventions that you follow automatically in person get sidestepped. Just be aware that this is a possibility and move slowly. You'll be glad you paused to review what you said before pressing **Return** to send that e-mail message. It takes only a moment, and it can save face if you tend to react too quickly.

Introductions

As a participant in an existing conversation or conference, you can do your part to make new people feel welcome (if they are!) by doing what you would do in person: introduce people to each other.

Suppose you're on an IRC channel and see a message like:

Blondie has joined Channel: #vine

If you know who Blondie is (a friend, perhaps, or someone you met on another conference), then you can mention to others on the conference or IRC channel who Blondie is, how you know this person, and any special interests she may have. This helps others understand who they are talking to.

Showing Emotions

As we have said, the text-oriented screen tends to cause some isolation among Internet users. It is easy for conversations to become rather staid. Over the years, conventions have evolved for showing emotions that can spice up your conversation and help others understand your current state of mind.

Probably the most common symbol for showing emotions that you're likely to see is the smiley face:

:)

Sometimes you get a variation on the basic face:

:-)

Or a winking smiley face:

;-)

Or one with glasses:

8-)

Then of course, when things aren't going too well, or the topic is a sad one (such as "I have a dental appointment after school"):

:(or :-(

By convention, these *emoticons* are also used:

(@@)	you're kidding
:-1	smirk
:-D	said with a smile

You may see others. Different groups use different symbols. Use your imagination, squint a little, and you'll be able to understand what is being said.

You can also specify emotions by spelling out a word. Usually you surround the emotion in asterisks:

grins
sigh
poor me
giggle

You get the idea. As you are talking, or within e-mail messages, you can tell the other person what you are feeling with one or two word statements like this surrounded in asterisks.

You can also explain actions, either to be funny or to describe what is happening on your end. Suppose you just spilled a coke on your keyboard:

***ACTION: Clumsily Tom knocks over the glass.

Or someone on your link says something that makes you happy ("I'm sending you a report that will answer all those questions and more."):

***ACTION: Tom stands up, jumps up and down, shouts!

As you get more experience with real-time links you will become creative in expressing yourself. It adds life to the conversation and makes you and the people you meet more relaxed. Just remember the first rule we mentioned earlier—be polite, reasonably reserved, and slow to jump in. Once you have gotten "in" with a group, however, be yourself, say what you feel, and show what you feel. It's fun!

GAMES

Just traveling around the Internet is fun, even if all you do is poke around looking at conversations and finding files. However, there are other things you can do besides talk with other travelers. There are interactive games you can play by yourself or with others.

What would traveling be like without games? Your family vacation is headed for problems if there aren't enough games in the back seat to keep the kids happy in the car. Your Internet travels also lack something if you don't investigate the games you can find there. We can't possibly show you where all the games on the Internet are, but we can point you in the right direction.

Here's one way to start researching Internet games on your own with Archie.

At your local host, execute the Archie client, if you have access to one. (If you don't know what this means, re-read the discussion of Archie in Chapter 4.) If you don't have a client, telnet to one of the available Archie sites. Once you are in Archie (or the client), issue this command:

prog game

You should get a familiar Archie list of hosts, directories, and files similar to Figure 5.7.

Figure 5.7

Portion of Archie
PROG game
search results

```
>prog game
Processing Case Insensitive Substring Search for 'game'

Host iamsun.unibe.ch

Location: /
        DIRECTORY drwxrwxr-x          512  Aug 24 1992  games

Host hpcsos.col.hp.com

Location: /mirrors/.scsi5/386BSD/0.1-ports
        DIRECTORY drwxr-xr-x         1024  Jun 16 02:16  games
Location: /mirrors/.scsi5/hp95lx
        DIRECTORY drwxr-xr-x         1024  Aug 30 01:36  games

Host inf.informatik.uni-stuttgart.de

Location: /pub/archive/comp.sources/amiga
        DIRECTORY drwxr-xr-x          512  Mar 30 11:02  games
Location: /pub/archive/comp.sources
        DIRECTORY drwxrwxr-x         4608  Sep  1 00:04  games

Host irisa.irisa.fr

Location: /pub
        DIRECTORY drwxr-xr-x          512  Jul  2 15:49  games

Host grasp1.univ-lyon1.fr

Location: /pub/faq-by-newsgroup/rec/rec.games.empire
        DIRECTORY drwxrwxr-x          512  Aug  6 23:20  games
Location: /pub/faq-by-newsgroup/rec/rec.games.frp.announce
        DIRECTORY drwxrwxr-x          512  Feb  7 00:00  games
```

The listing in Figure 5.7 is a partial one. Notice how many of the directories in the list have the name **games**. There's no real way to know exactly what is in there, but the parent directories (the ones above the games directories) give you some hints. Notice the series of directories at the **grasp1.univ-lyon1.fr** host, for example. (This domain name indicates that the host is in France at the University of Lyon.) There are several game directories that have **/pub/faq-by-newsgroup/rec** as the parent. You can guess that the directories under this parent will deal with recreation topics (**rec**), and that it includes newsgroups and will deal with frequently asked questions (**faq**) stored in a public directory (**pub**).

If you ftp to this site, then change to one of the game directories under this parent, you can use **ls** to see what is there. Here's the complete process from your local host. Enter these commands and you should get the results we show. Remember to turn on screen capture or a log file within your communications package to save information to disk. (We have eliminated some of the login banners for clarity.)

> **telnet archie.sura.net**

login: **qarchie**

>**prog game**

Processing Case Insensitive Substring Search for 'game'

This will produce the listing shown in Figure 5.7. When the listing is through, exit Archie by typing **quit** at the prompt:

> **quit**

Now you are back at your local host and you're ready to use ftp to get some of the information you've found. Try any directory you like, but here's one sample series of commands that will show you how to explore these game directories on your own:

> **ftp grasp1.univ-lyon1.fr**
Name (grasp1.univ-lyon1.fr:tbadgett): **anonymous**
331 Guest login ok, send your complete e-mail address as password.
Password:

At the **Password:** prompt, enter your complete mailing address. The system will display the **ftp>** prompt and wait for your command. Enter the following:

ftp> **cd /pub/faq-by-newsgroup/rec/rec.games.netrek/games**

250 CWD command successful.

ftp> **ls**
200 PORT command successful.
150 Opening ASCII mode data connection for file list.
netrek
226 Transfer complete.
8 bytes received in 3e-06 seconds (2.6e+03 Kbytes/s)
ftp> **cd netrek**
250 CWD command successful.
ftp> **ls**
200 PORT command successful.
150 Opening ASCII mode data connection for file list.
faq
server-list
ftp-list
226 Transfer complete.
28 bytes received in 0.02 seconds (1.4 Kbytes/s)
ftp> **get faq**
200 PORT command successful.
150 Opening ASCII mode data connection for faq (17844 bytes).
226 Transfer complete.
local: faq remote: faq
18279 bytes received in 1.8 seconds (9.8 Kbytes/s)

Now you have the file **faq** on your local host. This file is a text file that includes the answers to many questions about the networked game Netrek, which is played by teams of players simultaneously. Follow the same procedure to get the remaining files in this directory, and you have the basis for learning about playing an interactive, multi-user Star Trek-type game over the Internet. When you have all the files you want from this server, type **close** to stay in ftp but disconnect from the Univ-Lyon1 host. Now you can use the **open** command to attach to another ftp site and browse for more files or games. If you are through with ftp, type **quit** to return to your local host.

There are many other networked and single-user games you can play on your PC, Amiga, or Macintosh. Simply use ftp to get to the listed site, use **cd** to change to the directory that contains the information you want, then use **get** to copy the files from the remote host to your local host. If you want to get the games over to your own desktop Macintosh or PC, use Kermit, ZMODEM, or another protocol. See the discussion of protocol transfers in Chapter 4.

To find out more about Internet game playing, get onto IRC (see discussion earlier in this chapter) and look for a discussion group about games or entertainment. Join the conference and ask a lot of questions. With few exceptions, the people on the Internet are more than willing to help you find what you're looking for.

If you look around you'll find servers for popular board games such as chess, bridge, go, backgammon, and maybe Scrabble. Use Gopher or Archie to scan the network for games or game topics that interest you. See the Internet Reference Section in Chapter 6 for a listing of other games available on Internet.

What You Learned

This has been a fairly focused chapter. We have discussed how to talk to other users directly, either by using Talk or Send for one-on-one communications, or by using IRC for general discussion with many users. These facilities are useful additions to the general network features of e-mail and file storage. They bring the Internet alive, making it full of people with feelings, skills, and interests that match your own or lead you into entirely new directions.

These facilities, like most of what you'll find on the Internet, are best learned with hands-on practice. That should be your next step after studying this lesson: get on the Internet and try talking to someone or joining an IRC channel. This is how you find your way through new territory.

In the next chapter we will show you some specific places to look for interesting conversations or files to read. Chapter 6 will serve as an on-going reference as you use the Internet to search for specific information. You can also use the reference information in Chapter 6 to get you started with your Internet travels.

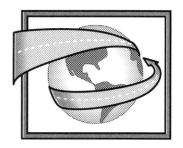

Chapter Six

COLLECTING SOUVENIRS ON THE INTERNET

As you roam around the Internet you will find interesting reference files, graphics images, sound files, names and addresses, and other items of interest. In addition, you can start with an idea of something you'd like to find or learn, then go to the Internet to search it out.

This chapter can serve as a reference of interesting and educational items you might want to look for on the Internet. Pick some items at random and practice your searching skills, then refer back to this chapter as you think of specific areas you want to research or learn.

In this chapter we're going to list and describe many of the souvenirs and treasures we have found on the Internet as a way of helping you find your own collectables. We can't possibly show you everything that's out there—and our treasures may be your junk—but from our descriptions and road maps you can get into areas you might not have found alone.

We have organized information into groups analogous to the USENET newsgroups we described earlier—with some poetic license. You will find Internet resources grouped under these headings:

◆ Computers

◆ Science and Other Technology

◆ Recreation

◆ Commercial and Business

◆ Religion

◆ Education

◆ Government

◆ Reference

◆ Art

◆ Miscellaneous

We have one or more subgroups within some of these broad areas. The groups and subgroups are set up as table of contents entries, so you can turn back to the table of contents for a quick outline-type summary of what you might find in this chapter. In addition, the index lists most of the items you'll find here by topic and description. And, of course, you can just turn through the pages and see what names, headings, or descriptions capture you attention.

Some of the entries will show you simply where to find the information on the Internet. With some entries we'll provide descriptions depending on the information we have and, frankly, on our level of interest in the topic. Most of the resources we mention are accessible via ftp or by sending an e-mail message asking for more information. Others are reached with telnet.

Use this listing as you would any telephone directory or catalog, remembering that things on the Internet change rapidly. If we tell you how to find something and you can't locate it where we said, you can assume that it has been removed or moved. If it has been removed, there's not much you can do. If, on the other hand, it has been moved, you might look around and find it. We have discovered, for example, that as the number of files in a particular area gets larger, system managers frequently create another subdirectory for that group of files.

So, if we tell you that a series of files on baboon feeding habits is at a certain host in the subdirectory **/pub/sci/animal** and you can't find them there, try another directory. It might be that the diversity of the animal directory grew to the point that a separate directory was created for **baboons**. Use **ls** to see what files are there, then try **cd** to change to the baboons directory if it is listed. Then your files would be in the directory **/pub/sci/animal/baboons**.

With most systems, when you enter via ftp you have a fair amount of freedom to move among directories and look for entries. Before you leave where you are, use **pwd** to list the current directory. Then you can try **whereis** to look for files of interest on that system.

If, after trying all this, the files you thought should be there can't be found, you might as well go on to another topic. In all likelihood the files have been moved to another system or deleted. Sorry! But the dynamic nature of the Internet is one of its many appeals, isn't it?

We also urge you to try Gopher, Archie and other tools you'll find along the way. Browsing the Internet is like looking up something in an encyclopedia. You start out looking for one thing and end up finding something else as well.

Because you most likely are dealing with UNIX-based systems as you travel the Internet, remember that what you enter at any prompt is probably case sensitive. If we tell you to look for something in the **/pub/libraries/INFO.net/Files** directory, for example, you must enter the path exactly as indicated, using the same upper and lower case combinations. Otherwise, you probably will get an error message indicating that no such file or directory exists.

The directories and resources we list are only a small portion of what any listed server has available. Once you have connected to an ftp site to download one specific file, look around and see what else is there. Chances are that there are lots of additional offerings you might want as well.

INTERNET TOOLS: A REFRESHER

We've already shown you how to use Archie, Gopher, and WAIS to locate information on the Internet, and we've discussed ftp as a way to download that data. For full details on these topics, refer to Chapter 4. Here we will present a quick reference to finding an information searching server, so you'll have it here, with the information we discuss in this chapter.

Archie Reference

Archie is a facility for searching Internet files for words or characters that you specify. It is a way of finding all files that deal with a specific topic.

You usually access Archie through a local client that attaches to a remote server. To get to your client, try one of the following commands: **Archie, QArchie,** or **XArchie.**

If none of these work, contact your service provider to see if there is another Archie command that you should use. If not, you can access an Archie server directly via telnet. The syntax is **telnet ArchieServerName,** where **ArchieServerName** is the address shown in the list.

When you have established a connection to an Archie server, either via telnet or through a local client, use **prog text** to find a topic, where text is a one-word topic you'd like to find. This will locate the names of files that include the text you specified.

You can narrow the search by adding additional parameters to the search line, as we showed in Chapter 4.

If you don't find what you want by searching for file names, try the **whatis** command, which searches a database of topics instead of file names. For example, a file named **elemedu** may contain information about elementary education, but if you conduct an Archie file search for **education** or **elementary,** you won't find it. The subject database will list this file along with the topics it contains.

Gopher Reference

The Gopher utility presents a menu-driven interface that lets you browse for topics. Like Archie, Gopher is accessed through a local client that attaches to a remote server (in most cases). The command **gopher** (or **xgopher**) at your local prompt should get you on-line with a Gopher server. If not, contact your service provider.

You can use Gopher itself to find out more details about Gopher. For example, if you launch Gopher at **gopher.tc.umn. edu** (University of Minnesota—a popular Gopher server), you can select "All the Gopher Servers in the World/" under "Other Gopher and Information Servers/" from the main menu. This will lead you down a winding path of server site and Gopher information.

You can also ftp information about Gopher by using the following commands:

ftp rtfm.mit.edu
cd /pub/usenet/news.answers
get gopher-faq

WAIS Reference

WAIS (Wide Area Information Servers) is another searching tool. WAIS—pronounced "ways"—accesses information like Gopher but provides a searchable user interface more like Archie. Try **wais** or **swais** at your system prompt to access a local client that will attach automatically to one of the available WAIS servers. If that doesn't work, use Archie and **prog wais** to locate a WAIS server. Then you can use telnet to attach to WAIS.

ftp Reference

When you find a file with Archie, you have to use ftp to get it to your system where you can read it. You may also use ftp with Gopher and WAIS, or you may be able to download files directly inside these utilities.

To use ftp, first identify the host name where the information you want to access is located. Then use this command:

ftp hostname

When the host answers and displays a **login:** prompt, type **anonymous** or **ftp** (these terms are synonymous). Use your full mailing address as the password. You should see a prompt such as:

ftp>

Now you can set the current directory with the **cd** command, list the files with **ls**, and use **get** to copy a file or files from the remote machine to the home directory on your machine.

Remember that ftp can transfer files in ASCII (text) or binary format, but that the default format is ASCII. Before you transfer a program file or any file with a **.Z**, **.ZIP**, or **.GZ** extension, type **binary** at the ftp prompt. This will change the ASCII default to binary, ensuring a reliable file transfer. If you fail to do this, compressed files will transfer as text, and you won't be able to uncompress them once you have them copied.

INTERNET REFERENCE GUIDE

In this section we'll show you a sampling of information available on the Internet, organized by major topics. Practice using Archie, Gopher, WAIS, and ftp with the files and addresses we provide here. Then you can go out on your own looking for topics we didn't include for you.

Computers

It is appropriate that the network that ties together so many different computer systems would provide a lot of information about the technology it serves. From computer games and technology, to software, security and networking data, you can find a lot of information about computers on the Internet.

Computer Security

```
ftp cert.sei.cmu.edu
cd /pub
```

Use **dir** or **ls** to locate a variety of files and directories. You can find a variety of information from CERT, the Computer Emergency Response Team, a federally-funded group that works in the field of computer and network security.

Computer Ethics

```
ftp ariel.unm.edu
cd /ethics
```

Use **ls** or **dir** to find a variety of files that deal with computer use and ethics. The data includes a bibliography of Canadian and U.S. articles, the Bitnet abuse policy, and information on laws that cover computer crime.

Archive/Compression Information

```
ftp ux1.cso.uiuc.edu
cd /doc/pcnet
get compression
```

This file lists in a table form the various archive and compression utilities available for MS-DOS and UNIX platforms. In addition to providing an excellent reference to programs and file types, this file points you in the right direction to finding the software for yourself.

Free Computer Software

```
ftp prep.ai.mit.edu
cd /pub/gnu
```

This directory contains a number of "public" software offerings, primarily for UNIX platforms. This software is offered under the umbrella of the Free Software Foundation (FSF), an organization that creates and distributes software without fee or license restrictions.

Get the file COPYING for information on the "general public license," under which this software is distributed.

You can get more information by sending e-mail to gnu@prep.ai.mit.edu.

MS-DOS ARCHIVE

If you are into studying MS DOS machines and learning what others are saying about MS DOS and doing with it, send an e-mail message to **listserv@TACOM-EMH1.Army.Mil**. Place the command **subscribe msdos-ann** in the body of the message. This will get you on the MS DOS mailing list. Remember, if you want to turn off your subscription, send an e-mail message to listserv@TACOM-EMH1.Army.Mil and include the message **unsubscribe msdos-ann**.

INTERNET

ftp nic.funet.fi
get README.FILETYPES
From the default (/) directory. Common Internet file types. Useful reference.

ftp nic.sura.net
cd /pub/nic/internet.literature

Use **ls** to view available files and directories.

ANNOTATED LIST OF PUBLIC, OPEN ACCESS UNIX SITES

ftp gvl.unisys.com
cd /pub/pubnet
get nixpub.long

This is an excellent list of UNIX systems that may be useful to you in arranging SLIP/PPP or other dial-in access to the Internet. In addition to the NIXPUB file, you'll find a number of other interesting postings at this location.

KNOWBOT

As you roam the Internet you'll encounter interesting characters with "bot" in their name, or who introduce themselves as **some-**

thing bot. These are software robots that are written to perform a variety of information services, such as automatically logging onto a service, searching for certain strings of characters and providing a pre-programmed response, and other jobs.

One interesting bot is the KnowBot Information Service. It is really a database of Internet services, hosts, and users that you can search for data. Here's how to get to it:

telnet regulus.cs.bucknell.edu 185

You don't have to log on; you are attached automatically to the KnowBot server.

The number after this telnet command (185 in this case) is a port number. This is a way of entering a remote host in a special way, triggering onsite software to handle the logon. Usually when you telnet to a specific port number, the remote host will log you on automatically and launch a specific utility or service. In this case, it is the KnowBot service.

Figure 6.1 show the opening screen, while Figure 6.2 lists available commands on this service.

Figure 6.1	
| Opening KnowBot screen | ```
Connected to regulus.bucknell.edu.
Escape character is '^]'.
Knowbot Information Service (V1.0). Copyright CNRI 1990. All Rights Reserved.
Try ? or man for help.
>
``` |

Type **man** at the KnowBot prompt to display a manual entry telling you how to issue commands and find the data you want to locate.
```

```
Queries must be longer than one character, must start with an alphabetic
character, and cannot be a common word such as netaddress, whois or finger.

Commands are:
-------------
service   service@host [service@host ...]
services
org       organization
country   country
echo      [on|off]
ident     service-specific-identifier
print
query     username
username  (where ``username'' is the name
          to be searched for
help, ?   print this summary
man       print manual page entry
quit
exit
```

SOUND FILES

Look for an increasing number of picture, sound, and motion video files on the Internet. These are just a portion of what's out there. Download these **.au** files for use directly on a Sun or compatible workstation. To play them on a PC or anything else, you'll need to convert them. A program called SOX will do this. Get it in the **/pub/SoundConversion** directory. Get the file appropriate for your system. **sox7dos.zip**, for example, is the current MS-DOS version. Be sure to get **sox.doc** for information on using the programs as well.

Here are a few representative sounds you can find out there. If you're using MS Windows you can use SOX to convert to .WAV format, then use these sounds in your Windows programs, including Media Player. You can use the **.au** files directly on your Sun workstation.

```
ftp sunsite.unc.edu
cd /pub/multimedia/sun-sounds/startrek
get energy_loss.au

ftp athena.sdsu.edu
cd /.1/sound_effects
get Tire_skids.au
```

cd /.1/cartoons/simpsons
get Krusty-Hey_Kids.au
get Gracie_Films.au

Also check out the **/Sounds** and **/.1/cartoons** directories for more sounds.

ftp ftp.cica.indiana.edu
cd /pub/pc/win3/uploads/JUN93
get jurassic.txt
get jurassic.zip
(Contains WAV files from the movie *Jurassic Park*)

ftp sunsite.unc.edu
cd /pub/multimedia/chinese-music/Traditional_Music
get E05.Life_Of_Leisure.au

ftp athena.sdsu.edu
cd /.1/movies
get You_a_college_boy_.au

ftp ftp.luth.se
cd /pub/sounds/athena.sdsu.edu/.0/rem
get religion.au

Network Information

As you might expect, you can use the resources of the Internet to learn about the Internet and other network resources. For example, suppose you want to send e-mail to someone on FIDOnet, but you don't know their address. Use the **fidonet-nodelist** entry in WAIS to search for the name, then get the list.

Here are some other network information resources you can access on Internet.

ftp ftp.msstate.edu
cd /pub/docs
get internetwork-mail-guide

This is an on-line mail guide to help you use the mail facilities of the Internet, particularly internetwork mailing. Also try **get finding-addresses** for additional information. And:

```
cd internet
get college-mail-addresses
get internet.library

cd bitnet
get HANDBOOK
get bitnet.intro
get bitnet.servers
get where.to.start
```

This series of files will give you a good overview of bitnet and get you started with it.

```
ftp nic.ddn.mil
cd /rfc
```

Use **dir** to list the files there, a series of rfcs (request for comment). These are files that describe how the Internet works, how to use it, and what its future might be. You'll find files in various formats here, from text to PostScript. This is a large directory with over 1,300 files when this book was written. Obviously, this is a dynamic resource that changes as new comments are added. The files are named with numbers, so there's no way to know from the file name what the topic of the file might be.

You can get a clue to what's here with the **fyi-by-title.txt file** and the **fyi-index.txt file**. Use **get** to download them to your system, then use **!cat** to view them, or exit to your local host and use an editor to look at them.

```
ftp boulder.colorado.edu
cd /pub/news-talk
get What_is_USENET?
```

This is a file that gives you some insight into USENET (as the title suggests). It is a good place to start understanding this sometimes slippery world of the Internet. And, there are a number of other USENET-related files in this subdirectory.

Freenets

Remember that the majority of freenets are configured similarly, using the "city" metaphor. Look for interesting or useful information according to its location within the city.

telnet freenet-in-a.cwru.edu

You will get an opening screen. Just follow directions. As with many freenets, there is a maximum number of users. If the system is full, you will receive a message telling you to try again later.

Heartland Free-Net

Peoria - 674-1100 Bloomington-Normal - 438-2300
telnet heartland.bradley.edu
login: bbguest

This is a freenet funded by a variety of private and public sponsors, including, Caterpillar, Inc., Illinois State University, Peoria Journal Star, Illinois Bell, and others.

Through this system you can browse as a visitor, or access more facilities as a registered user. Either way, there's no charge, except that out of state residents must pay a $5.00 registration fee. Among the features of this freenet are:

1. Send and receive electronic mail from other Registered Users.
2. Link to Other Selected Computer Systems on the Internet.
3. Pose anonymous questions to experts in a field within the Free-net system to which you may not normally have access.
4. Exchange ideas with other users in the Public Forum or in any of the Open Discussion Areas of the Free-net.

Youngstown Freenet

telnet yfn.ysu.edu
login: visitor

As a guest you can browse the freenet and read messages. However, to post any messages of your own, you'll need to register. The system is offered at no charge under the sponsorship of the St. Elizabeth Hospital Medical Center and Youngstown State University. After a brief opening message, you'll see the main menu screen shown in Figure 6.3.

Figure 6.3

Main Youngstown Freenet menu screen

```
<<< Main Menu >>>

 1 Administration
 2 Post Office
 3 The Public Square
 4 The Communications Center
 5 The Animal Hospital
 6 The Business & Industrial Park
 7 The Computer Center
 8 The Courthouse
 9 The Government Center
10 The Hospital
11 The House of Worship
12 The Human Services Building
13 The Teleport
14 The USA/Today Headline News
15 Youngstown State University
16 Academy One
--------------------------------------------------
h=Help, x=Exit YFN, "go help"=extended help

Your Choice ==>

ALT-Z FOR HELP|VT100|FDX|57600 N81 |LOG CLOSED | PRINT OFF | ON-LINE

—
```

NATIONAL CAPITAL FREENET

telnet freenet.carleton.ca
login: guest

The main National Capital Freenet menu screen is shown in Figure 6.4.

VICTORIA FREENET

telnet freenet.victoria.bc.ca
login: guest

The main Victoria Freenet screen is shown in Figure 6.5.

Figure 6.4

National Capital
Freenet main menu
screen

```
        <<< NATIONAL CAPITAL FREENET - MAIN MENU >>>

     1 About The National Capital Freenet...
     2 Administration...
     3 Post Office...
     4 Public Discussion...
     5 Social Services, Health, & Environment Centre...
     6 Community Associations...
     7 The Government Centre...
     8 Science, Engineering and Technology Centre...
     9 Schools, Colleges and Universities...
    10 The Newsstand...
    11 Libraries...
    12 Special Interest Groups...
    13 Communications...
    14 Professional Associations...
    15 Help Desk...
    16 Menu en francais (en developpement)
    17 Federal Election All Candidates Meeting...
    ------------------------------------------------------
    h=Help, x=Exit FreeNet, p=previous menu, m=main menu
    Your Choice ==>

    ALT-Z FOR HELP | VT100|FDX|57600 N81|LOG CLOSED|PRINT OFF | ON-LINE
```

Figure 6.5

Main Victoria
Freenet screen

```
                    Welcome to the VICTORIA FREE-NET

    *** MAIN MENU ***
    ==> go main

      1 Victoria Free-Net Headquarters (Register Here)
      2 Commerce Building
      3 Douglas & Yates ... the Hangout!
      4 Government Building
      5 House of Worship
      6 Library and Information Services
      7 Local/Global Community Centre
      8 Medical Centre
      9 Post Office
     10 Schoolhouse
     11 Science and Environment Centre
     12 Special Interest Groups (SIGs)
     13 Help Desk
     14 >>> FEDERAL ELECTION 1993 <<<
    ----------------------------------------------------------------------
    ------
    h=Help, x=Exit Free-Net, m=Main Menu, p=Previous Menu, "go
    help"=Extended Help

    Your Choice ==>

    ALT-Z FOR HELP| VT100| FDX|57600 N81 | LOG CLOSED | PRINT OFF | ON-LINE
```

TALLAHASSEE FREENET

telnet freenet.scri.fsu.edu
login: visitor

This freenet is sponsored by a number of public and private institutions, including IBM, DEC, the City of Tallahassee, Florida State University and Apalachee Federation of Jewish Charities. This information is shown in the opening screen (Figure 6.6).

Figure 6.6

Opening Tallahassee Freenet screen

```
                    Welcome to Tallahassee Free-Net

                           Sponsored by:

        Apogee Systems                   Cabletron
        Centel                          City of Tallahassee
        Digital Equipment Corporation   Florida State University
        I B M                           Leon County
        Leon County Public Library      Sun MicroSystems
        Xyplex


                  With additional support provided by:

                Apalachee Federation of Jewish Charities
                         Broad and Cassel
                        Computer 101, Inc.
                        Leon County Schools
                      Williams, Cox, Weidner & Cox

       ... Press the <Return> or <Enter> key to continue ...
       ALT-Z FOR HELP|VT100|FDX|57600 N81 | LOG CLOSED | PRINT OFF | ON-LINE
```

The main menu for this system is shown in Figure 6.7.

For other freenet information, send e-mail to bbslist@aug3.augsburg.edu. Just a mail message is all that is required, no subject or body necessary. This will get you three very interesting lists.

Figure 6.7

Main Tallahassee
Freenet menu screen

```
TALLAHASSEE FREE-NET MAIN MENU

  1.   All About Free-Net
  2.   Mail Service for Registered Users
  3.   Social Services and Organizations
  4.   Business & Professional Services
  5.   Medical & Health Services
  6.   Agriculture Center
  7.   Government Complex
  8.   Education Complex
  9.   Religion Center
 10.   Science and Technology Center
 11.   Home and Garden Center
 12.   Library Complex
 13.   Community Center
 14.   Disabilities Information
 15.   Free-Net Information & Messages from 9/7/93


(x) Exit
Your Choice:


SNAPSHOT   | VT100 | FDX | 57600 N81 | LOG CLOSED | PRINT OFF | ON-LINE
```

Science And Other Technology

Weather

WEATHER SERVICE

telnet downwind.sprl.umich.edu 3000

Offers city and state weather forecasts, ski conditions, earthquake reports, and other weather information. You are logged on automatically (without a username or password) to the University of Michigan WEATHER UNDERGROUND. At the first prompt you can enter the three-digit identifier for your location (these are FAA and Weather Service identifiers that usually are related to the local weather station or airport). You will see a weather summary like the one in Figure 6.8.

```
Weather Conditions at 5 PM EDT on 13 SEP 93 for Knoxville, TN.
Temp(F)    Humidity(%)    Wind(mph)    Pressure(in)    Weather
====================================================================
  86          42%          SW at 9       30.16      Mostly Cloudy


KNOXVILLE AND VICINITY FORECAST
NATIONAL WEATHER SERVICE KNOXVILLE TN
515 PM EDT MON SEP 13 1993

  TONIGHT...FAIR AND NOT AS COOL. LOW IN THE MID 60S.  WIND SOUTHWEST 5 MPH.
  TUESDAY...PARTLY SUNNY WITH A 20 PERCENT CHANCE OF AFTERNOON THUNDERSTORMS.
HIGH IN THE UPPER 80S.  WIND SOUTHWEST 10 MPH.
  TUESDAY NIGHT...SCATTERED SHOWERS AND THUNDERSTORMS.  LOW IN THE MID 60S.
RAIN CHANCE 40 PERCENT.
  WEDNESDAY...RAIN LIKELY AND NOT AS WARM.  HIGH IN THE LOWER 80S.
RAIN CHANCE 60 PERCENT.


  EXTENDED FORECAST...
    Press Return to continue, M to return to menu, X to exit:
  ALT-Z FOR HELP | VT100  | FDX | 57600 N81 | LOG OPEN  | PRINT OFF | ON-LINE
```

The service is menu driven after that. You can display the three-digit city codes to help you find yours. You can print climactic data for a selected city, and so on.

Below are sources for additional weather information.

> ftp lemming.uvm.edu
> cd /pub/rec.windsurfing
> get net-weather

Rec.windsurfing is a newsgroup directory that includes a lot of information on windsurfing as well as on the weather. Additional subdirectories under this one contain .GIF and .JPG images (See INDEX.gif for a visual index) as well as a series of files about windsurfing destinations and, of course, the weather information we promised.

WEATHER MAPS

You can also access weather maps via Internet provided as GIF files. Try:

> ftp vmd.cso.uiuc.edu
> cd /wx

Use **ls** or **dir** to view available information. See also Aviation listings.

ENERGY REFERENCE

> ftp plaza.aarnet.edu.au
> cd /usenet/FAQs/sci.energy

Use **ls** to view available files.

> ftp world.std.com
> cd /obi/Economics/energy
> get energy.zip

> ftp cobalt.cco.caltech.edu
> cd /pub/bjmccall/Clint.pos
> get energy.txt

> ftp bruno.cs.colorado.edu
> cd /pub/cs/distribs/energy-shootout

Use **ls** to view file names.

> ftp sunsite.unc.edu
> cd /pub/academic/environment/alternative-energy/miscella-
> neous/sci.energy

Use **ls** to view file names.

> cd /pub/academic/geography/COGS/Oil_n_Gas
> get energy.doc
> cd /pub/academic/political-science/speeches/clinton-positions
> get energy.txt

> ftp lth.se
> cd /pub/netnews/sys.sun/volume91/jun
> get SCSI.II.literature

OBSERVATORY DATA

You can access some U.S. Naval Observatory files via the Internet. The information is varied, from gps (Global Positioning System) to LORAN navigation data. Not only can you access the standard time services, but also learn a lot about the Observatory. Here's how to get there:

ftp tycho.usno.navy.mil
cd /pub

Then use **dir** to list the files and directories there. For the most part the file names are obvious. You can use **cd** to move into any directory that promises to deliver information you might be interested in.

Space

NASA SPACELINK

telnet spacelink.msfc.nasa.gov

SpaceLink is a space-related information database provided by the educational affairs division of NASA and operated by the Marshall Space Flight Center. You'll be given a one-screen introduction to this service, then prompted for a user name. Enter the user name you normally use on-line, then a password. On your first visit you will be asked some additional questions for registration. After that, just use the same name and password for direct access.

This is a menu-driven system. The main menu looks like the sample in Figure 6.9.

Figure 6.9	
NASA SpaceLink opening menu	

```
NASA/SPACELINK     MENU SYSTEM      Revision:1.67.00.00  [@TCON11
NETWORK]

NASA Spacelink Main Menu

1.   Log Off NASA Spacelink

2.   NASA Spacelink Overview
3.   Current NASA News
4.   Aeronautics
5.   Space Exploration: Before the Shuttle
6.   Space Exploration: The Shuttle and Beyond
7.   NASA and its Centers
8.   NASA Educational Services
9.   Instructional Materials
10.  Space Program Spinoffs/Technology Transfer

Enter an option number, 'G' for GO TO, ? for HELP, or
  press RETURN to redisplay menu...
ALT-Z FOR HELP | VT100    | FDX | 57600 N81 | LOG OPEN   | PRINT OFF | ON-LINE
```

This is an interesting resource for anyone who wants to keep up with the shuttle launch schedule, research space topics, or learn more about NASA.

NASA NEWS

Finger nasanews@space.mit.edu

Turn on a log file or screen capture before issuing this command. Once the Finger command attaches to the host, you'll get several screens of data that scroll by. This is a daily bulletin that varies in length and changes topics according to what is current. This material reads like a press release or a newspaper or wire story. It is interesting, timely, and gives you the feeling of keeping up with the space program in a direct way. Try it, you'll like it.

NASA LUNAR AND PLANETARY INSTITUTE

telnet lpi.jsc.nasa.gov
Login: lpi

Look for the Lunar & Planetary Information Bulletin. Also, you can access a bibliographic database of planetary information. This is a research service from NASA and is targeted at researchers in the field. However, as a teacher or student, you may find some of the information here of interest. Figure 6.10 shows the LPI opening menu.

Figure 6.10

NASA Lunar and Planetary Institute main menu

```
          ┌─LUNAR AND PLANETARY INSTITUTE MAIN MENU─┐
          │ General Information                      │
          │                                         │
          │  Information and Research Services       │
          │                                         │
          │  Lunar and Planetary Bibliography        │
          │                                         │
          │  Image Retrieval and Processing System (IRPS) │
          │                                         │
          │  Meeting Information and Abstracts       │
          │                                         │
          │  Mars Exploration Bulletin Board         │
          │                                         │
          │  Lunar and Planetary Information Bulletin │
          │                                         │
          │  Help                                   │
          │                                         │
          │  Exit and Logout                        │
          └─────────────────────────────────────────┘


  Alt-Z FOR HELP│ VT100 │ FDX │ 57600 N81 │ LOG CLOSED │ PRINT OFF │ ON-LINE
```

NASA EXTRAGALACTIC DATABASE

telnet denver.ipac.caltech.edu
Login: ned

A database of astronomical facts and figures, plus a bibliography of astronomical publications. You'll be advised about an x-based graphical user interface, decide whether you want results e-mailed to you, then you will see the main NED screen shown in Figure 6.11.

Figure 6.11

NASA Extragalactic database menu

```
********************************************************
!!!!!           ATTENTION NED USERS            !!!!!
********************************************************
YOU ARE INVITED TO PREVIEW THE NED X-WINDOW GRAPHICAL USER INTERFACE

   The new interface can be accessed over the INTERNET by typing:

                   telnet ned.ipac.caltech.edu

                   and responding with

                   USERNAME:  xned

     Simply follow the new on-screen instructions thereafter.

   Your comments on the new interface and the resultant new capabilities
                   will be most welcome.

   If you have problems, questions or suggestions, e-mail:
ned@ipac.caltech.edu
   or contact by phone G. Helou, B. Madore or M. Schmitz at (818) 397-9594

           ========= Press RETURN to proceed =========     (Sept 27,
1993)

ALT-Z FOR HELP|VT100 | FDX |57600 N81 | LOG CLOSED | PRINT OFF | ON-LINE
```

The database, according to a NASA notice on one of the opening screens, "is an on-going effort, funded by NASA to make available over computer networks the rapidly accumulating literature on EXTRAGALACTIC objects."

You can use the database to search for bibliographic references associated with extragalactic objects, abstracts of recent journal articles, and published notes.

HUBBLE TELESCOPE INFORMATION

ftp stsci.edu

Several directories with information about the Hubble space telescope experiment. You can find instrument reports, faq lists, plans for the future, software, and more.

Use **ls** or **dir** to view the files and directories in the default directory, then use **cd** to change to a directory that looks interesting to you. Remember, the ftp **get** command copies specified files to your local host.

SHUTTLE AND SATELLITE IMAGES

ftp sseop.jsc.nasa.gov

Large selection of .GIF and .JPG images. Get on and browse. Fun!

ftp ames.arc.nasa.gov
cd /pub/GIF

Use **ls** or **dir** to view available images. You should be able to download these images for use in word processors and other applications that support graphics. There are other directories on this host that also contain interesting information and images. Try:

cd /pub/SPACE/GIF
cd /pub/space/CDROM

telnet sanddunes.scd.ucar.edu

You'll need login information and a password to access this facility. You can probably get authorized. Simply e-mail kelley@sanddunes.scd.ucar.edu and request information on accessing this host.

ftp pioneer.unm.edu
cd /pub/info

Download **beginner.info** first with the **get** command. Then use **!cat** beginner.info while still at the ftp prompt to view the file. This will give you valuable help in finding and using data on this host.

ftp iris1.ucis.dal.ca
cd /pub/GIF

Restricted use. Access only between 1700 and 2000 Eastern time.

NASA SERVERS

Want to know where NASA maintains servers on the network? That information is available through WAIS. Look for NASA-directory-of-servers.

Technology

EARTHQUAKE INFORMATION

Just in case you'd like to know current earthquake information (location, time, magnitude of recent quakes), here's how to find it:

finger quake@geophys.washington.edu

This is an immediate-response list that scrolls up your screen. Turn on screen capture or be prepared to press **Ctrl-S** and **Ctrl-Q** to stop and start the display. Figure 6.12 shows a portion of the earthquake information file you get from this resource.

Figure 6.12

Earthquake file fragment

```
finger quake@geophys.washington.edu
[geophys.washington.edu]
Login name: quake      In real life: Earthquake Information
Directory: /u0/quake           Shell: /u0/quake/run_quake
Last login Mon Sep 13 10:05 on ttyq2 from vml.yorku.ca
New mail received Mon Sep 13 07:10:33 1993;
  unread since Sun Sep 12 00:59:33 1993
Plan:
Information about Recent earthquakes are reported here for public use.
Catalogs are available by anonymous ftp in geophys.washington.edu:pub/seis-net
DATE-TIME is in Universal Stardard Time which is PST + 8 hours, LAT and
LON are in decimal degrees, DEP is depth in kilometers, N-STA is number
of stations recording event, QUAL is location quality A-good, D-poor, Z-from
automatic system and may be in error.

Recent events reported by the USGS National Earthquake Information Center
  DATE-TIME (UT)  LAT    LON    DEP   MAG        LOCATION AREA
 93/09/11 06:14   4.7S   76.3W  120   5.7   NORTHERN PERU
 93/09/11 19:29  14.0N   92.2W   33   5.6   NEAR COAST OF CHIAPAS, MEXICO
 93/09/12 08:22  29.3S  177.3W   33   5.7   KERMADEC ISLANDS, NEW ZEALAND
 93/09/12 03:22  13.2N   90.3W   70   5.8   NEAR COAST OF GUATEMALA
 93/09/13 12:37  29.1S  177.4W   33   6.0   KERMADEC ISLANDS, NEW ZEALAND
```

Technical Reports

> ftp daneel.rdt.monash.edu.au
> cd /pub/techreports/reports

Use **ls** or **dir** to view the files there. This directory is a repository of interesting technical information from private companies and universities about a broad range of topics. Among the findings here are bibliographies that refer you to published articles about a variety of technical topics.

Miscellaneous

Network Addresses

A WAIS resource will help you locate very specific addresses. Look for **biologists-addresses** (net.bio.net) on the main WAIS topic list. You can search this database, or if you want to browse through the list, enter a period or any other general key word and you will be shown the catalog for that section.

You can get biologists address and other information from this host via ftp.

> ftp net.bio.net
> cd /pub/BIOSCI

Use **dir** to view available files and directories. The topics are varied and interesting. Just browse around and locate files you'd like to see.

Nutrition Information

You can find a variety of nutrition information on the Internet. For example, to get a file on cholesterol that tells you what it is and other information, do this:

> ftp coos.dartmouth.edu
> cd /pub/Chance/Cholesterol
> get cholesterol's_new_image_.bin

You'll find a number of other files in this directory that deal with this topic. In addition, take a look at the Chance parent directory.

The list of directories there looks like the one in Figure 6.13.

Figure 6.13

Directory List from
coos.dartmouth.edu

```
dir
200 PORT command successful.
150 Opening data connection for /bin/ls (128.169.92.86,3532) (0 bytes).
total 23
drwxr-xr-x  2 281     15          512 Sep 24  1992 AIDS
drwxr-xr-x  2 281     15          512 Sep 24  1992 Bibliography
drwxr-xr-x  2 281     15          512 Sep 24  1992 Cholesterol
drwxr-xr-x  2 281     15          512 Aug 26  1992 Clinical_trials
drwxr-xr-x  3 281     15          512 Sep  4  1992 DNA_fingerprinting
drwxr-xr-x  2 281     15          512 Sep 15  1992 Deming_quality_control
drwxr-xr-x  2 281     15          512 Sep 24  1992 Micellaneous
drwxr-xr-x  2 281     15          512 Sep 18  1992 SAT
drwxr-xr-x  2 281     15          512 Sep 10  1992 Statistics_packages
drwxr-xr-x  2 281     15          512 Aug 22  1992 Syllabi
drwxr-xr-x  2 281     15          512 Sep  4  1992 Tversky
drwxr-xr-x  2 281     15          512 Aug 22  1992 Video_material
drwxr-xr-x  2 281     15          512 Sep 24  1992 Weekly_news
drwxr-xr-x  2 281     15          512 Sep  4  1992 bootstrap_method
drwxr-xr-x  2 281     15          512 Sep 15  1992 cancer
drwxrwxrwx  2 281     15          512 Nov 16  1992 common
drwxr-xr-x  2 281     15          512 Sep  7  1992 earthquake_prediction
drwxr-xr-x  2 281     15          512 Aug 26  1992 environmental_risks
drwxr-xr-x  2 281     15          512 Sep 24  1992 gender_issues
drwxr-xr-x  2 281     15          512 Sep 18  1992 paradoxes
drwxr-xr-x  2 281     15          512 Sep 15  1992 political_polls
drwxr-xr-x  2 281     15          512 Aug 26  1992 shuffling
drwxr-xr-x  2 281     15          512 Sep 24  1992 stock_market
226 Transfer complete.
1579 bytes received in 0.44 seconds (3.5 Kbytes/s)
ftp>
```

And,

> ftp flubber.cs.umd.edu
> cd /other/tms/veg
> get PCRM.cholesterol

Also in this directory are many other files that deal with nutrition. The directory looks like the one in Figure 6.14.

For some general information, get **FAQ.rec.food.veg.**

CRYONICS

> ftp charon.mit.edu
> Directory: /pub/usenet-by-group/sci.cryonics
> File: Cryonics_FAQ_3:_Philosophy_Religion

Figure 6.14				
Directory from flubber.cs.umd.edu				

```
total 393
-rw-r--r--  1 483       200         26450 Feb 24  1993 ADA.position
-rw-r--r--  1 483       200          5576 Sep 25  1992 B12
-rw-r--r--  1 483       200         19751 Feb 24  1993 BeyondBeefBackground
-rw-r--r--  1 483       200          4747 Feb 24  1993 BeyondBeefBarnard
-rw-r--r--  1 483       200          5190 Feb 24  1993 BeyondBeefBello
-rw-r--r--  1 483       200         12725 Oct 19  1992 BeyondBeefEnvironment
-rw-r--r--  1 483       200          5961 Feb 24  1993 BeyondBeefFarm
-rw-r--r--  1 483       200         11628 Feb 24  1993 BeyondBeefHealth
-rw-r--r--  1 483       200          4702 Feb 24  1993 BeyondBeefHoyt
-rw-r--r--  1 483       200         12033 Oct 19  1992 BeyondBeefQuotes
-rw-r--r--  1 483       200          8312 Feb 24  1993 BeyondBeefRifkin
-rw-r--r--  1 483       200         11648 Feb 24  1993 China.study
-rw-r--r--  1 483       200         38172 Sep  9 01:19 FAQ.rec.food.veg
-rw-r--r--  1 483       200         14869 Oct 19  1992 Gandhi
-rw-r--r--  1 483       200          2292 Mar  4  1993 Index
-rw-r--r--  1 483       200          2234 Feb 24  1993 Index-
-rw-r--r--  1 483       200          2800 Feb 24  1993 PCRM.B12
-rw-r--r--  1 483       200          3710 Mar  4  1993 PCRM.McDonalds
-rw-r--r--  1 483       200          7297 Feb 24  1993 PCRM.calcium
-rw-r--r--  1 483       200          9510 Feb 24  1993 PCRM.cancer
-rw-r--r--  1 483       200          9109 Feb 24  1993 PCRM.cholesterol
-rw-r--r--  1 483       200          6186 Feb 24  1993 PCRM.dairy
-rw-r--r--  1 483       200          5317 Oct  5  1992 PCRM.diabetes
-rw-r--r--  1 483       200          3446 Oct  5  1992 PCRM.hypoglycemia
-rw-r--r--  1 483       200          6348 Oct  2  1992 PCRM.milk.press-release
-rw-r--r--  1 483       200          4816 Oct 19  1992 PCRM.protein
-rw-r--r--  1 483       200         10848 Oct 19  1992 PCRM.veg.food
-rw-r--r--  1 483       200          4419 Oct  5  1992 PCRM.weight
-rw-r--r--  1 483       200          4382 Feb 24  1993 Xian.veg
-rw-r--r--  1 483       200         18968 Oct  6  1992 animal.ingredients
-rw-r--r--  1 483       200          2741 Sep 25  1992 beef
-rw-r--r--  1 483       200          8570 Sep 25  1992 brethren
-rw-r--r--  1 483       200          6529 Feb 24  1993 comstock
-rw-r--r--  1 483       200         21131 Feb 24  1993 fat.land
-rw-r--r--  1 483       200         15094 Jul 30 13:21 leather.alternatives.FAQ
-rw-r--r--  1 483       200         15154 May 28 14:46 leather.alternatives.FAQ~
-rw-r--r--  1 483       200          4452 Sep 25  1992 osteoporosis
-rw-r--r--  1 483       200          4689 Feb 24  1993 self.sufficiency
-rw-r--r--  1 483       200          3631 Feb 24  1993 singer
-rw-r--r--  1 483       200          4436 Feb 24  1993 son.sue
-rw-r--r--  1 483       200         10148 Oct 14  1992 viva
226 ASCII Transfer complete.
2823 bytes received in 1.4 seconds (2 Kbytes/s)
```

Recreation

RECREATION DATABASE

ftp ftp.cs.dal.ca
cd /comp.archives

Use **ls** to show the available directories under this one. This is a gold mine of useful files and pointers to other information. Data is stored by topic, and the number of files is large. You might want to turn on a log file (screen capture) and issue several **ls** commands:

ls rec.*
ls rec.arts*
ls rec.aviation*
ls rec.bicycles*
ls rec.food*
ls rec.games*
ls rec.music*

```
ls rec.radio.amateur*
ls alt.*
ls comp.*
ls soc.*
```

Once you have identified a directory you want to explore, use **cd dirname** to make that directory current, then use **ls** again to view the names of the available files or directories. If you're not sure which names are files and which are directories, use **dir** and note the first character in the file description at the left of the display. If it is a **d**, then the name at the end of that line represents a directory.

Movies

```
ftp grasp1.univ-lyon1.fr
cd /pub/faq-by-newsgroup/rec/rec.arts.movies/movies
get faq
Get trivia-faq
get bladerunner-faq
```

These files give you information on a broad set of movie topics. You'll also get pointers toward other files that might be of interest. These files are configured as a series of common questions and trivia about movies of all kinds. For example, "who was the voice of Jessica Rabbit in the film *Who Framed Roger Rabbit*, or when is George Lucas going to make more Star Wars films? Whether you're a dedicated movie fan who studies every new film and star or just someone who likes to watch movies, you'll find some interesting facts and figures here.

Games

Information about games on the Internet is available from a variety of sources. A good place to start (as always) is Archie. Log on to an Archie server through your local client, and search for games (**prog games**). You'll get a fairly long list of directories named games. Try some of these and you'll find faq files about a variety of game topics. Some of the files in the Archie list will be grouped by topic, so you can locate video game faqs or pinball faqs, and so on. As with nearly anything on the Internet, the key to finding what you want (or to serendipitously finding something you didn't know about) is to poke around, ask questions, and see what you can find.

You'll uncover at least three types of game information on the Internet:

1. PC, Macintosh, and other microcomputer games you can download and play on your own machine.

2. Interactive, networked games that you play with many users simultaneously across the Internet.

3. Text files that contain game hints, conversations about games, and directories for locating games.

In this section we will list a few of the game resources you can find on the Internet, just to get you started.

FLIGHT SIMULATORS

> ftp cs.dal.ca
> cd /comp.archives/rec.aviation.simulators

Use **ls** to view available files. Also, search any ftp site for the directory **news.answers** (probably under the **/pub** directory) for faqs about flight simulators and a variety of other game topics.

PINBALL

There is a surprising amount of interest on the Internet in discussing pinball—both electronic, computer-based versions, and the old, klunky, mechanical machines once so popular in diners and clubs. If you're interested in learning more about pinball, do an Archie search for pinball as a place to start. Also, you can try these files:

> ftp grasp1.univ-lyon1.fr
> cd /pub/faq-by-newsgroup/rec/rec.games.pinball/games
> get part1
> get part2

Not only will you get an interesting discussion of pinball, but also a list of current pinball magazines and newsletters. You can e-mail Andy Oakland, who maintains this monthly posting, at **sao@athena.mit.edu**, for additional information.

TAKING CARE OF BUSINESS

ftp potemkin.cs.pdx.edu
cd /pub/frp/stories/business

Use **ls** to view filenames. This is a series of compressed files about business. **get** the **business.intro.Z** file first. Use **uncompress** to expand it, and then use cat to view it. This is a very specialized, text-based role playing game. We'll say no more, but you might find the exchanges interesting.

STAR TREK

We started working with computers in about 1975—first Digital Equipment Corporation PDP-11-series minicomputers, then a variety of microcomputers. This was *long* before the IBM PC was designed and before Apple had a popular machine. But nearly every computer in those days had some form of Star Trek game. This was in the days of text-based displays, remember. There were almost no graphics applications, and certainly no real-time, flight-simulator-type, joystick controlled games.

Star Trek certainly would have been an excellent graphics game, but those early versions were played with Xs, plus signs and some text hints. And you know what? Some seventeen years later, Star Trek—not shoot-em-up color graphics versions, but the old text games—are still popular on UNIX machines and across the Internet.

There are several places to look for Trek games. The first place may be on your local host. From your home directory, try cd **/usr/games**. You should see a list of several game files, including one called trek. Type **trek** with the games directory selected, and see what happens. You will be asked for game length and skill level. Answer **s** for short and **n** for novice (unless you want something else), then supply a password at the prompt. You are asked for a command. That's all—a simple **Command:** prompt and you're into the game. You can enter a question mark to get a list of possible commands, similar to the list in Figure 6.15.

```
> trek

   * * *   S T A R   T R E K   * * *

What length game: s
What skill game: n
Enter a password:
Enter a password: pass
5 Klingons
3 starbases at 0,3, 2,6, 6,5
It takes 250 units to kill a Klingon

Command: h
invalid input; ? for valid inputs

Command: ?
        abandon       capture        cloak      computer
        damages       destruct         dock         help
        impulse         lrscan         move       phasers
            ram           dump         rest        shell
         shield         srscan       status     terminate
        torpedo         undock       visual         warp

Command:
ALT-Z FOR HELP|VT100|FDX|57600 N81|LOG CLOSED|PRINT OFF|ON-LINE
```

You can find out the status of your game by typing **status** at the **Command:** prompt. Your screen should look something like the one in Figure 6.16.

You can spend some time with this local game to get an idea of how Trek is played, then you can branch out and look for network versions. Where do you look? Try:

ftp soda.berkeley.edu
cd /pub/netrek
get netrekFAQ
get netrekFTP
get netreklist

The netrekFAQ and netrekFTP files are particularly useful for beginning Netrek players. Download them and study them. Try some of the sources listed for more information. At some point, you will be ready to try your hand at the game yourself.

Figure 6.16

Typical Text-based
Trek screen

```
Command: status
stardate       3700.00
condition      DOCKED
position       0,3/7,2
warp factor    5.0
total energy   5000
torpedoes      10
shields        down, 100%
Klingons left 5
time left      8.00
life support   active
current crew   387
brig space     400
Klingon power 250
Length, Skill short, novice

Command:
ALT-Z FOR HELP|VT100|FDX|57600 N81|LOG CLOSED|PRINT OFF |ON-LINE
```

These files will give you answers to a lot of questions about netrek, the networked version of Star Trek, and also show you where you can find Netrek servers. To access a network game, telnet to one of the listed servers (be sure to include the port number).

MUD

The MUD game, available in many varieties on many hosts, is a multiuser role playing game like Dungeons and Dragons. MUD stands for multiuser dimensions or multiuser dungeons. One place to find a version is on your local host. Again, try the **/usr/games** directory. There may be a version of MUD there, and that's a good place for some hands-on experience. Also, you can ask other users on your system about using the local MUD and about finding a MUD server popular with the users on your system.

You can get information about MUD servers with an Archie search. Log on to an Archie server and issue a **prog mud** search. Here's one resource:

ftp netcom.com
cd /pub/pdh/lpmud
get mudlist

This will show you a very long list of MUD servers, places you might be able to find out more about MUD, and where you might play the game.

If you're familiar with Dungeons and Dragons, you have an idea how MUD works. There can be many variations of the game, each with a different set of characters, and different worlds or scenes. Once you join a MUD game, you are a character in a MUD dimension and can interact with other characters in that dimension.

Usually there is a quest to solve or another adventure. The players who solve the quest become wizards who often get the ability to program part of the game. They just take a room or other place and start programming from there. They may make a new exit to the East or West, add a teleporter—you name it.

When you go into their part of the game, they can have their own programs there that do what they want. Suppose you are playing a Startrek MUD and end up in an area that is a holo-deck. When you are a wizard you can change the holo-deck to whatever you want. The fun is that you become a part of the creation of the game. For others who are not on that level, the fun is playing a game that people you know made, and seeing their creativity.

Each MUD server has different help files and different forms of the game.. If you'd like to try one MUD, try this:

ftp pa.itd.com 9999

This is a system called "After Five," which means what it says. This system is open after five PM and all day weekends. Like many MUD games, it attracts a wide variety of players and personalities. You are liable to see anything, so adults should monitor how children use MUD and other interactive games and conversations In fact, one prompt as you join the conversations cautions, "Remember, After Five is *not* a game, it is a method of conversation." This is true for this MUD implementation. Other versions of MUD are different. Experiment to find a MUD that you enjoy.

You log on automatically and will be asked for a name. You can either **continue** an existing character or **create** a new one. If you haven't logged on to this particular MUD server before, you'll need to create a character. The MUD playing screen is made up of prompts and a blank line at the bottom of the screen. You enter commands on this blank line. Type **create charactername** to create a new identity on this MUD. Next you'll get a screen welcoming you to the MUD. The system knows you are a new player and steps you through several screens of information where you describe your character any way you like. Then you will be asked if this is a male of female character, and other questions.

This is a well-prompted system that shows you how the command structure works. For example, you are shown how to specify the gender of your character with **@sex me=<male/female/neuter>**. This is typical of these MUD command. Start with a commercial at sign (@), enter the command followed by **me** to identify that the command works against your own character, enter the **equal sign,** then enter the description or other command information.

When the questions are over, you are sent into one of the "rooms" where other players are passing information back and forth, asking questions, and moving through the game. A typical screen from this MUD looks like the one in Figure 6.17.

Figure 6.17

Typical MUD Exchange

```
Corner of Bourbon St. and Canal St.
As you gaze about you see the Woolworth building squatting on the corner of the
street.  Its not terribly impressive.  Along either side of the block you see
all manner of stores ranging from clothing to liquor to cheap electronics.
Garish neon signs blaze forth causing strange shadows as people pass you by.  A
bum sits in the corner of one store front begging for money.  You also notice a
group of young teenagers laughing and cutting up.  A twang cracks through the
air and moments later a trolley clatters along its rails behind you.
You can go "north" further up Bourbon Street, "south" onto a trolley,
"west" or "east" down Canal Street.
Contents:
Sandra
Saralynii
Fishhook
Batman
Antiwolf
Maxwell_Smart
Kari
Snag
Technomaster
LiquidMax
A bench
Kari is dying to sing this song...heh
Saralynii says, "dune MUSH is Cool too"
Sandra(#2393P) looks at you.
LiquidMax says, "The 4hr cut is better."
```

You can return to your "home" room and QUIT the game at any time. Follow the instructions and move around until you've had enough, then move on.

OTHER ROLE PLAYING

MUD isn't the only role-playing activity you can find on the Internet. Keep your eyes open as you browse IRC and conferences. Also, you can try some of the BBS sources listed through Gopher. From the main Gopher menu, choose Fun & Games, then select games/Fantasy Role-Playing Games, then BBSes from the next menu. You can get a list of active BBSes that conduct role-playing.

Hobbies

If you think about it a moment, you realize that the folk, like you, who use the Internet have a wide range of interests. It is only natural, then, that a lot of discussions, files and articles you will come across on the Internet have to do with hobbies of one kind or another. We'll list some sample hobby-related files in this section.

For example, are you a cook? Do you like to get recipes from other cooks? Use Gopher and select Fun & Games from the main menu, then choose Recipes from the next menu. You can search for recipes or get a menu-driven list of menus by topic.

Aviation

The field of aviation is changing rapidly. It is more difficult than ever to keep up with technology and regulations. Some of the information on the Internet can help and, we predict, that as more pilots and others interested in the field access the Internet, this area of on-line data will grow apace.

AERONAUTICS ARCHIVES

ftp rascal.ics.utexas.edu
cd /misc/av

Use **ls** and **dir** to find what you want. You will find rec.aviation newsgroup postings, for one thing, but there is a lot more as well. For example you will find FARs (Federal Air Regulations), specifications for a variety of aircraft, reviews of flight simulation software and more.

RESOURCES FOR PILOTS

telnet duat.contel.com

If you are a licensed pilot, you can use this database for weather briefings and flight planning services. Student pilots can use a portion of this facility as well:

telnet duats.contel.com

If you are a registered user, you will be asked to enter an ID or your last name at the login prompt. To login for the first time, enter **new** at the initial prompt. You will be asked for your pilot certificate number, or press **Return** if you are not a licensed pilot.

The main menu for this system is shown in Figure 6.18.

Figure 6.18	
DUAT main menu screen	

```
                    DUAT Main Menu

        Weather Briefing                    1
        Flight Plan *NEW! Flt Planner*      2
        Encode                              3
        Decode                              4
        Modify Screen Width/Length          5
        Golden Eagle Services (tm)          6
        Service Information *NEW*           7
        Extended Decode                     8
        FAA/NWS Contractions                9

        Select function (or 'Q' to quit):
        ALT-Z FOR HELP|VT100|FDX | 57600 E71 | LOG CLOSED | PRINT OFF | ON-LINE
```

The flight planner is one interesting service provided by this service. You can enter the departure and destination points, departure time and other information, for a pretty-good automated flight planner. Other features for pilots are available here as well. See also Weather Service listings.

Flying is a popular recreation/hobby topic on the Internet. You can find someone to talk to you on IRC or on conferences. There are some interesting files you can check out as well. Here are some samples:

    ftp ftp sol.cs.ruu.nl
    cd /pub/AIRCRFT-IMAGES

Use **ls** or **dir** to view the available files. You'll see a series of .jpg-format graphics images of a variety of aircraft, from a MiG-29 to a Tiger Moth.

Bicycling

FREQUENTLY ASKED QUESTIONS

    ftp athene.uni-paderborn.de
    cd /doc/FAQ/news.answers/bicycle-faq

Use **ls** to display available files (there are five files in .gz format as this book is written), Use **get** to download the ones you want.

The **/doc/FAQ/news.answers** directory is rich in frequently-asked question files and directories. Once you get to this ftp site, study it carefully. Use **ls** to display the contents of **/doc/FAQ** for more bicycle information.

Other faq files about bicycles are located as follows. We are sure there is some duplication here:

    Host: rzsun2.informatik.uni-hamburg.de
    Directory: /pub/doc/news.answers/bicycles-faq

    Host: procyon.cis.ksu.edu
    Directory: /pub/mirrors/news.answers/bicycles-faq

    Host: charon.mit.edu
    Directory: /pub/usenet-by-group/news.answers/bicycles-faq
    Directory: /pub/usenet-by-group/rec.answers/bicycles-faq

Directory: /pub/usenet-by-group/rec.bicycles.misc

Host: animal-farm.nevada.edu
Directory: /pub/guitar/k/Kotte
File: BustedBicycle.ptab

Host: relay.cs.toronto.edu
Directory: /pub/usenet/news.answers/bicycles-faq

GEAR RATIO CALCULATIONS

ftp uceng.uc.edu
cd /pub/wuarchive/systems/mac/umich.edu/hypercard/fun
get bicyclegearcalc4.0.cpt.hqx

Ham Radio

Amateur radio operators, or "hams," have been on the leading edge of communications technology for nearly three-quarters of a century. These private citizens have spent their own money, time, and expertise to develop communications hardware and procedures for personal communications, emergency services, and research. The ham community has launched over a dozen satellites, for example, and there are radio servers that "talk" TCP/IP and can access Internet addresses. You'll find ham radio talk and information in many Internet locations. Here are some to try:

ftp world.std.com
cd /pub/hamradio

Use **dir** or **ls** to view the files and subdirectories there. You'll find information about amateur testing, organizations, using computers with radio, radio TCP/IP, and more.

cd /pub
get morsecode1.0.sit.hqx
get morsetrainer1.03.sit.hqx
Apple users utilities.

HAM RADIO CALLBOOK

telnet callsign.cs.buffalo.edu 2000

You are logged on automatically and receive a double chevron prompt: **>>**. Type **help** at the prompt for information on searching the database. Basically, this is an electronic version of a licensed amateur radio operators' call book. You can search by call sign, city, surname, zip code, and other criteria. A sample record is shown in Figure 6.19 (the actual information was changed for this example):

Figure 6.19

Sample callbook entry

```
        info                    - get info about server
        more rows               - set number of terminal rows
        name [filters] surname  - lookup last name
        quit                    - exit the server
        set name|data|raw|addr  - set the display mode
        zip [filters] zipcode   - lookup zip code

    Available regular expression filters:
        -c   filter by callsign
        -f   filter by first name
        -l   filter by last name
        -a   filter by street address
        -z   filter by zip code
        -t   filter by town
        -s   filter by state (or province)

    For information on regular expressions:
        help regexp
    >> call k8ao
    Call-Sign: K8AO                    Class: EXTRA
    Real Name: JOHN T BADGETT          Birthday: SEP 14, 1944
    Mailing Address: 7042 FRANKLYN RD, CORRIGAN, TN  37722
    Valid From: AUG 23, 1988           To: AUG 23, 1998
    >>
    ALT-Z FOR HELP|VT100 | FDX | 57600 N81 | LOG CLOSED | PRINT OFF | ON-LINE
```

The American Radio Relay League is the premier source of information about the state of ham radio, about current happenings, and about laws and technology. ARRL has moved with current technology to support the hams they serve. The organization operates radio packet stations, publishes QST, a monthly journal, and is active on the Internet. The ARRL Internet postings are a good place to start if you need information on ham radio.

Start by sending e-mail to **info@arrl.org**. When you do, you'll get a document that includes this ARRL ham radio information guide, shown in Figure 6.20.

Figure 6.20

ARRL information
guide

```
Each line of the message should contain a single command as shown below. You may place as many
commands in a message as you want. Each file you request will be sent to you in a separate
message. Only ASCII text files are supported at present.

Valid INFO commands:

help          Sends this help file

index         Sends an index of the files available from INFO

send <FILENAME>  Sends "FILENAME" example: send PROSPECT

quit          Terminates the transaction (use this if you have
              a signature or other text at the end of the message.)

reply <address>  Sends the response to the specified address. Put this
              at the BEGINNING of your message if your From: address
              is not a valid Internet address.

Note: your message will *not* be read by a human! Do not include any requests or questions
except by way of the above commands. Retrieve the "ARRL-EMAIL-ADR" file for a list of
addresses of ARRL HQ people.

Also, note that this message is from info-serv@arrl.org.  DO *NOT* USE YOUR MAILER'S "REPLY"
FUNCTION TO SEND YOUR NEXT REQUEST! Generate a new message addressed to info@arrl.org instead.
We set it up this way to prevent failed mail from looping endlessly, annoying system
administrators.  Mail sent back to info-serv@arrl.org ends up in the bit bucket.

Your From: field or Reply-to: field in your header should contain a valid Internet address,
including full domain name.  If your From: field does not contain a valid Internet address,
the answer will not reach you. However, we have recently added a reply function as a server
command. If needed, the REPLY command should be the first command in your message.

      syntax: reply mailaddr

Where mailaddr is a valid Internet mail address (either user@domain or bang address accepted.)
An invalid address generates an error. A wrong address results in non-delivery of your
response.

The address given in the reply command is the address to which all subsequent requests in the
message will be sent.
```

In addition, this file will show you some sample files available from ARRL, including the ones shown in Figure 6.21.

Figure 6.21

ARRL available file list

```
FILENAME        SIZE   DATE    DESCRIPTION
--------------- ----  ------   --------------------
#Note - If you are not yet an Amateur Radio operator retrieve the
#file prospect (send prospect) for information on how to easily get
#started in this fun hobby.

PROSPECT        2k    930514   How to get your Amateur Radio license
EXAM-SCHEDULE   52k   930629   Current exam schedule info - updated bi-weekly
EXAM-INFO       9k    921020   Examinations - what to bring - requirements
ARRL-EMAIL-ADR  6k    930119   List of HQ Email addresses
ARRL-CATALOG    39k   930709   Catalog of ARRL Publications - commercial content
ARRL-JOIN       2k    930621   How become an ARRL member
ARRL-SERVICES   5k    930621   A condensed list of ARRL membership services
ARRL-TOUR       28k   930621   An electronic tour of ARRL Headquarters
VISIT-HQ        5k    930310   Visiting ARRL HQ - diretions and tour information
BANDS-HF        7k    921203   Breakdown of users of HF spectrum
Q-SIGNALS       1k    921203   ARRL list of Amateur Radio Q-signals
W1AW-SCHEDULE   2k    930120   W1AW schedule of transmissions and operation
BEST-RIG-1      12k   930227   Which rig is best? Part 1 - QST Lab Notes
BEST-RIG-2      22k   930227   Which rig is best? Part 2 - QST Lab Notes
EMI-GEN         37k   930120   How to solve an EMI/RFI problem - QST Lab Notes
EMI-SOURCE      13k   930607   Where to buy filters - EMI-proof telephones etc.
ADDRESSES       16k   930318   Lots and lots of ham/electonic company addresses
KITS            6k    930430   List of companies that sell kits
BBS             12k   930601   List of ham-radio land-line bulletin boards
FAQ-1           25k   930707   Introduction to the FAQ and Amateur Radio
FAQ-2           45k   930707   Amateur Radio Orgs, Services and Info Sources
FAQ-3           32k   930707   Amateur Radio Advanced and Technical Questions
```

As the note suggests, the PROSPECT file is a good place to start if you re not yet a licensed amateur radio. Next, study the three FAQ files. After that, follow the thread that best fits your needs for ham radio information.

As we have mentioned, there are other locations for information on ham radio as well. A rich resource are the new group postings (some of which are available from ARRL archives as well). Start by searching these directories:

rec.radio.amateur
digital.misc
rec.radio.info
rec.answers
news.answers

on any newsgroup server. These directories and associated ham radio information should be available on the following ftp sites:

ftp.cs.buffalo.edu
rtfm.mit.edu (pub/usenet/news.answers directory)

In addition, there is a mail server on **rtfm.mit.edu**. You can address this server as **mail-server@rtfm.mit.edu**. For details on how to operate this server, send a message to that address with the word "help" in the BODY of the message.

SCUBA

SCUBA activities are among the rapidly growing leisure time activities at seashore locations and inland as well. It is natural that Internet travelers would share what they know about this fascinating topic. Here are some SCUBA references we came across. You can find your own with an Archie search, by using Gopher, or by simply posting questions on bulletin boards and conferences.

ftp ames.arc.nasa.gov
cd /pub/SCUBA

Use **dir** or **ls** to list the files available in this directory. This is a rich repository of comments and personal experiences, from diving reports on specific locations to schedules and suggestions. These are mostly text files which you can access easily.

One file you might enjoy seeing, if you're a Macintosh user, is **dive-log-15.hqx**. Download it, expand it, and see what you have.

ftp sol.cs.ruu.nl
cd /pub/NEWS.ANSWERS
get scuba-faq

This is just one of hundreds of faq files in this directory. Use **get** to copy the file to your local host, then you can use **cat** to look at it or use a protocol to download it to your own system.

Astronomy

Whether as a hobby or a profession, the field of astronomy is a fascinating topic. You'll find discussions and references of one kind or another on this topic if you use Internet resources to scope it out. However you approach the topic, you can find information of interest on the Internet. As with other specialized topics of this sort, the best advice is to use Archie, Gopher, and WAIS for generalized searches to get you started. Then access some or all of the sites you locate. From these first contacts, you will get other information that will send you in different directions. We'll list a few resources here to get you started.

```
ftp mandarin.mit.edu
cd /astro

ftp pomona.claremont.edu
cd /yale_bsc

ftp world.std.com
cd /pub/astronomy
```

Use **dir** or **ls** to view available files. These are mostly program files designed to help in astronomy activities. For example, you can find a file that shows librations (oscillations) of the moon, and a C program that computes ephemerides of sun, moon, planets, comets, and stars.

Other Recreation

COLLECTING

```
ftp grasp1.univ-lyon1.fr
cd /pub/nfs-mounted/ftp.univ-lyon1.fr/usenet-stats/groups/rec
get rec.antiques
```

ELECTRICAL INFORMATION

ftp athene.uni-paderborn.de
cd /doc/FAQ/misc.answers
get electrical-wiring.gz
cd /doc/FAQ/misc.consumers.house
get electrical_Wiring_FAQ.gz
get rec.woodworking_Electric_Motors_Frequently_asked_
Questions.gz

BULLETIN BOARDS

telnet spacemet.phast.umass.edu

Simply press Enter when you are connected. No logon is required except that you will be asked for your first and last names. You can enter GUEST to tour the facility with limited access.

The initial screen is shown in Figure 6.22.

Figure 6.22

Initial Spacemet BBS screen

```
***********************************************
                SPACEMET INTERNET
***********************************************
This electronic bulletin board offers access to various Message Areas
plus text and program FILES which you can upload or download.  Any
terminal or micro can be used to read text files and access the forums.
Program files only run on the computers which are indicated in their
descriptions.

We hope you will find this BBS an exciting and useful way to share
teaching ideas and materials.  If you have any suggestions or questions,
leave a "message for SYSOP" as you sign off.

Contact:
  Helen Sternheim
  Department of Physics and Astronomy
  Lederle Graduate Research Center 426
  University of Massachusetts
  Amherst, MA 01003
  413-545-1908, 3697

This completes the new-user introduction to
      SPACEMET INTERNET
More [Y,n,=]?
ALT-Z FOR HELP|VT100| FDX | 57600 N81 | LOG CLOSED | PRINT OFF | ON-LINE
```

This is a BBS dedicated to space information and targeted at the science educator. Help with curriculum planning, plus information on NASA plans and schedules. After you complete registration, you will see a screen similar to the one in Figure 6.23.

Figure 6.23

BULLETIN MENU
from Spacemet

```
This is the BULLETIN MENU
  (to return here later, enter B in Main Menu)

Select one of these:
  U) USA Today News
  W) UMassK12 Internet BBS Workshops 10/21, 11/2, 11/16, 11/30
  5) Five College/UMass Public School Partnership Events
  F) Five College Calendar of Events
  D) 5C/5E 1993-1994 Meeting Schedule
  A)ppeal for SpaceMet Monetary Contributions
  C)urrent workshops, courses, lectures, etc.
  R)edisplay Bulletin Menu
  Q)uit (go to the Main Menu)



Select (R=Redisplay Bulletin Menu, Q=Go to Main Menu):




ALT-Z FOR HELP|VT100 | FDX | 57600 N81 |LOG CLOSED|PRINT OFF | ON-LINE
```

KIDS BBS

telnet kids.kotel.co.kr
login: kids

You will be asked to register by entering NEW at the User ID prompt. This system periodically fills up and you will be told there is no room for new users. You can try again at a later time to see if there is room.

QUARTZ BBS

telnet quartz.rutgers.edu
Login: bbs

This is a message-only board with no files available. But you can find a variety of interesting topic areas to browse and study.

ISCA BBS

> telnet bbs.isca.uiowa.edu
> Login: **New** to open a new account; **Guest** to look around

This is certainly among the largest BBS systems on Internet. You may find as many as 300 participants at any given time. You can find somebody on here to talk about just about anything.

For a list that contains many interesting and unusual BBS services available through Internet, send an e-mail message to **bbslist@aug3.augsburg.edu**. You don't need to include a subject or any message in the body. In return, you'll receive three useful lists of resources.

PRISM BBS

> telnet bbs.fdu.edu
> Login: bbs

A general purpose bbs with a "room" motif. You will be asked to enter a "handle" to use on the system, then some real information about you. After that, you are presented with a command-oriented bbs for messages and discussions. Different activities and topics are covered in different rooms. Which rooms are available is dynamic, but you can get a list of current rooms, as shown in Figure 6.24.

See also Sunset and Quartz BBS information. They are tied with this one, at least logically.

SUNSET BBS

> telnet paladine.hacks.arizona.edu
> login: bbs

A programming project of the University of Arizona Hardware and Computer Knowledge Society in Tucson. Like PRISM, this is a room-oriented bbs designed for conversation and e-mail.

See also PRISM and Quartz BBS information. These bbs services are open to anyone, but there is a slant toward local university users. This also is a command-oriented bbs, with commands shown in Figure 6.25.

```
Ground Floor:The End> Known Rooms

Rooms on this floor with new messages:
  The End>  Open Discussion>  New Users>  PrismBBS Help>  Suggestion
Box>
  Hand Me the Flyswatter>

No unseen messages in:
  Mail>

Other floors with new messages:
  Arts & Entertainment:(19/19)  Silly Stuff:(19/19)  Fun and
Games:(11/11)
  Physical:(15/16)  Metaphysical:(10/10)  Science & Technology:(10/10)
  Breaking News:(2/2)  Discussions:(14/18)  Emotions:(7/7)
  Education:(9/9)  Business:(4/4)  NetLife:(7/7)  Music:(13/13)
  New Jersey:(1/1)  Computing:(15/16)

Uneventful floors:
  Arts & Entertainment:  Silly Stuff:  Fun and Games:  Physical:
  Metaphysical:  Science & Technology:  Breaking News:  Discussions:
  Emotions:  Education:  Business:  NetLife:  Music:  New Jersey:
Computing:



Ground Floor:The End>
ALT-Z FOR HELP|VT100|FDX | 57600 E71 | LOG CLOSED | PRINT OFF | ON-LINE
```

```
+------------------------------------------------------------------------+
|                      Sunset BBS Quick Reference                        |
+------------------------------------------------------------------------+
| READING COMMANDS    N: Next Message    F: Forward All    O: Old Reverse |
|     L: Last 5       #: Last x          R: All Reverse    S: Stop        |
+------------------------------------------------------------------------+
| ROOM COMMANDS          G: Goto Next rm w/ New msgs  N: Read New Messages |
| E: Enter Message       U: Ungoto/Back to prev room  K: List Rooms        |
| S: Skip rm/all unread  A: Abandon room/rest unread  Z: Zap (forget) Room |
| J: Jump to named room  I: Read Room Info            -: Upload Message    |
+------------------------------------------------------------------------+
| MISC COMMANDS      T: Terminate (Logout)       H: Help                  |
| Y: Your Fortune    W: List online users        D: Date / Time Info      |
| P: Profile User    X: Change "what" column      V: View System Config    |
| &: Remote Who                                                            |
+------------------------------------------------------------------------+
| CONFIGURATION MENU:   Hit C followed by...      C: Screen/Reading Config |
| R: Registration Information      P: Password    B: Biography/Profile     |
+------------------------------------------------------------------------+



Lobby>
ALT-Z FOR HELP | VT100     | FDX | 57600 E71 | LOG CLOSED | PRINT OFF | ON-LINE
```

Commercial and Business

INTERNET BUSINESS JOURNAL

A relatively new effort that may generate real interest across the Internet, is the Internet Business Journal. This is an electronic publication targeted at an international business audience which deals with topics about the Internet business community. You can find it through Gopher (depending on your Gopher server and client). Look under Electronic Information or a similar title. For information about access, e-mail Editor-in-Chief Christopher Locke at **chris@avalanche.com**, or write Avalanche Development, 947 Walnut Street, Boulder, CO 80302, 303-449-5032.

AGRICULTURE

telnet isn.iastate.edu (129.186.99.8)

At the **DIAL:** prompt, enter **scholar**. Press **Return** at the **Enter terminal type: (default=VT100)** or enter the terminal type if different from VT100. At the **Command:** prompt, enter **scholar** again. At the **Database Selection:** prompt, type **ICAT**. You will see the prompt screen shown in Figure 6.26.

Figure 6.26

Scholar's ICAT database screen

```
                        WELCOME TO SCHOLAR'S ICAT DATABASE

        ICAT contains records for library materials cataloged since 1978, and all
        cataloged serials. Pre-1978 books are continually being added to the database.

             To search for:       Use command:               Example:
                keywords               k            k lasers         <ENTER>
                titles                 t            t war and peace  <ENTER>
                authors                a            a bronte c       <ENTER>
                subjects               s            s acid rain      <ENTER>
                call numbers           c            c jc571z45x 1990 <ENTER>

        For more information on SEARCHING, press <ENTER>.
        For INFORMATION about the Library, type exp info and press <ENTER>.
        For DATABASE SELECTION menu, type cho and press <ENTER>.
        --------------------------------------------- + Page 1 of 4 ------------
                             Enter search command               <F8>  FORward page
                             NEWs


        NEXT COMMAND:
        ALT-Z FOR HELP  | VT100   | FDX | 57600 N81 | LOG CLOSED | PRINT OFF | ON-LINE
```

AGRICULTURE DATABASE

```
ftp sunsite.unc.edu
cd /pub//academic/agriculture/sustainable_agriculture
get INDEX
```

This text file lists the currently available agriculture-related files in this directory. There are other agriculture files in directories close to this one as well. Use **cd ..** to back up a directory, and then **ls** to find out what else is there.

AGRICULTURE INTERNET SERVERS (NOT JUST COWS)

```
ftp aun.uninett.no
cd /uninettinfo/nettinfo
get agriculture-internet.servers
```

A fairly comprehensive guide to Internet/BITNET resources in agriculture. You can download this list to help you find other agriculture resources on the Internet. You can find out more from the report's author:

```
Wilfred Drew
Serials/Reference Librarian
State University of New York
Morrisville College of Agriculture and Technology
Morrisville, New York 13408
BITNET:  drewwe@snymorva.bitnet
Voice:      315-684-6055
FAX:        315-684-6115
```

LIVESTOCK REPORTS, MARKET PRICES

```
telnet psupen.psu.edu
```

At the **Username:** prompt, enter the two-digit abbreviation for your state. This gives you access to PENpages (college of Agricultural Sciences at The Pennsylvania State University), and to TEACHER*PAGES (The Pennsylvania Department of Education). The system is entirely menu-driven and provides a number of search and database services that you may find useful. For example, in PENpages, you can access the International Food & Nutrition Database, files on Small and Part-Time

Farming, information on the National Family Database and the 4-H Development Database, and more. A PENpages menu screen is shown in Figure 6.27.

Figure 6.27

PENpages menu screen

```
                        *** PENpages Main Menu ***

    PENpages User Information         Databases
    ---------------------------       --------------------------------------------
    1..How to Use PENpages            5..International Food & Nutrition Database
    2..Recent Changes                 6..Information on:
    3..Recent Changes - Market News      MAPP - National Family Database
    4..PENpages Announcements            Senior Series
                                         The 4-H Youth Development Database

    National & International News and Information
    ---------------------------------------------------------------------------
    7..Ag*SAT                          13..PDA Ag & Weather Statistics
    8..Colorado                        14..PA Calendars & Events
    9..Rutgers, New Jersey             15..PA Market News
    10..West Virginia University       16..PA News & Newsletters
    11..USDA                           17..PA Drought Information
    12..Small & Part-Time Farming      18..PSU College of AG Information

                       * To EXIT press Control-E *
                * <PF1> then 7 to go to a known page number *

                    C h o i c e :
    ALT-Z FOR HELP | VT100  | FDX | 57600 N81 | LOG CLOSED | PRINT OFF | ON-LINE
```

USDA files available through this system include the Farm Broadcasters Letter, Market Reports, News Releases, and more.

When you select TEACHER*PAGES you can access a WHAT'S HERE menu like the one in Figure 6.28.

Figure 6.28

TEACHER*PAGES WHAT'S HERE menu

```
                    ================================
                    WHAT'S HERE AND HOW TO USE IT
                    ================================

    1...Welcome to TEACHER*PAGES!
    2...Hardware and Software Selection for TEACHER*PAGES
    3...Configuring Your Equipment for TEACHER*PAGES
    4...TEACHER*PAGES Public Access Locations and Telephone Numbers
    5...How to Use Keyword Search
    6...TEACHER*PAGES Command Reference
    7...TEACHER*PAGES Quick Command Reference


                            TO EXIT
                        PRESS <CONTROL>E




                    C h o i c e :
    ALT-Z FOR HELP|VT100 | FDX | 57600 N81 |LOG CLOSED | PRINT OFF | ON-LINE
```

TEACHER*PAGES is a full-text database of information of interest to teachers. New data is added daily and is available for viewing and downloading without a subscription fee. Data is accessed primarily through keyword search.

AMWAY (NETWORK MARKETING)

> ftp netcom.com
> cd /pub/noring/amway

Get one or more of the files you find there with the **dir** command.

This is a series of newsgroup discussions on small business and entrepreneurs with an Amway network marketing focus. Interesting reading, but take this material with a pound of salt. There are highly personal opinions here, but it shows the kind of far ranging discussions you can find on nearly any topic.

> ftp plaza.aarnet.edu.au
> cd /usenet/FAQs/alt.business.multi-level
> get alt.business.multi-level_FAQ_(Frequently_Asked_Questions)

> ftp kekule.osc.edu
> cd /pub/russian/business/ukraine
> get commercial.directory

This is an example of how businesses and individuals can use the Internet for the advancement of business, and for the advancement of communications among different countries. This file is a list of at least 165 e-mail addresses of business firms from 19 regions of the Ukraine. The compiler of the list says it is designed to enhance communications among businessmen of Poland and the Ukraine for the development of a market economy.

BIG SKY TELEGRAPH

> Telnet 192.231.192.1 or bigsky.bigsky.dillon.mt.us
> Dial direct: 406-683-7680 (300/1200 bps)
>   406-683-7685 or 406-683-7686 (2400 bps)
>   406-683-7880 (9600 bps)
> Type **hrn** at login.

The Headwaters Regional Network (hrn) is a commercial and educational service (see separate listing under Education) that provides conferencing, Internet access, and other services. In all, there are five on-line services under the Big Sky Telegraph umbrella:

+ System One: Type **bbs** for rural education and the on-line class.

+ System Two: Type **hrn** for rural economic development and community services.

+ System Three: Type **wmc** for Western Montana College campus activities, clubs and classes.

+ System Four: Type **gold** for rural peer counseling.

+ System Five: AKCS is our professional computer conferencing global system connected to USENET, BITNET, Internet and FIDOnet. Subscribers only.

Religion

JEWISH AND OTHER SPECIAL INTEREST FILES

ftp nctuccca.edu.tw
cd /USENET/comp.archives/auto

Use **ls soc.culture.*** to view the culture directories. Change to a directory of interest with **cd**. For example, to view Jewish information, use **cd soc.culture.jewish**, then use **ls** again to see a list of the files there. Use the ftp **get** command to copy over the files you want. You will find dozens of files and programs here, including pictures (most in .GIF format).

Many of these files are "gz" zip files. The required **GUNZIP.EXE** file may be somewhere on nctuccca, but we know it is at host **ftp.uni-kl.de** in subdirectory **/pub0/bio/0uti**. You can ftp there and download it with the **get** command.

ftp cs.dal.ca
cd /comp.archives

Use ls to view available directories. Among the ones you'll find are: soc.religion.christian
         soc.religion.islam

ftp world.std.com
cd /obi/Quotes
get religion

ftp athene.uni-paderborn.de
cd /doc/FAQ/soc.religion.quaker
get soc.religion.quaker_Answers_to_Frequently_Asked_
Questions.gz

ftp cs.bu.edu
cd /CN/keywords

Use ls to view files within this Copt-Net archive. These files help you locate topics within the archive, available via ftp from **pharos.bu.edu**. Copt-Net is a Christian fellowship serving the emigrant Coptic (Egyptian) Orthodox community.

Education

One useful aspect of the Internet is the amount of educational and reference material you can find there. Colleges and universities, government agencies, students, writers—lots of Internet users—place information files where you can find them. Some of these files are personal research projects—information that is gathered by an individual who has an interest in a particular area. This includes Internet references that show you where to find games or other information. Universities, through their researchers, place files on the Internet that discuss an aspect of their studies or list resources in a particular field.

As you browse the Internet, you'll find data that fits right into something you're working on now, and you'll locate files that are serendipitous, happenstance findings that you download and read simply because it is interesting. Use this information as a place to start your own research.

DISTANCE LEARNING

Among the more popular "trends" or topics in education is "distance learning." People are busy today, they move around, they work long hours. It is important for institutions of higher learning to respond to individual needs for instruction. One way to do this is with television classes, and on-line instruction. The facilities of the Internet are an obvious tool for this type of instruction.

Here is one place to learn about distance learning on the Internet:

ftp acsvax.open.ac.uk

At the Login prompt, enter FTP, and use FTP at the Password prompt as well. Once you are logged onto the system, type: **get ICDLINFO**. This file will give you background and current information on the services of Commonwealth of Learning information services at the British Open University.

NATIONAL EDUCATION BBS

This is one of several bulletin board services you can find that support educators through discussions, suggestions, training and the like. To access this bbs, do the following:

telnet nebbs.nersc.gov
Login: new

The stated purpose of this bbs is "to support education by providing access to advanced computational and network resources for students in grades K through 12."

This is a command-driven system, but there are prompts and help screens to help you learn you way around. For example, the default command on the first screen is **HELP**, which produces the display shown in Figure 6.29.

This system is divided into "boards" for different topics. When you issue the **Boards** command by typing **B** at the prompt, you will see a list similar to the one in Figure 6.30.

```
National Education BBS                      Current Board = 'general'
Enter Command: Help


HELP SCREEN
  (I)nfo              Get Version and Copyright Information
  (B)oards            List boards on system
  (C)ount             Count posts by board
  (D)ist              Distributed Processing menu
  (S)elect            Select current board
  (R)ead              Enter multifunction Read Menu
  (T)alk              Enter Talk Menu (Talk, Chat, Query, User List)
  (G)oodbye           Leave This BBS
  (H)elp              Get this Help Screen





    ALT-Z FOR HELP  |VT100|FDX|57600 N81|LOG CLOSED|PRINT OFF | ON-LINE
```

```
National Education BBS                      Current Board = 'general'
Enter Command: Select

List of Boards (* = zapped board)
  Name                Title
  Announcements       Official NESP / BBS Information
  General             Main BBS Board - General Use
  Network             Network Information - Sites, Archives & Services
  Libris              Library and Information Science
  Math                Mathematics Discussion Board
  Science             General and Interdisciplinary Science
  Physics             Physics and Computational Physics
  Programming         General Computer programming
  Macintosh           Discussion of Macintosh computers and programming
  PC                  PC and Compatable computers
  Politics            Political Issues of the Day
  Poetry              Sharing and discussing Poetry
  Philosophy          Philosophical Discussion
  Sysop               Messages to the system operator
  Chemistry           Computational Chemistry



    ALT-Z FOR HELP| VT100 | FDX | 57600 N81|LOG CLOSED | PRINT OFF | ON-LINE
```

Educational Software

SOFTWARE LISTINGS

> ftp swdsrv.edvz.univie.ac.at
> cd /mac/info-mac/info/app
> get educational-software-kids.txt

Literature

LITERATURE LISTS

    ftp ren.css.itd.umich.edu
    cd /poli/mim.d
    get _literature.list

    ftp nic.cic.net
    cd /pub/nircomm/gopher/e-serials/alphabetic/m/mim
    get README.literature.list.Z

LITERATURE REVIEWS

    ftp ski.utah.edu
    cd /net
    get literature_reviews

ONLINE LITERATURE

    ftp top.magnus.acs.ohio-state.edu
    cd /pub/library/books
    get as-you-like-it.text
    get peter_pan

There are other interesting on-line literature offerings. Use Gopher and access Libraries from the main menu, then choose Electronic Books. From there you can read literature including *Alice in Wonderland*, the *CIA World Factbook*, the *Bible*, *Moby Dick*, and lots more. You won't find everything you might ever want to search from the world of literature, of course, but there certainly is an interesting cross section of information here.

Libraries

BASIC LIBRARY INFORMATION

You can use Gopher to find out how to access card catalogs from a number of colleges and universities around the country. From the main menu, choose Libraries, then choose Library Catalogs via telnet. You'll get a menu of available card catalogs.

In addition, you can retrieve a list of useful library information via ftp:

ftp ftp.utdallas.edu
cd /pub/staff/billy/libguide

Use **dir** or **ls** to view available files. The list is separated by country. To get information about available on-line libraries in America, for example, get **libraries.america**. For Asian libraries, get **libraries.asia**.

Figure 6.31 shows a sample entry from these files.

```
                              Bond University
        Location:  Gold Coast, Queensland, Australia
        Catalog: URICA

        To access:

        1.     Type TELNET LIBRARY.BU.OZ.AU.
        2.     At the login prompt, type opac.

        To exit, type OFF on main menu

        Contact:
           Joanna Richardson
           <richardj@surf.sics.bu.oz.au>
           075 95 1401
        IP address:  131.244.7.7


                           Charles Sturt University

        Location: Bathurst and Wagga, New South Wales Australia
        Catal
         ALT-Z FOR HELP| VT100 | FDX| 57600 N81| LOG CLOSED| PRINT OFF | ON-LINE
```

telnet access.usask.ca

Log in as **hytelnet**. You should see the screen shown in Figure 6.32.

This is an on-line library reference service that provides menu-driven reference to Internet-accessible library services. In addition to running this reference software on-line, you can download PC, Macintosh, UNIX, and VMS versions for use on your own system. The author requests a $20 donation.

To download software:

ftp access.usask.ca
cd /pub/hytelnet/<pc, mac,unix, vms, amiga>
get 00readme
!cat 00readme

Figure 6.32

**Sample opening
Screen from Hytelnet**

```
                        Welcome to HYTELNET
                          version 6.5.x

              What is HYTELNET?          <WHATIS>
              Library catalogs           <SITES1>
              Other resources            <SITES2>
              Help files for catalogs    <OP000>
              Catalog interfaces         <SYS000>
              Internet Glossary          <GLOSSARY>
              Telnet tips                <TELNET>
              Telnet/TN3270 escape keys  <ESCAPE.KEY>
              Key-stroke commands        <HELP>
     ..................................................................
     Up/Down arrows MOVE      Left/Right arrows SELECT     ? for HELP anytime
          m  returns here     i  searches the index        q  quits
     ..................................................................
          We are now using a new version of the Hytelnet Software
            For information on the new features see <CHANGES>
     ..................................................................

               HYTELNET 6.5 was written by Peter Scott
               E-mail address: aa375@freenet.carleton.ca


    ALT-Z FOR HELP  | VT100 | FDX | 57600 N81 | LOG CLOSED | PRINT OFF | ON-LINE
```

This displays the **00readme** file on your host system, if it is a UNIX system. (For other systems, issue the appropriate text file display command). This file will tell you which file or files you need to download to support your particular system.

ERIC

ERIC (Educational Resources Information Center) has been around university libraries for a long time. It is a database of educational articles, abstracts, and summaries of doctoral dissertations, master's theses and other research and publications. It is a good source of published and unpublished information that is excellent because it comes from front line researchers and is usually very current.

You can access ERIC through WAIS. Once you have the WAIS search screen displayed (See Chapter 4 for information on accessing WAIS), look for **ERIC.archive**. Press **Enter** to select that entry and enter a key word to look for.

There are other ERIC resources also available on WAIS. Look for these sections:

AskERIC-Infoguides
AskERIC-Lesson-Plans
AskERIC-Minisearches
AskERIC-Questions

LAW LIBRARY

This is one more of the almost unbelievable assets you can reach on line through the Internet. You'll have more luck accessing this system after hours, as during regular business times you frequently get "Sorry load too great" messages and you are disconnected.

> To access the Liberty legal system:
> telnet liberty.uc.wlu.edu

Log in as **lawlib** and you will be presented with a welcome screen and instructions.

> ftp sulaw.law.su.oz.au
> cd /pub/law

Use **dir** or **ls** to view available files and directories. You can find here laws for each state, computer law information, and more. Most of these files have been compressed with COMPRESS (.Z extension) or combined with tar. You'll have to uncompress them and separate them before you can access the information.

> ftp ftp.cwru.edu
> cd /hermes

Use **ls** or **dir** to find out what files and directories are available. Among the reference material you should find here are ASCII files of U.S. Supreme Court rulings. You can also download WordPerfect and Xywrite versions of these files. Download the **Index, INFO,** and **README** files to get more information about this repository.

Periodicals

You can find listings of periodicals as well as on-line material by searching the Internet. Use Gopher to find on-line magazines. Try Archie (**prog periodical**) and see what you find. Here are some sample references.

> ftp world.std.com
> cd /periodicals

Use **dir** or **ls** to view the additional directories. You can look at the Network-World or Middlesex-News directories, for example, to find various articles and news.

USA Today

You can get to USA Today, headline news, and other on-line references through some freenets. Try:

> telnet hela.INS.CWRU.Edu
> log in as **visitor**.

This is a busy freenet system. If you get a busy message, try the Youngstown freenet listed below.

> telnet yfn.ysu.edu
> log in as **visitor**.

This is the Youngstown Free-Net, provided free of charge by St. Elizabeth Hospital Medical Center and Youngstown State University. This is a menu-driven system that includes entries for administration, business & industrial, The Government Center, etc. This is typical of freenets, which frequently are set up as small towns, with different types of information and services set up in different "rooms" or areas. The YFN main menu is shown in Figure 6.33.

Figure 6.33

YFN main menu screen

```
<<< Main Menu >>>

 1 Administration
 2 Post Office
 3 The Public Square
 4 The Communications Center
 5 The Animal Hospital
 6 The Business & Industrial Park
 7 The Computer Center
 8 The Courthouse
 9 The Government Center
10 The Hospital
11 The House of Worship
12 The Human Services Building
13 The Teleport
14 The USA/Today Headline News
15 Youngstown State University
16 Academy One
------------------------------------------------
h=Help, x=Exit YFN, "go help"=extended help

Your Choice ==>

ALT-Z FOR HELP|VT100|FDX|57600 N81 | LOG CLOSED | PRINT OFF | ON-LINE
```

Notice that this menu includes the USA Today and Headline News. This area is further divided into snapshots, sports, and other areas which, again, you can access via the menu.

LISTSERV INFORMATION, GENERAL

Mailing lists are an important way to keep current on happening in a variety of fields, but how do you know what any individual list server has available, and how do you find list servers? Here are some things that will help. You can send an e-mail message to any known listserver with the message **list global**. You should get a response with the resources of that list server. In addition, there are some fairly complete lists of available list servers out on Internet. Here's a place to start:

FTP KSUVXA.KENT.EDU

        cd library

Use **ls** or **dir** to view available files. You should find acadlist.file1 through acadlist.file7, and acadlist.readme and an index file.

        get acadlist.readme
        get index

Use **!cat** to view these files and decide what else you want to download.

PC MAGAZINE

        ftp wuarchive.wustl.edu
        cd /mirrors/msdos/pcmag

Online versions of the popular Ziff-Davis publication, PC Magazine. This is one of many sites. Find others with **prog pcmag** from within Archie.

JOURNALIST FILES & RESOURCES

The Internet is a rich resource for journalists. Any of the resources mentioned elsewhere could serve as a starting point for article or book research. So, it is natural that journalists gather on the Internet to support each other in their efforts. Here's an excellent resource that points you toward dozens of mailing lists, discussion groups, data bases and more of interest specifically to journalists. Send an e-mail message to **verbwork@access.dig ex.net** and ask for the Journalism List.

You'll receive a long list of resources that you'll have to investigate on your own to determine whether they are what you need. To join any of the discussion groups that use listserv, send e-mail to **listserv@domain** where **domain** is the addressed provided in the list you are sent. In the body of the e-mail message, say **sub listname** followed by your first name and last name. Your actual mail list will be provided in the header of the e-mail message. For Internet mailing lists, send e-mail to **listname-request@domain** and in the text, type **sub firstname lastname**.

Internet References

You'll find a number of rather good on-line publications about the Internet as you browse around. Most of them are available in multiple locations. Among the earliest (and somewhat outdated but still an easy to read, well-done book) is *Zen and the Art of the Internet*. Look for it in several forms, PostScript, ASCII and more. Here's one place to get it:

> ftp ftp.cs.widener.edu
> cd pub/zen
> get README

Then use **!cat README** to scan this file for additional information. There are several versions of this Internet guide in the directory. One quick and easy way to get a copy of the guide is to get zen-1.0.PS. This is a PostScript version of the file. Then simply copy it to a PostScript printer using the appropriate command for your computer system. The guide will print with page formatting and be ready for hole punching and inserting in a three-ring binder.

"Kids" General

These listings contain files of general interest to or about kids. ftp to the specified site, change to the listed directory (**cd directory-name**), and get the file shown. Use **ls** to display a list of available files in the listed directory. Host: athene.uni-paderborn.de

> Directory: /doc/FAQ/misc.answers
> File: misc-kids-FAQ.gz

> Directory: /doc/FAQ/misc.kids
> File: Welcome_to_Misc.kids_FAQ_File_Index_(Updated_6_2
> 9_93).gz

> Directory: /doc/FAQ/news.answers
> File: misc-kids-FAQ.gz

> Host: cs.dal.ca
> Directory: /comp.archives/alt.missing-kids

Sharing Educational Resources

BIG SKY TELEGRAPH

> Telnet 192.231.192.1 or bigsky.bigsky.dillon.mt.us
> Dial direct: 406-683-7680 (300/1200 bps)
>   406-683-7685 or 406-683-7686 (2400 bps)
>   406-683-7880 (9600 bps)
> Type **bbs** at login.

Big Sky Telegraph is a consortium of educators interested in sharing resources and information about computers and on-line education. The group claims to have more than 600 lesson plans on-line, and solicits lesson plans, ideas, and other resources from the education community for K-12 age groups. Among the resources you can get on-line is a course titled "Microcomputer Telecommunications," which covers the basics of telecomputing and modem use for connection to any of 60,000+ systems for users on a limited budget. A number of other on-line classes—some that qualify for teacher re-certification–are available through BST. A companion commercial service is available. (Log in as **hrn** instead of **bbs** for a look at the commercial offerings.)

Questions? Contact:
franko@bigsky.dillon.mt.us
Frank Odasz, Director of BST
Western Montana College
710 S. Atlantic
Dillon, MT 59725
Voice: 406-683-7338
Fax: 406-683-7493
Modem: 406-683-7680

KIDSPHERE EDUCATIONAL NETWORK

ftp animal-farm.nevada.edu
cd /pub/ccsd/KIDSPHERE
get one or more files:
    kidsnet.9212
    kidsnet.9301
    kidsphere.9302
    kidsphere.9303
    kidsphere.info

Postings from Kidsphere, a group established to stimulate development of an international network for kids and teachers. Use **get** to download the **Kidsphere.info** file first. This will provide a lot more information. You can join mailing lists for Kidsphere information through one of the following:

kidsphere-request@vms.cis.pitt.edu [Internet]
joinkids@vms.cis.pitt.edu   [Internet]
joinkids@pittvms   [BITNET]

KIDS is a list of mail postings from kid-to-kid. To receive postings, use one of the joinkids addresses above. To post information to the Kidsphere list, send mailings to:

kidsphere@vms.cis.pitt.edu   [Internet]
kidsphere@pittvms   [BITNET]
kids@vms.cis.pitt.edu   [Internet]
kids@pittvms   [BITNET]

OPERATION UPLINK

> ftp ftp.OpUp.Org
> cd /pub/library/Opup
> get edu.networking

This file provides a basic introduction to on-line education. The offerings in this directory will grow rapidly, so check frequently. Operation Uplink is an innovative elementary and secondary educational program run within Knoxville, TN public schools, but operated with teachers and professionals from around the world. Funding for the program is mostly private.

Operation Uplink uses computers—and particularly the Internet—to link youngsters with other students and with adults in a sharing, learning environment. You can usually find V_Kids (a multi-user UNIX machine that puts up to 13 kids on the Internet at once) on IRC in #vine or #UpLink channels. Questions? e-mail **Towne@OpUp.Org**.

> ftp aramis.rutgers.edu
> cd /pub/watrous
> get kids.quotes

> ftp animal-farm.nevada.edu
> cd /pub/ccsd/EDUC.LISTSERV.INFO
> get k12.listserv
> (A fairly comprehensive list of K-12 e-mail lists.)

> ftp casbah.acns.nwu.edu
> cd /pub/ltp
> et computers.in.literature.teaching

Government

NATIONAL SCIENCE FOUNDATION

The National Science Foundation is among the founders of the Internet as we know it today. It should not be surprising, then, that you can access NSF information via Internet. Here's how:

> telnet stis.nsf.gov
Login: Public

You will see a welcoming screen, then a login prompt. Enter **new** if you've never accessed this facility before. Then you will be prompted for the ID you want to use on the system and you will be asked a few more questions to register with this system.

Now you can access this host to perform sophisticated text searches on NSF Publications as well as a database of award abstracts. The screen should look like the one in Figure 6.34.

Figure 6.34

NSF Main menu screen

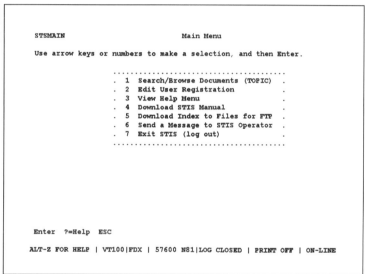

```
STSMAIN                        Main Menu

Use arrow keys or numbers to make a selection, and then Enter.

                  ............................................
                  . 1  Search/Browse Documents (TOPIC)  .
                  . 2  Edit User Registration           .
                  . 3  View Help Menu                   .
                  . 4  Download STIS Manual             .
                  . 5  Download Index to Files for FTP  .
                  . 6  Send a Message to STIS Operator  .
                  . 7  Exit STIS (log out)              .
                  ............................................




      Enter  ?=Help  ESC

      ALT-Z FOR HELP | VT100|FDX | 57600 N81|LOG CLOSED | PRINT OFF | ON-LINE
```

The search engine is TOPIC, from Verity, Inc. You can download a user's guide for TOPIC from the host, or call 202-357-5000, and request a printed copy of NSF publication NSF 91-19.

You can also access information from this host through anonymous ftp and the Internet Gopher.

FEDERAL INFORMATION EXCHANGE

You can access the Federal Information Exchange (fedix) from a variety of sources, including Gopher. You can also get to it via telnet or through a dialup 800 number (shown in Figure 6.35).

For telnet access, issue this command:

telnet fedix.fie.com

You will get a logon banner that looks something like the one shown in Figure 6.35.

Figure 6.35

FEDEX opening screen

```
         FFFFFFFF EEEEEEEE DDDDDDD  IIIII  XXX    XXX
         FFF      EEE      DDD DDDD III    XXX XXX
         FFF      EEE      DDD  DDD III     XXXXX
         FFFFF    EEEEEEE  DDD  DDD III      XXX
         FFF      EEE      DDD  DDD III     XXXXX
         FFF      EEE      DDD DDDD III    XXX XXX
         FFF      EEEEEEEE DDDDDDD  IIIII  XXX    XXX


logged in on - /dev/ttyp6
Internet


        F E D E R A L   I N F O R M A T I O N   E X C H A N G E

        555 Quince Orchard Road      dialup..: (800) 783-3349
        Suite 200                    internet: fedix.fie.com
        Gaithersburg, MD  20878      helpline: (301) 975-0103
```

As you can see, you can use Internet or direct dialup. The first time you access the service logon as NEW and follow directions.

What is on Fedix? A variety of federal information services, including:

1. Federal Opportunities (FEDIX)
2. Minority College & University Capability Information (MOLIS)
3. Higher Education Opportunities for Minorities & Women (HERO)

As you work through the menu system, you will learn that Fedix is "an on-line information service that links the higher education community and the federal government to facilitate research, education, and services. The system provides accurate and timely federal agency information to colleges, universities, and other research organizations."

Information from at least nine federal agencies is available on-line, including data from The Department of Energy (DOE), Office of Naval Research (ONR), National Aeronautics and Space Administration (NASA), Air Force Office of Scientific

Research (AFOSR), and Federal Aviation Administration (FAA) are providing comprehensive education- and research-related agency information, while the National Science Foundation (NSF), Department of Housing and Urban Development (HUD), Department of Commerce (DOC) and the U.S. Agency for International Development (AID), are providing minority information, exclusively. But the list is changing, so consult the on-line list for current availability.

U.S. FEDERAL REGISTER

You can find the U.S. Federal Register through some Gopher clients. You'll have to access it through an educational institution or company, unless you're up for some fairly stiff fees. A campus license, for example, is $4,500, and non-educational licenses go as high as $10,000. However, you can get access via telnet for around $10 per hour.

For information about accessing the Federal Register, send e-mail to: **fedreg@internet.com**.

PRESIDENTIAL ADDRESSES

The following are the e-mail addresses for the executive branch. Use your local mail system to send messages to the listed addresses.

U.S. President	PRESIDENT@WHITEHOUSE.GOV
U.S. Vice-President	VICE.PRESIDENT@WHITE-HOUSE.GOV

OTHER GOVERNMENT AGENCY ACCESS

Through Gopher or WAIS, you can find access to various governmental offices (or rather the information they produce), including the Commission on Civil Rights, the Federal Communications Commission, and the Patent and Trademark

Office. In addition, you can find a collection of Presidential Documents. Access depends on your Gopher server; just search Gopher for Government topics.

FOOD AND DRUG ADMINISTRATION

The FDA offers news releases, AIDS information, consumer information, and more through its fdabbs. You can reach it through telnet:

telnet fdabbs.fda.gov

At the **login:** prompt, enter **bbs**. You'll see the screen shown in Figure 6.37.

Figure 6.37

FDA BBS initial screen

```
Escape character is '^]'.

 UNIX System V  R.3 (WINS) (FDABBS)

login: bbs
UNIX System V Release 3.2.3 AT&T 3B2
FDABBS
Copyright (c) 1984, 1986, 1987, 1988, 1989, 1990 AT&T
All Rights Reserved
Login last used: Mon Sep 13 15:09:43 1993

        @@@@@  @@@@@@    @
        @      @      @  @ @                    THE FDA
        @@@@@  @      @ @@@@@        ELECTRONIC BULLETIN BOARD
        @      @@@@ @ @        @

    Welcome to FDA's electronic bulletin board, a service of the Food and
    Drug Administration.

        UNAUTHORIZED USE IS PROHIBITED BY TITLE 18 OF U.S.C.


Please enter your name (first and last) ==>
ALT-Z FOR HELP | VT100 | FDX || 57600 N81 | LOG CLOSED | PRINT OFF | ON-LINE
```

You'll be asked for your first and last name, company or organization, and an address and phone number to register for the FDA electronic BBS. The topics you can search are shown in Figure 6.38.

Figure 6.38

FDA BBS Topic list

```
         TOPICS         DESCRIPTION

   *  NEWS          News releases
   *  ENFORCE       Enforcement Report
   *  APPROVALS     Drug and Device Product Approvals list
   *  CDRH          Center for Devices and Radiological Health
   *  BULLETIN      Text from Drug Bulletin
   *  AIDS          Current Information on AIDS
   *  CONSUMER      FDA Consumer magazine index and selected articles
   *  SUBJ-REG      FDA Federal Register Summaries by Subject
   *  ANSWERS       Summaries of FDA information
   *  INDEX         Index of News Releases and Answers
   *  DATE-REG      FDA Federal Register Summaries by Publication Date
   *  CONGRESS      Text of Testimony at FDA Congressional Hearings
   *  SPEECH        Speeches Given by FDA Commissioner and Deputy
   *  VETNEWS       Veterinary Medicine News
   *  MEETINGS      Upcoming FDA Meetings
   *  IMPORT        Import Alerts
   *  MANUAL        On-Line User's Manual


   FOR LIST OF AVAILABLE TOPICS TYPE TOPICS
   OR ENTER THE TOPIC YOU DESIRE ==>
   ALT-Z FOR HELP| VT100| FDX| 57600 N81 | LOG CLOSED | PRINT OFF | ON-LINE
```

PROJECT GUTENBERG

Through Project Gutenberg you can access the latest U.S. Census information, articles, reference material, and more. It may be on your Gopher. If it isn't, you can ftp directly to it:

ftp mrcnext.cso.uiuc.edu
cd etext/etext91

Use **dir** to list files. There is an INDEX file in each of these directories. You can use **get** to copy it to your system, then **cat** to look at it to find out what each of these files means. Then go on to other directories:

cd etext/articles
cd etext92
cd etext93

You can find interesting books, articles, and reference material in these directories.

CIA INFORMATION

We want to get this straight. The Central Intelligence Agency is one of this country's spy groups, right? Well, maybe "spy" is a little harsh, but at least it is a sort of secret, governmental agency that collects data about all kinds of things around the world. You wouldn't expect to be able to get to their information, would you? You can.

There are at least a couple of CIA resources you can locate in various places on the Internet: the CIA World Map and the CIA Factbook. In fact, if you want to see something interesting, use Archie to do a substring search for **cia**. You'll get a number of resources from the CIA.

Here's one place to get the CIA World Fact Book:

ftp world.std.com
cd /obi/World.Factbook
get world11.txt.Z

As for the CIA World Map, try:

ftp relay.cs.toronto.edu
cd /doc/geography/CIA_World_Map

Within this directory are a number of additional directories. Start by getting the file README. Use **!cat README** to view this file and find out what you need to do. This is actually an archive that contains map drawing programs that use the CIA World Map data.

SOCIAL SECURITY ADMINISTRATION

Whether you're near retirement or merely curious about what is current in the Social Security Administration, this can be an interesting resource.

ftp soaf1.ssa.gov
cd pub

Then use dir to find out what is there. It is a mixed bag. Just browse around by using **cd** and a directory name, then **dir** to look for files and directories that make sense. One interesting resource is the **ssa.phone.book.Z** file located in the **/pub** directory. Use **get** to download this file to your local host, then use **UNCOMPRESS** to unpack it. There are a number of speech files that offer some data. You can start with the **README.1st** file, or one of the abstract files to get you underway here.

Congress

Ever want to contact your congressman? You can get the address information for any member of congress through WAIS. Once on WAIS, locate the **US-Congress-Phone-Fax** entry on the main list. Highlight it, press **Space** and enter the name you are looking for. WAIS will search the database and display a list of any entries that match. Figure 6.34 shows the results of a search for duncan, congressman from Tennessee.

Figure 6.34

WAIS Congress
Search: Duncan

```
SWAIS                    Document Display            Page:  1
R TN Duncan Jr., John J.      1-202-225-5435  1-202-225-6440
  p st representative           phone           fax
```

If you only know the last name of the person you're looking for, enter that and then choose the correct one from the list on the next screen.

There are other reference sections you'll find close to the congressional entry. For example, there is a file for us-judges and you can reference the **US-Budget-1993** or **US-Gov-Programs** sections for some interesting information. Figure 6.35 shows a sample screen from the budget file.

You can look at political speeches through WAIS as well. Just open the main WAIS screen, then look for clinton-speeches, bush-speeches, and the like. (We found these with the sunsite.unc.edu WAIS client SWAIS). You can ftp to this information as well:

ftp sunsite.unc.edu
cd /pub/docs/speeches

Figure 6.35

Sample Screen from
US-Budget-1993 file

```
Document # 44
Headline: Executive-Office-of-the-President The-Points-of-Light-Foundation
DocID: 0 391 /b/FEDERAL-PROGRAMS-BY-AGENCY-AND-ACCOUNT/Executive-Office-of-the-P
resident/The-Points-of-Light-Foundation

Document # 45
Headline: Executive-Office-of-the-President Summary
DocID: 0 679 /b/FEDERAL-PROGRAMS-BY-AGENCY-AND-ACCOUNT/Executive-Office-of-the-P
resident/Summary

Document # 46
Headline: Funds-Appropriated-to-the-President Unanticipated-Needs
DocID: 0 380 /b/FEDERAL-PROGRAMS-BY-AGENCY-AND-ACCOUNT/Funds-Appropriated-to-the
-President/Unanticipated-Needs

Document # 47
Headline: Funds-Appropriated-to-the-President Investment-in-Management-Improveme
nt
DocID: 0 338 /b/FEDERAL-PROGRAMS-BY-AGENCY-AND-ACCOUNT/Funds-Appropriated-to-the
-President/Investment-in-Management-Improvement

Document # 48
Press any key to continue, 'q' to quit.
```

Use **dir** to find out what is there. The directory should look like Figure 6.36.

Figure 6.36

Directory at
sunsite.unc.edu

```
ftp> dir
200 PORT command successful.
150 Opening ASCII mode data connection for /bin/ls.
total 52
-rwxr-xr-x  1 root     daemon       1262 Mar 18  1993 .cache
drwxr-xr-x  2 root     daemon        512 Jul  6 20:31 .cap
-rw-r--r--  1 root     daemon       3616 Aug 26  1992 ABOUT.NPTN.TXT
-rw-r--r--  1 root     daemon       2484 Aug 26  1992 CAMPAIGN.92.TXT
-rw-r--r--  1 root     daemon        613 Jan  4  1993 INDEX
-r--r--r--  1 root     daemon       5206 Oct 28  1992 INDEX.BUSH
-r--r--r--  1 root     daemon      13177 Nov  2  1992 INDEX.CLINTON
drwxr-xr-x  2 root     daemon        512 Mar  4  1993 Perot
-rw-r--r--  1 root     daemon        124 Jan  4  1993 README
drwxr-xr-x  2 root     daemon       3584 Mar 18  1993 bush.dir
-r--r--r--  1 root     daemon       3003 Oct 19  1992 c199.txt
drwxr-xr-x  2 root     daemon        512 Mar  4  1993 clinton-positions
drwxr-xr-x  2 root     daemon       9216 Mar  4  1993 clinton.dir
drwxr-xr-x  2 root     daemon        512 Oct 21  1992 debates
drwxr-xr-x  2 root     daemon        512 Aug 26  1992 demo-conv
drwxr-xr-x  3 root     daemon        512 Jun  3 21:24 kibo-for-prez
226 Transfer complete.
1057 bytes received in 0.32 seconds (3.2 Kbytes/s)
ftp>
```

Download INDEX or INDEX.CLINTON first. That will point you in the right direction toward finding the files you want. Then use CD **clinton.dir**, for example, to access actual speeches.

Use WAIS to locate the **White-House-Papers** entry, then search for entries by keyword, or enter a space to get a directory list. You can ftp to this information as well:

ftp sunsite.unc.edu
cd /pub/academic/political-science/whitehouse-papers/1993

Use **dir** to see how this directory is structured. You will find a separate directory for each month, then files about different topics. You can use **get** to download these files for your own reference.

Reference

DICTIONARY

Until recently you could access a dictionary and thesaurus on-line from Rutgers University. The provider of the dictionary recently restricted on-line access to Rutgers students and faculty and members of other New Jersey institutions. You can still find items of interest at the Rutgers INFO project, however:

telnet info.rutgers.edu

Logon is automatic and the system is menu driven. Among the information you can find is the Federal Fedix database, the NIH Guide for Grants database, Rutgers library information, and more. Simply type the appropriate menu command at the **Menu>** prompt.

For another dictionary reference, try this:

telnet moose.cs.indiana.edu 2627

THESAURUS

Use WAIS and look for the thesaurus entry in the Source list. At the Keyword: prompt, enter the word you want to look up. WAIS displays the files that seem to fit your request. Again, remember that the number under Score shows how closely the listed item meets your search request. Figure 6.37 shows the first screen of results on a search for **network**. Figure 6.38 shows the detailed entry.

```
Searching: thesaurus Found 2 items. SWAIS Search ResultsItems:  2
  #    Score SourceTitle  Lines
001:   [1000] (roget-thesaurus)#59a. Complexity -- N. complexity;      11
002:   [1000] (roget-thesaurus)#219. Crossing. -- N. crossing &c.      29001:
[1000] (roget-thesaurus)
```

```
#59a. Complexity -- N. complexity; complexness &c. adj.; complexus;
complication, implication; intricacy, intrication; perplexity; network,
labyrinth; wilderness, jungle; involution, raveling, entanglement; coil &c.
(convolution) 248; sleave, tangled skein, knot, Gordian knot, wheels within
wheels; kink, knarl; webwork.
Adj.  knarled. complex, complexed; intricate, complicated, perplexed,
involved, raveled, entangled, knotted, tangled, inextricable; irreducible.
```

UPI NEWS (UPI NEWSWIRE)

Use Gopher to locate the News entry and select **UPI News.** You
can view a short description of what UPI News is, and see a
menu for UPI News access. You may not be able to get to some
of this information (except the About UPI News Introduction)
unless you are accessing the information from on the campus.

This information is provided (at least where we found it)
through a site license purchased by the University of Minnesota.
UPI and other news services are offering similar licenses to colleges and universities as well as businesses which use it for
research and general information. This is provided through a
facility called Clarinet, a commercial information provider.

You can search the database for information by topic and
receive a list of available stories, like the one shown in Figure
6.39.

ZIP CODE LIST

> ftp top.magnus.acs.ohio-state.edu
> cd /pub/library/lists
> get US_zip_codes

This will give you an excellent reference list for U.S. zip codes.

Figure 6.39

Typical UPI News
Story List After Search

```
Client v1.11Search Today's News: india

 --> 1.  1993/Sep/Sep 30/news/New Navy Chief takes charge in India : From: .
 2.  1993/Sep/Sep 30/news/India quake toll mounts to 6,200 : From: clar.
 3.  1993/Sep/Sep 30/news/India quake toll rises to 6,513 : From: clari.
 4.  1993/Sep/Sep 30/news/A UPI News Update [Sep 30 8 am PDT] : From: c.
 5.  1993/Sep/Sep 30/news/A UPI News Update [Sep 30 9 am PDT] : From: c.
 6.  1993/Sep/Sep 30/news/A UPI News Update [Sep 30 10 am PDT] : From: .
 7.  1993/Sep/Sep 30/news/A UPI News Update [Sep 30 11 am PDT] : From: .
 8.  1993/Sep/Sep 30/news/A UPI News Update [Sep 30 12 pm PDT] : From: .
 9.  1993/Sep/Sep 30/news/The UPI Afternoon Report [Sep 30 12 pm PDT] .
10.  1993/Sep/Sep 29/local/UPI Midwest Farm Report : From: clarinews@cl.
11.  1993/Sep/Sep 29/local/Georgia Second News In Brief [Sep 29 7 am P .
12.  1993/Sep/Sep 29/news/India sets up human rights commission : From:.
13.  1993/Sep/Sep 29/news/Inter-tribal warfare spreads in India's nort .
14.  1993/Sep/Sep 29/news/Earthquake measuring 6.4 hits southern India .
15.  1993/Sep/Sep 29/news/500 trapped under debris after quake in Indi .
16.  1993/Sep/Sep 29/news/A UPI News Update [Sep 29 8 pm PDT] : From: c.
17.  1993/Sep/Sep 29/news/A UPI News Update [Sep 29 9 pm PDT] : From: c.
18.  1993/Sep/Sep 29/news/Quakes jar western India, killing as many as .

Press ? for Help, q to Quit, u to go up a menuPage: 1/2
```

Books and More

NEW YORK CITY (MANHATTAN) BOOKSTORES

ftp rtfm.mit.edu (18.172.1.27)
cd /pub/usenet/news.answers/books/stores/north-american
get nyc.Z

or

Send e-mail to **mail-server@rtfm.mit.edu** with the subject line "send usenet/news.answers/books/stores/north-american/nyc", leaving the body of the message empty.

This is an annotated list of Manhattan bookstores by section of town. The author describes the store, mentions any special information that may be useful ("identify the mystery quote of the day and get an additional 20% off your purchase"), and shares personal experiences.

DINOSAURS

ftp wiretap.spies.com
cd /Library/Article/Misc
get dinosaur.fly

A brief discussion of which dinosaurs were able to fly.

ftp ftp.uni-kl.de
cd /pub0/humor/funnies
get dinosaurus.jokes.Z

ftp wasp.eng.ufl.edu
cd /incoming/BarneyTheDinosaurMeetsWOLFE
get NSTEIN.txt
get NSTEIN.voc

ftp swdsrv.edvz.univie.ac.at
cd /mac/info-mac/grf
get jurassic-park-logo-icon.hqx
cd /pc/windows/win3/desktop
get jurassic.zip

COLLEGE LISTS

ftp ftp.denet.dk
cd /pub/wordlists/places
get Colleges.Z

Art

If you have even a passing interest in art, you can find some interesting resources on the Internet. One place to start is with a simple Archie search. Once you are inside Archie, use **Set Search Exact** at the prompt to narrow the search, then use **prog art** to produce a list of files with the name art. What you'll get is several pages of host and directory names. Some are obvious, and others require a little imagination or a hands-on check to find out what's really there.

Images

For example, one listing is at host **sunbane.engrg.uwo.ca** in the directory **/pub/gifpics/art**. It is fairly obvious that this is some kind of digital image repository, in .GIF format and, perhaps, the images are art related. We used **ftp** to attach to this host, then did a directory listing (**dir** at the ftp prompt) to see what was there. We got the file list shown in Figure 6.40.

Figure 6.40
Sunbane.engrg.uwo.ca Directory

```
> dir
200 PORT command successful.
150 Opening ASCII mode data connection for /bin/ls.
bathrs.gif        31885   (null)
creationii.gif    57980   (null)
escher3           12855   (null)
landscape         70888   (null)
monalisa         161512   (null)
order.chaos       25906   (null)
reptiles          24840   (null)
venus             91244   (null)
waterfall         21740   (null)
226 Transfer complete.
297 bytes received in 0.08 seconds (3.6 Kbytes/s)
```

Notice that some of these files do not carry the .GIF extension, but they are, indeed, .GIF files. To use them on your system you may have to rename them, adding the .GIF extension, for your application software to recognize the file format. These are mostly well-known artistic images—Mona Lisa, for example—that can be fun to work with in your word processor or graphics manipulation package.

If you back up one directory on this host, you'll find some additional image possibilities. Simply issue the **cd ..** command and then use **dir** again. The file names that end with a forward slash (/) are directories. You can use **cd** to find out what they contain as well.

That's a start. Here are some additional art resources from our cursory search of the Internet. You can use Archie and other tools we described earlier in this book to find your own art information or images.

What about medical images? You can start looking at:

ftp athene.uni-paderborn.de
cd /pcsoft3/mac/misc/medical/art

Issue the dir command and you will get a list like the one in Figure 6.41.

Figure 6.41

File List from
athene.uni-
paderborn.de

```
dir
200 PORT command successful.
150 Opening ASCII mode data connection for /bin/ls.
total 851
drwxr-xr-x    2 Software Admin        512 Sep  8 08:38 .AppleDouble
-rw-r--r--    1 Software Admin        450 Jul 13 03:56 00readme.txt
-rw-r--r--    1 Software Admin       7565 Feb  5  1993 abdomaorta.gif.hqx
-rw-r--r--    1 Software Admin      16293 Jun 29  1992 cranialnerves.cpt.hqx
-rw-r--r--    1 Software Admin     343877 May 31  1992 histology.cpt.hqx
-rw-r--r--    1 Software Admin      31849 May 31  1992 medsymbols.cpt.hqx
-rw-r--r--    1 Software Admin      74204 May 31  1992 torsoanatomy.cpt.hqx
-rw-r--r--    1 Software Admin     225844 May 31  1992 upperextrem.cpt.hqx
-rw-r--r--    1 Software Admin     132570 May 14 20:31 ysmicons1.0.cpt.hqx
226 Transfer complete.
```

Obviously, these are .hqx files (Macintosh format).

These files are typical of the type of sharing that goes on over the Internet.

ftp world.std.com
cd /pub/ClipArt

Use **dir** to view the available files. These are clip art samples compiled by William Phillips at ShoeString Projects in Cambridge, MA. It is "shareware," in that you can download these images in pcx or tiff format, but a "small contribution" is requested

The following are additional resources for discovering pictures and graphics.

ftp nic.switch.ch
cd /mirror/hp95lx/pcx
get dinosaur.pcx
cd /mirror/info-mac/Graphic/Quicktime
get dinosaur-glares.hqx

cd /mirror/info-mac/Graphic/qt
get dinosaur-glares.hqx

ftp sunsite.unc.edu
cd /pub/academic.medicine/mac-medical
cd /pub/multimedia/pictures/smithsonian

An interesting collection of art images is available in the /pub/art directory of host biome.bio.dfo.ca. Files are in .gif and .jpg format.

ftp biome.bio.dfo.ca
cd /pub/art

Use **dir** to get the file list shown in Figure 6.42.

Figure 6.42

File List from biome.bio.dfo.ca

```
> dir
200 PORT command successful.
150 Opening ASCII mode data connection for '/bin/ls'.
Index             899
README            140
botti4.jpg     111272   Botticelli: Virgin on the Half-Shell
botti5.jpg     153352   Botticelli: Dancing Nymphs
loacoon.jpg    122531   Laocoon Statue (with snakes)
michela2c.jpg  135082   Michelangelo: Woman reading scroll
michela3b.jpg  189733   Michelangelo: Old woman reading book
michela7.jpg   117546   Michelangelo: God
mntlunch.jpg   428986   Monet Picnic
monet1.jpg      70098   Monet: Women and Children in Poppy Field
monet2.jpg      67899   Monet: Cathedral, very dark
parisien.gif   191957   Parisienne in Blue Dress
redcanna.jpg    72589   Georgia O'Keefe: flower painting, Red Canna
renoir.gif     175385   Renoir: Young woman with daughter or young sister
skull.gif       88738   da Vinci: drawing of a skull
226 Transfer complete.
805 bytes received in 0.84 seconds (0.94 Kbytes/s)
ftp>
```

Here's an interesting resource, the "Bryn-mawr-classical-review." Access it through WAIS and enter search key words. This on-line publication consists of articles about a number of "classical" topics, and it fully-searchable.

Television

Its an age-old question that we won't try to resolve here: Is television art? Whatever the answer to that, you can find out more about current and past television programs over the Internet. Here's how:

ftp ftp.uu.net
cd /usenet/rec.arts.tv

Use **dir** to find out what's there. This is a dynamic database that comes from a variety of sources. There is data and comments here about past and present shows. You'll find both files and directories of files in this subdirectory. Many of the files are compressed. (You can tell which ones: those whose file names end in **.Z**.)

Those topics that have grown rather large earn their own subdirectory. Simply use **cd** again to make the desired directory current, and use **dir** again to see what you have available.

For example, if you change to the **twilightzone** subdirectory, you'll find the Vidiot directory and inside that directory are two more subdirectories, each with a handful of files about Twilight Zone. Some of these files are in **ps** format (the file names end in **.ps**), which means they will print directly on a PostScript printer.

Music

Under the art category you may also discover some music files and information. At the **biome.bio.dfo.ca host**, for example, you can find a list of music-related information in the **/pub/music** subdirectory like the one shown in Figure 6.43.

Figure 6.43

Music List at
biome.bio.dfo.ca

```
ftp> dir
200 PORT command successful.
150 Opening ASCII mode data connection for '/bin/ls'.
Concerts            2971   Concerts and other musical events
FAQ                12217
Index                388
Lyrics.Z           35921
SITES               1997
lehrer.tom/            =
mail-order         12898
summerschools.uk    2340   Summer Schools in Cambridge, England
226 Transfer complete.
```

Try the mail-order file (**get mail-order**). It contains a number of mail-order resources for music, CDs, tapes, and the like.

You'll find even more music information here:

ftp cs.uwp.edu
cd /pub/music

This archive, at the University of Wisconsin-Parkside, contains a variety of music-oriented information, including data on CD collections, lyrics, guitar chords, and graphics files that contain pictures of some artists. The directories that were in this location as this book was written are shown in Figure 6.44.

Figure 6.44

Directories in /pub/music at host cs.uwp.edu

```
dir
200 PORT command successful.
150 Opening ASCII mode data connection for /bin/dl.
CHANGES          1126
GOPHER.README    2023
README.CORRUPT   2611
SITES            2387  Other music-related FTP archive sites
artists/           =  Artists- Archives by Artist name
classical/         =  Classical Buying Guide
composition/       -  Articles of Music Composition
database/          =  Music Database program
faqs/              =  Frequently Asked Questions files
folk/              =  Folk Music Files and pointers
guitar/            =  Guitar TAB files from ftp.nevada.edu
info/              =  rec.music.info newsgroup archives
kurzweil/          =  Kurzweil K2000 Archives
lists/             =  Mailing lists archives
lyrics/            =  Lyrics Archives
midi/              -  Some midi files
misc/              -  Misc files that don't fit anywhere else
pictures/          =  GIFS, JPEGs, PBMs and more.
programs/          -  Misc music-related programs for various machines
releases/          =  USA release listings (now info/releases)
reviews/           =  rec.music.reviews archives
uap/               -  Usenet Artist Polls
226 Transfer complete.
1140 bytes received in 0.38 seconds (2.9 Kbytes/s)
ftp>
```

Simply use **cd** to change to the directory you're interested in, and use **dir** to list the available files and directories. One interesting resource here is the music database, located in the **/pub/music/database** subdirectory. First, **get README** and look at it to determine how to use the files here. Among the information here is a database of over 700 CDs, plus an executable program to manage this database. You can use the Albums program to retrieve CD information by title or artist and there is even a routine to help you determine how many songs from a given album will fit on a cassette tape. Useful stuff!

You'll also want to look at the **/pub/music/artists** subdirectory. Here you'll find 26 subdirectories, one for each letter of the alphabet. This is an interesting archive because the alphabetical subdirectories contain links to the other resources on this host. That means you can use **cd /pub/music/artists/p** and then **dir** to get a list of all artists catalogued there. Each of these subdirectories contain additional information. So, for example, if you **cd presley.elvis** and use **dir**, you'll see additional subdirectories, including **guitar, lyrics**, and **pictures**.

Check out the lyrics under many of the artist's directories. You'll find compressed files designed to be used in Windows (crd format), so you can create your own database of artists and lyrics.

In many ftp systems, you don't need to issue the entire path command to get to a specific subdirectory. Simply use **cd presley.elvis** at any local directory (for example) and you should be transferred immediately to the specified directory without entering the entire path. This may not work on all systems.

Other music resources include:

ftp casbah.acns.nwu.edu
cd /pub/acoustic-guitar/digests

Among the items you'll find here is the Acoustic Guitar Digest. This information is not new, but it might be useful to you.

Also in the acoustic-guitar directory, are subdirectories for **misc** files (these include PostScript files with scales, staff paper, and more), and transcriptions (a series of text files that hold the lyrics and guitar chord designations for a number of songs).

Here's one final music resource:

Use WAIS to locate the Sheet_Music_Index.

TOP 10 MUSIC LIST

This is the top ten music list compiled by Billboard Magazine, the publication many radio stations use to help them determine which songs to play and which artists are climbing up the chart. Get your own top ten list:

finger buckmr@rpi.edu

You'll get an immediate list like the one shown in Figure 6.45.

Figure 6.45

Top Ten list from Billboard

```
*** PROVIDED FOR PERSONAL EDUCATIONAL USE ONLY ***

Here is an update on the available charts for the week ending 09/04/93:
Copyright Billboard Magazine (1993)

To see the latest Billboard chart info try "finger buckmr@rpi.edu".
? = previous position unknown
- = no previous position
-----------------------------------------------------------------

U.S. Top Pop Singles:
    1. (01) UB40  --  Can't Help Falling in Love [SEVENTH week at #1]
    2. (03) MARIAH CAREY  --  Dreamlover
    3. (02) TAG TEAM  --  Whoomp! (There it is)
    4. (04) JODECI  --  Lately
    5. (05) SOUL ASYLUM  --  Runaway Train
    6. (07) JANET JACKSON  --  If
    7. (1?) SWV  --  Right Here/Human Nature
    8. (??) MICHAEL JACKSON  --  Will You Be There
    9. (06) THE PROCLAIMERS  --  I'm Gonna Be (500 Miles)
   10. (09) TONY! TONI! TONE!  --   If I Had NoLoot
```

Miscellaneous Resources

Sure, we probably could have found a specific topic under which to place these resources, but it would have required a number of different resource names, and some would have had only one or two listings. Anyway, here's a list of Internet resources you can reference when you don't find what you wanted elsewhere in this resource chapter.

Here's a miscellaneous listing under the miscellaneous heading. You can find programs, text files and graphics images about a very broad range of topics here.

ftp athene.uni-paderborn.de
cd /pcsoft3/mac/misc

Use **dir** to discover the many subdirectories that exist under this one. You can find information and Macintosh files about everything from astronomy to medicine to physics. Enjoy.

You don't have a Macintosh? Try the **/pcsoft** directory. You'll see the banner shown in Figure 6.46.

Figure 6.46

PCSOFT Directory
Banner

```
ftp> cd pcsoft
250-()===============================================================()
250-|| PPP    CC    SSS  OO  FFFF TTTTT    Software for Personal Computers ||
250-|| P  P C  C S     O  O F      T       DOS/WINDOWS/OS2/LINUX/AMIGA/ATARI ||
250-|| PPP  C     SS  O  O FFF     T                                        ||
250-|| P    C  C   S O  O F        T          Mirrors + Local specialities  ||
250-|| P     CC  SSS  OO  F        T                                        ||
250-()===============================================================()
250-|| MS-DOS    ->    cd msdos    (Simtel+More)        ||
250-|| WINDOWS   ->    cd windows  (Cica)               ||
250-|| PC-Games  ->    cd pc-games (Ulowell)            ||
250-|| OS/2      ->    cd os2      (RUS/IBM-Watson)      ||
250-|| LINUX     ->    cd linux    (sunsite/tsx/cdrom)   ||
250-|| AMIGA     ->    cd amiga    (Aminet+More)        ||
250-|| ATARI-ST  ->    cd atari                         ||
250-()===============================================================()
```

Now you can use the specified commands to find resources for your specific machine. Note that some of these directories are mirror images of the **wuarchive.wustl.edu** archives. You can attach directly there, as well:

ftp wuarchive.wustl.edu

Issue the dir command to find out which directories are available. Among the ones you might find interesting are **graphics, multimedia,** and **packages.**

Many local hosts mirror this archive so you can access the local host and retrieve images as if they were in the local directory.

Here's another one:

finger yanoff@csd4.csd.uwm.edu

This will tell you how to get a comprehensive list of Internet resources.

Here's a resource for a wide range of information, much of which will also show up on other systems around the Internet. Try this:

ftp ftp.uu.net
cd /usenet

In this subdirectory you'll find a number of other subdirectories, most named after the USENET recreation topics. You can see how the list looked as this book was written by studying Figure 6.47.

```
total 552
-rw-r--r--    1 3      archive       88 Jun 16 17:34 .message
drwxrwxr-x    2 3      archive      512 Sep 21 15:26 comp.risks
drwxrwsr-x    5 81     archive      512 Jul 29  1992 comp.sources.3b1
drwxrwsr-x    6 107    archive      512 Dec 21  1992 comp.sources.amiga
drwxrwsr-x   25 33     archive     1024 Jul 20 19:18 comp.sources.games
drwxrwsr-x   41 78     archive     1024 Oct  1 23:00 comp.sources.misc
drwxrwsr-x    2 216    archive      512 Mar  9  1993 comp.sources.postscript
drwxrwsr-x    5 91     archive      512 Mar 14  1993 comp.sources.reviewed
drwxrwsr-x    6 50     archive      512 Jul 29  1992 comp.sources.sun
drwxrwsr-x   29 3      archive     1024 Aug 21 00:17 comp.sources.unix
drwxr-xr-x   24 32     archive      512 Sep 25 23:00 comp.sources.x
drwxr-sr-x   23 86     archive     1536 Jul 15 14:55 comp.std.unix
drwxrwsr-x  179 6      archive     3072 Sep 30 17:23 control
drwx--s--x    2 0      0           8192 Jul 29  1992 lost+found
-rw-r--r--    1 3      archive   477717 Oct  2 15:37 ls-lR.Z
drwxrwsr-x    2 50     archive     1024 Jul 29  1992 net.sources
drwxrwsr-x   19 27     archive     1024 Sep 25 16:12 news.announce.newgroups
drwxrwsr-x  188 3      archive     7680 Oct  1 00:20 news.answers
drwxrwxr-x    2 3      archive     4608 Sep 28 23:53 news.lists
drwxr-sr-x    2 192    archive      512 Jan  8  1993 rec.arts.movies
drwxr-sr-x    5 251    archive      512 Sep 30 16:49 rec.arts.movies.reviews
drwxrwsr-x   13 192    archive      512 May 14 18:34 rec.arts.startrek
drwxr-sr-x    2 192    archive     6144 Jan 25  1993 rec.arts.startrek.current
drwxr-sr-x    2 192    archive     2048 Jan 25  1993 rec.arts.startrek.fandom
drwxr-sr-x    2 192    archive      512 Jan 25  1993 rec.arts.startrek.info
drwxr-sr-x    2 192    archive     8704 Jan 25  1993 rec.arts.startrek.misc
drwxr-sr-x    2 192    archive     2560 Jan 25  1993 rec.arts.startrek.tech
drwxr-sr-x   26 192    archive     5120 Jul 28 15:13 rec.arts.tv
drwxr-sr-x   24 188    archive     1024 Aug 11  1992 rec.food.recipes
drwxr-sr-x    2 50     archive      512 Jul 29  1992 rec.juggling
drwxr-sr-x    5 98     archive      512 Feb 16  1993 rec.music.gaffa
drwxrwsr-x    7 50     archive      512 Jul 29  1992 uunet.tech
```

PUBLICATIONS

The *Wall Street Journal, USA Today*, and numerous other newspapers are either on-line or are experimenting with offering some on-line offerings. Use WAIS to search for **wall-street-journal-sample**.

ASTROLOGY

You can find newsgroup discussions and conferences on astrology. Do an Archie search or use Gopher to find general information and the location of files that include frequently asked questions and copies of running discussions on a variety of astrology topics. Here are some places to start:

    ftp hilbert.maths.utas.edu.au
    cd /pub/astrology
    get faq
    cd /pub/astrology/alt.astrology

Use **ls** for a long list of available files.

EMPLOYMENT

There are a number of job reference files. Some are fairly localized and others are more general. On The Well, for example, you can find conferences dedicated to job searches. Savvy employers scan these files looking for people with certain skills. You can upload a file of information about yourself and wait for the call. Here are a few job-related files to get you started.

```
ftp ftp.concert.net
cd /triangle.jobs
get INDEX
```

This directory contains a continuously updated list of files (dozens and dozens of them) listed by number and date. Use the **dir** command to get a list that shows the file date. The INDEX file will also describe these files so you can get an idea of what's there. Some are very local and time sensitive ("I need a ride to DC"). Others discuss job offerings in a variety of fields. This set of files certainly won't answer all your needs for a job, but it is another resource you can tap as you start your research.

One series of files you can find there, for example, is staff openings at the University of North Carolina. There are several files that detail opportunities, requirements, salary, and so on. Full-time as well as part-time opportunities are posted. Jobs in one listing we saw ranged from secretarial to administrative, from carpenter and security to accounting and programming. Look for similar files on other systems as you browse through Internet facilities.

You can also use Gopher (at whatever site) to look for any entry that lists positions or campus information. Many Gopher servers are run by a university. As part of the general campus information offered by the school, there frequently will be a current job listing.

In addition, you can use WAIS for job openings. Try the **AAS_jobs listing** on the main WAIS menu as a place to start. This is maintained by NASA (ndadsb.gsfc.nasa.gov).

You can look for job opportunities with lawyers, again with WAIS. Search for the **law-employers** (pegun.law.columbia.edu) entry on the WAIS topic list.

WHAT YOU LEARNED

What you got from this chapter depends to some extent on how willing you were to put your hands on the keyboard and try out some of the resources we suggested. We reviewed the use of Archie, Gopher, WAIS, and ftp to help you find and access information on the Internet. Then we showed you specific examples of resources you can find within specific topic areas, including Science, Recreation, Commercial and Business, Art, Education, Government, and Computers.

Remember that in addition to the specific files or databases we listed, you may also find information about specific topics in IRC (Internet Relay Chat). Simply sign onto an IRC server and use **/list** to display the current discussion topics (Just skip over those that seem inappropriate for you, and there will be some). If one seems to be addressing something you're interested in right now, use **/join #name** to join the conference #name. Or, you can create your own conference with the /join command, then use **/topic text** to describe the topic you're interested in. For example, you could use:

/topic Info on hang gliding in Arizona, please?

Use this guide as an ongoing reference to some topics as you perfect your use of the Internet. But don't forget to check out the information in the appendices and glossary to help you prepare for your own journey.

EVERYTHING YOU NEVER WANTED TO KNOW ABOUT UNIX

The good news about using the Internet is that most of the hardware used to manage it and connect to it runs under UNIX, an almost universal operating system with a long history that manages networking and communications very well.

The bad news about using the Internet is that most of the hardware used to manage it and connect to it runs under UNIX, a ponderous, text-based, old operating system that is not used by very many people other than system designers, engineers, and programmers (of course X-Window and other graphical user interfaces help this traditional UNIX image). For people accustomed to Macintosh or Microsoft Windows user interfaces, the dial-up, text-based user interface common in UNIX is counterintuitive, obscure, and difficult.

However, you don't have to program in UNIX as a user of the Internet—you just have to interact with it a little. In this appendix we will show you how UNIX systems are structured, and will explain some of the more important commands and features you are likely to encounter during your Internet travels.

SIMPLE ESSENTIALS OF THE UNIX OPERATING SYSTEM

In some implementations of UNIX, up to 300 megabytes of storage space are required just to hold all the components of the operating system! Compared to a PC's requirements for 6 megabytes of storage for MS DOS, UNIX seems like a disk hog. (Even if you add Microsoft Windows and a number of applications, you still need only about a tenth as much space as UNIX requires.)

One reason UNIX needs so much room is that it is rich in features and facilities. Built into the operating system are applications to conduct most of the operations you need. As a casual user along the Internet, however, you will encounter only a small portion of UNIX.

What is UNIX

As we have said, UNIX is an operating system. If you know what that means, skip to the next section. If you don't, read on.

An operating system is the low-level software that conducts most of the housekeeping chores for a computer system. The operating system accepts input from the keyboard or mouse and sends it to applications or to other parts of the operating system. This software also is responsible for managing all output to the screen and to printers. In UNIX, the operating system also controls networking and other communications chores. The operating system manages the disk drives and other storage media, conducting all input and output operations. In addition, an operating system must provide links to other applications, so that a spreadsheet or database program, for example, can access the screen, load and store information to disk, and print.

UNIX is a multiuser and multitasking operating system, which means it will support more than one user and more than one program at the same time. The operating system includes numerous utility programs to send and receive mail, to show you who else is on the system, and to let you talk to other users.

UNIX also manages the log on and log off process and supports security features to protect the system.

As a user of a UNIX system on the Internet, it is these utility applications you are most likely to encounter, as well as disk and directory services. We will talk about some of these utilities—accessed as commands—later in this appendix.

Typical UNIX System Design

In your journey around the Internet you are likely to encounter a wide variety of UNIX systems, from a Digital Equipment Corporation VAX, to an IBM or HP minicomputer, to a Sun workstation. You won't always know what type of machine you are using, and it really doesn't matter. Until you get fairly deep into UNIX—enough to know the differences among different implementations—you don't need to know precisely which machine you are using.

Whatever the machine, however, there are general structures they have in common which you should understand to use the Internet efficiently.

UNIX, like most operating systems, uses a series of directories and subdirectories to store information on a hard disk. If the hard disk is analogous to a filing cabinet, then the directories are the drawers in the cabinet. Inside a file drawer is a series of folders, and each folder contains one or more pieces of paper with letters, reports, and other information. On a disk, the folders are files. Each file has a name, just as you might label a folder inside a file cabinet. If your file cabinet contained a drawer for EMPLOYEES, each folder inside the drawer might be labeled with an employee name: Able, Baker, Charles, Davis, Edwards, Franklyn, and so on. In fact, you might divide each drawer into alphabetic sections, and within each alphabetic division might be several folders: Able, Allison, Ashley, Axel, Azden. If you have more than one employee named Able, you could have multiple Able folders: Able, Bob; Able, Sarah; Able, Tom.

If you can understand that filing cabinet structure, you can understand the directory structure on a UNIX disk. The disk may be divided into any number of drawers, and each drawer can hold a varied number of subdivisions and folders.

On the disk, the first directory, which represents the entire file cabinet, is called the root directory. Under the root are all the subordinate directories. Any directory that has other directories under it is usually referred to as a *parent* and the directories under the parent are called *children* or *child directories*. You may hear other names for these directories, but the concept is the same. A hierarchy of directories and files to help the system administrator and the users keep straight all the information stored on the disk.

When you log on to a UNIX server, you probably are using a default directory that carries your logon name or nickname. That directory may be located in a directory off of the root called **usr** or **user**, or it may be several directories deep. In Figure A.1 we have shown one possible directory structure. This is a much simpler structure than you are likely to encounter on most UNIX systems, but it gives you an idea of how files are arranged.

Figure A.1	
Simplified UNIX directory structure	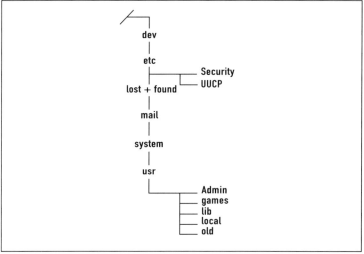

One job UNIX must conduct is managing security. You can imagine that with dozens or even hundreds of users accessing a system, you have to have a way to keep prying eyes and destructive fingers out of where they don't belong.

You probably have free privileges within your own directory: you can read, copy, and erase files at will. However, beyond that, you may have severely limited access to the rest of the system. Sensitive files are either stored on another physical disk or on another companion system, or the files and directories you don't have rights to see or manipulate are hidden or protected.

Still, you can poke around the system to get a feel for its structure. We'll show you how to do that in the next section, where we introduce a few of the important UNIX commands for Internet travelers.

IMPORTANT UNIX COMMANDS

When you log on to a UNIX system, one of two things may happen. Either you are placed at a command line prompt, or you are placed directly into a menu-driven system. If your service provider puts you into a menu system when you log on, then your need to know very much about UNIX is diminished—until you move off of the home system and out onto the Internet. Then it would be useful if you understood a few basic commands.

If the default operating environment for you is the UNIX command line, then you will see some form of prompt and a blinking cursor. A common prompt is a greater-than symbol and a blinking underline cursor:

> _

On some systems you may get a more elaborate prompt, such as the one from The Well:

OK (type a command or type opt for Options):

The Well calls this the "OK Prompt," but obviously you are given information about what to type if you need help with the commands. In this case, if you type **opt** and press **Enter**, a short menu is displayed that shows you some of the available conference commands. What you don't know, unless you have played with the system a little, is that there is another command, **help**, that will display a much longer list of available Well commands.

In fact, many systems offer a **help** command, so as you try to learn your way around a UNIX system, try **help** and see if you can display additional information about which commands are available to you. Remember, we said that for security reasons you may be restricted in the files and directories you can access. Likewise, some systems provide a limited command interface. They either lock out some UNIX commands, or substitute an entirely non-UNIX user interface with its own set of commands. Which you use depends on the system, so if you have problems with any of the UNIX commands we discuss here, call your service provider for help, or try to find some on-line assistance.

Whatever the command line prompt is, your system is not going to do anything until you issue a command. To do that, type the appropriate command and press **Enter** or **Return**. Following is a list of UNIX commands grouped by function. Find the function you need to perform, locate an appropriate command, then refer to the alphabetical listing in the next section to find out how to use it.

UNIX Commands by Function

In addition to UNIX commands, there are some keyboard conventions you should know. For example, the keyboard combinations **Ctrl-C**, **Ctrl-D**, and **Ctrl-Z** perform useful functions.

✦ **Ctrl-C** Use this combination to halt a running process. If you are in the middle of a command operation you don't want to finish, you can press **Ctrl-C** and (usually) the process will terminate right where it is. For example, if you use the **man** command and it produces a very long list that you don't want to view, simply hold down **Ctrl** and press **C**. You should be returned to the system prompt.

✦ **Ctrl-D** This is an input terminator. Sometimes it functions like **Ctrl-C**, but sometimes it won't halt a process when **Ctrl-C** will. You can use **Ctrl-D** to signify that you are finished entering data in some cases, for example.

✦ **Ctrl-Z** You sometimes can use it like **Ctrl-C** or **Ctrl-D**, but with many processes it signifies that you want to suspend the process. If you press **Ctrl-Z** while a UNIX program is running, for example, you will get a message like "Suspended," and the program stops. It has not gone away, but is waiting for you to start it up again. You can view all suspended jobs with the **jobs** command.

System Commands
bye
date
logout

File & Disk Commands
cd
cp
ls
mkdir
rm
tar (Tape Archiver)

Process Commands
kill
ps (Process Status)

Utilities
ed
mail
man
pwd
rx
rz

send
w
whereis
who

UNIX Commands: Alphabetical List

Obviously, these aren't all of the UNIX commands, but they are most of the ones you should need as a casual user of a UNIX system on the Internet. See especially the **man** command, which can give you more information on these and other UNIX commands whenever you need it.

Bye

Not necessarily a UNIX command, but one frequently used on UNIX systems to log off from a program or from the system. If bye doesn't work, try **quit, logout, logoff**.

cd

Change Directory. Makes the specified directory the current directory. Use **cd** with a full path name:

cd /usr/games

You might want to try looking at the directory specified in this example. Most UNIX systems automatically have some games installed. You can play with them!

N O T E

For MS-DOS users: Notice that the directory name separator in UNIX is a forward slash, not the backward slash you're used to in DOS.

---

cp

Copy a file or directory. To copy file1 to file2, enter the following:

cp file1 file2

This copies the contents of file1 to file2, overwriting file2 if it already exists.

date

Displays the current system date. As a casual user it is unlikely that you will be able to change the date, but the command structure for doing that is:

date yymmddhhmm

where yy = year

mm = month
dd = day
hh = hour (24 hour format)
mm = minutes

Use **date** to find out what the current date and time are and to verify that the computer knows the correct date and time. This is useful when sending and receiving mail, especially if you suspect that mail is being delayed somehow.

ed

Edit. This command launches the UNIX text editor. Use **man ed** to find out more about how the editor works. Also, there is a good probability that your system has implemented a more modern editor that will be easier to use and offer more features.

kill

Kill a process. Use **kill** if you have suspended a process with **Ctrl-Z** and don't want to restart it. Notice that you have to specify the process ID to kill a process. Use the **jobs** command to display a list of suspended jobs, then use **ps** to get the process ID. Then you can kill the process with **kill id**, where **id** is the numerical **id** displayed with **ps**.

logout

Terminate a current session. May be interchangeable with **bye** and **logoff**.

ls

List files. Displays files and directories in the current directory. To list files in a subordinate directory, use **ls directoryname**. You can display more information about a file by adding "switches" to the **ls** command. The switch you are likely to need is **-l**, which expands the directory listing to include file or directory type, size, and more.

mail

Display any pending mail. If you add a user ID to the mail command, you are placed into an editor to type the mail message. When you have entered the last line of the mail entry, enter a **period** on a line by itself.

man

Manual. Display on-line help in the form of manual pages for the specified command. **man intro** provides a general introduction to the on-line manual.

mkdir

Make Directory. Creates a new subdirectory under the current directory. This is helpful if you need to store a number of different files about different topics within your home directory. For example, **mkdir games** creates a new directory called **games** in your current directory.

ps

Process Status. Use this command to secure a process ID number, which you will need to kill a suspended process.

pwd

Displays the current directory. Use this command to find out what directory you are using.

rm

Remove. Use this command to remove a file or directory. For example, **rm newbooks.txt** erases the file **newbooks.txt** in the current directory.

rx

Receive XMODEM. Launches the XMODEM protocol application and prepares to receive a file.

rz

Receive ZMODEM. Launches the ZMODEM protocol application and prepares to receive a file.

send

Lets you send text to a specified user. **send userid** moves the cursor down one line where you can enter one or more lines of text. When you have entered all you want to send to the specified user, type a **period** on a line by itself.

tar

Tape Archiver. A utility that groups multiple files into a single file. While conceived as a tape archiver, it also is useful for transmitting files across the Internet. When you download a game application, for example, it frequently is in tar format, which means it contains more than one file. For example, to combine the entire directory **games** into a file called **games.tar,** use this command:

tar -cf games.tar games

In this example we use two of the available switches with the tar command, **-c** and **-f.** The **-c** switch tells tar to create a new file and start writing the files at the beginning of the tar file. The **-f** switch specifies that the next name on the command will be the name of the archive. (The **-f** switch is combined with **c** in this example. Only one switch symbol is needed.)

If you download a file called **games.tar** and you want to extract it, use the tar command this way:

tar -xf games.tar

Again, two switches were used with tar. The **-x** switch tells tar to extract the files contained in the file named after the **f** switch, in this example, **games.tar.**

w

A variation of **who.** Displays current user IDs and information about what each user is doing.

whereis

A useful utility that helps you find specific files anywhere on the current disk. Use **whereis filespec** to display the path to the specified file. If the same file exists in more than one directory, you will see every instance of the specified file.

who

Displays IDs of current users and shows other information about them, including their home system or directory.

How to Get More Information

As we said earlier, many systems include a help command that will display available commands. If so, there are probably sub-commands under the main help command. If you type **help** and get a screen full of available commands, you can either type one of those commands at the prompt (if it says something such as **Help on Topic?**), or you can type **help topic** at the command line, where **topic** is the command you want to know more about.

If you try help and get a bad command error, try preceding the command with an exclamation point:

!help

Some systems that use a shell of some kind to isolate the user from UNIX will send commands to UNIX if they are preceded with an exclamation.

In addition, one useful feature of UNIX is the on-line manual system. Most or all of the available commands should have a manual entry that you can display on your screen and capture to disk for future use. At the command prompt simply type **man command**, where **command** is the command you need help with. You should get a display of one or more pages that describe fully how the specified command works.

You could also call technical support at your service provider, or try talking to someone else on the system. Use **who** to find out who is currently logged on, then use **talk userid** to tap them on the shoulder and ask for help.

Appendix B

You Have Been Warned!

Unless you have never read a newspaper or magazine and your radio and television are permanently set to hard rock sounds instead of news, then you've heard about the threat of computer viruses. In fact, the Internet itself was infected in a serious way not too long ago. But our experience has shown that far too many computer users ignore the threat until they have experienced it first hand.

We can tell you—from first-hand experience—that viruses can cause real damage to your computer and data. Fortunately, there are numerous software utilities to scan your system for virus infection and to remove the infection. We can't cover every aspect of viruses here, nor can we tell you about every commercial product available, but we can alert you to the threat and show you how to inspect your system and rid it of a virus should you contract one.

WHAT IS A VIRUS?

A computer *virus* is a software program that is designed to install itself on a computer, then conduct various tasks depending on the programmer's design. The term "virus" was coined to describe how these programs work. They act a lot like a biological virus—like a cold or the flu—that attaches itself to certain cells within a living organism and causes distress.

Computer viruses do the same thing. They sneak into your system as part of a file you download from a network or bulletin board, or even on a commercial disk you purchase. You can't see the program by looking at a directory of the disk or program. Viruses are smart enough to hide themselves cleverly, even to the point of modifying the directory entry to show that the size of an infected file has not changed, when, in fact, it has.

If you think you can avoid a virus infection by dealing only with people or bulletin boards you know, or by carefully studying disk directories or any other kind of simplistic mumbo jumbo, you're setting yourself up for a fall. No computer system is immune, and the results of an infection can be catastrophic.

WHAT DO VIRUSES DO?

There are hundreds of strains of viruses. Many of them are similar, while others are frighteningly unique, so it is impossible to say with certainty exactly what a virus does. But here are some things they have done in the past:

✦ Reprogram the keyboard so the letters don't mean what they say.

✦ Freeze the computer system when certain characters are typed or when a date and time arrive.

✦ Play music or display a picture randomly or when certain events occur.

✦ Erase specific data files—or all of the files on a disk—after a pre-determined period of time or when a specific date and time arrive.

✦ Slowly change the size and contents of executable files until the program doesn't work because it grows too large or fails automatic error checks that the program conducts each time it executes.

Regardless of what it does, a virus is probably programmed to spread from disk to disk and from computer to computer. Once the virus program executes, it starts doing its work within the current system, but it also hides inside one or more applications. Some viruses, for example, install themselves in the boot record of your hard disk so that they reload each time the computer is started. Then every time a new program is executed, the virus code installs itself inside the executable program. If you move that program to another computer or copy it to another disk, the virus moves with it. When the program runs for the first time on a new computer, the virus checks to see if it already is running in memory. If not, it installs itself and starts the process all over again.

Some viruses are more aggressive in their attempts to expand. Once they are running, some viruses will scan the system looking for other disks or computers to infect. Suppose you are attached to a network and load a program that contains a virus. The virus infects your system, then looks for other disk drives to infect.

You can see that viruses are serious threats to your computer and its data. Even if the virus isn't designed to erase files, it can damage data by saving a piece of itself or some other code into a data file from the host application. The key is to avoid an infection in the first place.

You can do this by never installing foreign software and by never logging on to a network or bulletin board. Obviously, this is not a practical solution. But you can take steps to minimize the threat and to rid your system of a virus if you do get infected.

How to Tell if Your System Has Been Infected

Because there are so many kinds of viruses, there is no set, fool-proof formula for detecting a virus. In fact, many strains show absolutely no symptoms until it is too late. They may lie dormant inside an infected program waiting for a specific date to arrive, for example. They do nothing and cause no change in system performance until that date arrives, and then they systematically erase everything on your hard drive.

So even if you don't have any virus symptoms, it is a good idea to conduct regular scans for them. Use one of the software utilities listed in the next section to keep viruses from entering your system and to conduct regular scans to make sure you don't have any hidden infections.

Beyond that, be aware of how your system performs. If a virus is alive and operating in your system, there are some things that may happen to give you a clue. For example, if you notice an unusual amount of disk activity while you are running applications, you can suspect that a virus is saving the program file to store additional code.

Notice whether the sizes of program files change or the directory date changes. Most viruses that modify the application executable file are smart enough to hide file size and date changes, but some are not. Notice whether applications seem to be running more slowly or whether you get an unusual number of errors. Are you having problems with application areas that used to run, yet nothing that you're aware of has changed? Do you see messages that you've never seen before?

Any of these events could mean a virus attack. Of course they could also mean that you are having some kind of hardware problem. The only real way to find out is with some kind of virus detection and eradication software such as the ones we list later in this appendix.

VIRUS PROTECTION

The best way to protect your system against a virus infection is never to get one in the first place. There are software packages designed to do just that. If you have DOS 6 for your PC-compatible machine, for example, there is an included utility that loads and stays RAM-resident. It constantly scans the system looking for anything unusual and will alert you in the event that a suspected virus is detected. It isn't foolproof, but it may catch a virus as it loads from an infected program before it can do any more damage.

There are other, similar programs for PCs, Macintoshes and UNIX machines from a variety of vendors. Some programs will scan your system memory and all the programs on your disks to see if there are any known viruses already present. If any infections are found, these routines can eliminate them, or tell you to run another program that will take them out. After a virus has been detected and removed, you may not be able to run the infected program, however. In fact, it is always a good idea to re-install a program that has been infected by a virus.

As with data backup procedures, a good plan for virus prevention goes a long way toward protecting the integrity of your system. You should get in the habit of running a virus detection program every day when you boot your system. You should run a virus detection program on any new software you acquire, whether it is from a commercial vendor or from the Internet or another on-line service.

Anytime you have been on-line, whether or not you downloaded anything, run a virus utility before you go on with the rest of your work. All of this may seem tedious, and it is. But if you ever experience the anger, frustration, and lost time that a full-blown virus infection can cause, you'll gladly take these steps to keep from having to go through it again.

VIRUS PROTECTION SOFTWARE

Since the threat of virus infection has gotten so universal, a number of companies have started selling virus detection and eradication software. If you don't already have such software, get it. In this section we show you some of the available offerings. You'll have to decide for yourself which is best for you—based on your hardware, where you live or work, what features you need, and what other applications you already are running. The first step is to contact one or more of the vendors we list and ask them for a recommendation. Then pick a package, install it, and use it.

Note that many of these packages do much more than just offer virus protection. Some are full-fledged security systems; others are part of a package of utilities and tools. Contact the vendor for complete information.

PC (MS-DOS)-based Software

D-FENCE, SWEEP, AND VACCINE

Alternative Computer Technology, Inc.
7908 Cin-Day Rd., Ste. WB
West Chester, OH 45069
513-755-1957
FAX: 513-755-1958

INFORMATION SECURITY POLICIES MADE EASY

Baseline Software
PO Box 1219
Sausalito, CA 94966
800-829-9955; 415-332-7763
FAX: 415-332-8032

CENTRAL POINT ANTI-VIRUS (V.2.0), CENTRAL POINT ANTI-VIRUS FOR WINDOWS (V.1.4), SAFE SIX, SAFE SIX FOR WINDOWS

Central Point Software, Inc.
15220 N.W. Greenbrier Pkwy., Ste. 150
Beaverton, OR 97006
800-333-0744; 503-690-8088
Direct Sales: 800-445-4208
FAX: 503-690-8083

INOCULAN-THE NETWORK GUARDIAN, INOCULAN/PC

Cheyenne Software, Inc.
3 Expressway Plaza
Roslyn Hgts., NY 11577
800-243-9462; 516-484-5110
FAX: 516-484-3446

F-PROT PROFESSIONAL (V.2.07), FREEZE!, SECURITY GUARDIAN PLUS (V.3.65)

Command Software Systems, Inc.
1061 E. Indiantown Rd., Ste. 500
Jupiter, FL 33477
800-423-9147; 407-575-3200
FAX: 407-575-3026

DETECT PLUS (V.2.11)

Commcrypt, Inc.
10000 Virginia Manor Rd., Ste. 300
Beltsville, MD 20705
800-334-8338; 301-470-2500
Direct Sales: 800-683-1313
FAX: 301-470-2507

PC CANARY

Compass/New England
PO Box 117
Portsmouth, NH 03802
603-431-8030

VICTOR CHARLIE (VC) (V.5.0)

Computer Security Associates
738 1/2 Meeting St.
West Columbia, SC 29169
803-796-6591
FAX: 803-796-8379

PC/ASSURE (V.4.0)

Cordant, Inc.
11400 Commerce Park Dr.
Reston, VA 22091-1506
800-762-5632; 703-758-7000
FAX: 703-758-7380

SWIFT PROFESSIONAL VIRUS TERMINATOR (V.2.1), SWIFT PROFESSIONAL VIRUS TERMINATOR FOR WINDOWS (V.2.1)

Cosmi Corp.
2600 Homestead Place
Rancho Dominguez, CA 90220-5610
310-833-2000
FAX: 310-886-3500

VFIND

CyberSoft, Inc.
210 West 12th Ave.
Conshohocken, PA 19428-1464
215-825-4748
FAX: 215-825-6785

VACCINE (V.5.0), VACNET (V.5.0), VACWIN (V.5.0)

The Davidsohn Group
20 Exchange Place, 27th Fl.
New York, NY 10005
800-999-6031; 212-422-4100
Direct Sales: 212-363-3018
FAX: 212-422-1953

DATA PHYSICIAN PLUS! (V.3.1B)

Digital Dispatch, Inc.
55 Lakeland Shores Rd.
Lakeland, MN 55043
800-221-8091; 612-436-1000
FAX: 612-436-2085

PC DOCTOR

Diversified Computer Products and Services, Inc.
PO Box 579
Swampscott, MA 01907
617-592-9001

CODESAFE HD, VIRUSAFE-GOLD, VIRUSAFE-GOLD FOR WINDOWS

Eliashim Microcomputers, Inc.
520 W. Hwy. 436, Ste. 1180
Altamonte Springs, FL 32714
800-677-1587; 407-682-1587
FAX: 407-869-1409

SAFE (V.2.0), SEARCH & DESTROY FOR DOS AND WINDOWS, UNTOUCHABLE (V.1.13), UNTOUCHABLE FOR WINDOWS (V.1.12), UNTOUCHABLE NETWORK NLM (NETWARE LOADABLE MODULE) (V.1.1)

Fifth Generation Systems, Inc.
10049 N. Reiger Rd.
Baton Rouge, LA 70809-4562
800-677-1848; 504-291-7221

FAX: 504-295-3268

WATCHDOG (V.7.02), WATCHDOG VIRUS BUSTER

Fischer International Systems Corp.
PO Box 9107, 4073 Merchantile Ave.
Naples, FL 33942
800-237-4510; 800-331-2866 (FL); 813-643-1500
FAX: 813-643-3772

IBM ANTIVIRUS (V.1.0)

IBM (International Business Machines)
Old Orchard Rd.
Armonk, NY 10504
800-426-3333; 914-765-1900
Direct Sales: 800-426-2968 (IBM Direct)

COP (COMPUTER OWNER PROTECTION)

IDX Technologies, Inc.
14 Research Way
Setauket, NY 11733
800-626-6863; 516-689-9866
FAX: 516-689-1419

LANDESK VIRUS PROTECT (V.2.0), LANPROTECT (V.1.5)

Intel Corp.
(Personal Computer Enhancement Operation)
5200 N.E. Elam Young Pkwy.
Hillsboro, OR 97124
800-538-3373; 503-696-8080
FAX: 503-696-4633

VIRUSCURE PLUS (V.2.41

International Microcomputer Software, Inc. (IMSI)
1938 Fourth St.
San Rafael, CA 94901-2682
800-833-4674; 415-454-7101

Direct Sales: 800-833-8082
FAX: 415-454-8901

VIRUS-PRO (V.3.0)

International Security Technology, Inc.
99 Park Ave., 11th Fl.
New York, NY 10016
212-557-0900
FAX: 212-808-5206

PALLADIUM

Laser Digital, Inc.
1030 E. Duane Ave., Ste. H
Sunnyvale, CA 94086
408-737-2666
FAX: 408-737-9698

VIRUS BUSTER (V.4.0), VIRUS BUSTER FOR WINDOWS

Leprechaun Software International, Ltd.
PO Box 669306
Marietta, GA 30066-0106
800-521-8849; 404-971-8900
FAX: 404-971-8828

VIRUSALERT (V.2.08)

Look Software
PO Box 1356
Ogdensburg, NY 13669
800-267-0778; 613-837-2151
FAX: 613-837-5572

INTEGRITY TOOLKIT (V.3.7.7)

Management Analytics
PO Box 1480

Hudson, OH 44236
216-655-9770
FAX: 216-655-9776

CLEAN-UP, NETSCAN, NETSHIELD (V.1.51), PRO-SCAN (V.3.0), SCAN, SCAN FOR WINDOWS, VIRUSCAN (V.1.02), VSHIELD, WSCAN FOR WINDOWS

McAfee Associates, Inc.
2710 Walsh Ave., Ste. 200
Santa Clara, CA 95051-0963
408-988-3832
FAX: 408-970-9727

NET/DACS, PC/DACS (V.3.0)

Mergent International, Inc.
70 Inwood Rd.
Rocky Hill, CT 06067
800-688-3227; 203-257-4223
FAX: 203-257-4245

FULL ARMOR (V.2.0)

Micah Development Corp.
955 Massachusetts Ave., Ste. 302
Cambridge, MA 02139
800-653-1783; 617-489-5854
FAX: 617-489-5844

BIT-LOCK

Microcomputer Applications
3167 E. Otero Circle
Littleton, CO 80122
303-770-1917
FAX: 303-770-1863

VIRUSTOP PLUS

Multix, Inc.

4203 Beltway Dr., Ste. 7
Dallas, TX 75244
214-239-4989
FAX: 214-239-6826

FS SCANMASTER, PC SCANMASTER

NetPro Computing, Inc.
8655 E. Via de Ventura, Ste. E155
Scottsdale, AZ 85258
800-998-5090; 602-998-5008
FAX: 602-998-5076

DR. SOLOMON'S ANTI-VIRUS TOOLKIT (V.6.01), DR. SOLOMON'S ANTI-VIRUS TOOLKIT FOR WINDOWS (V.6.01)

Ontrack Computer Systems, Inc.
6321 Bury Dr., Ste. 15-19
Eden Prairie, MN 55346
800-752-1333; 612-937-1107
FAX: 612-937-5815

PC PASSKEY

Optimum Electronics, Inc.
425 Washington Ave., PO Box 250
North Haven, CT 06473
203-239-6098
FAX: 203-234-9324

VIRUCIDE PLUS (V.3.0)

Parsons Technology, Inc.
One Parsons Dr., PO Box 100
Hiawatha, IA 52233-0100
800-223-6925; 319-395-9626
FAX: 319-395-0217

DATA SECURITY PLUS (V.5.3), VIRUS PREVENTION PLUS

PC Guardian
118 Alto St.
San Rafael, CA 94901
800-288-8126; 415-459-0190
FAX: 415-459-1162

PS-LOCK, SECURE WRAP

PS Publishing, Inc.
25 S. Livingston Ave., Ste. A
Livingston, NJ 07039
800-777-2663; 201-740-1750
FAX: 201-740-9118

VI-SPY PROFESSIONAL EDITION (V.11.0)

RG Software Systems, Inc.
6900 E. Camelback Rd., Ste. 630
Scottsdale, AZ 85251
602-423-8000
FAX: 602-423-8389

DRIVE-IN ANITVIRUS (V.2.03), VIRUSNET (V.2.06), STOPLIGHT (V.1.71)

SafetyNet, Inc.
55 Bleeker St.
Millburn, NJ 07041-1414
800-851-0188; 201-467-1024
FAX: 201-467-1611

IRONCLAD (V.2.0)

Silver Oak Systems, Inc.
8209 Cedar St.
Silver Spring, MD 20910
301-585-8641
FAX: 301-588-6484

FLU SHOT PLUS (V.1.84)

Software Concepts Design
PO Box 908
Margaretville, NY 12455
607-326-4422
FAX: 607-326-4424

PROTEC (V.4.0)

SOPHCO, Inc.
PO Box 7430
Boulder, CO 80306-7430
800-922-3001; 303-530-7759
FAX: 303-530-7745

TNT ANTIVIRUS

SST (System Security Technology, Inc.)
3310 Berwyck St.
Las Vegas, NV 89121
800-782-9110; 702-454-7855
FAX: 702-454-7700

INTEGRITY MASTER (V.1.41)

Stiller Research
2625 Ridgeway St.
Tallahassee, FL 32310-5169
800-622-2793; 904-575-7884
Direct Sales: 708-397-1221

CERTUS (V.2.11), NORTON ANTIVIRUS (V.2.1), NOVI (V.1.15)

Symantec Corp.
10201 Torre Ave.
Cupertino, CA 95014-2132
800-441-7234; 408-253-9600
FAX: 408-252-4696

ANTIVIRUSPLUS (V.4.20.09), VIRAWAY

T.C.P. Techmar Computer Products, Inc.
98-11 Queens Blvd., Ste. 2-C
Rego Park, NY 11374
800-922-0015; 718-997-6606
FAX: 718-520-0170

PC RX ANTIVIRUS (V.2.65), PC-CILLIN (V.3.65), PCOPY (V.1.0), WIN RX ANTIVIRUS (V.1.4)

Trend Micro Devices, Inc.
2421 West 205th St., Ste. D-100
Torrance, CA 90501
800-228-5651; 310-782-8190
FAX: 310-328-5892

VIR-GUARD

uti-maco Safeguard Systems, Inc.
750 Old Main St.
Rocky Hill, CT 06067
800-394-4230; 203-257-4230
FAX: 203-257-8390

FAILSAFE COMPUTER GUARDIAN

Villa Crespo Software, Inc.
1725 McGovern St.
Highland Park, IL 60035
800-521-3963; 708-433-0500
FAX: 708-433-1485

VIRUS CHECK AND CURES

Wizardworks, Inc.
5354 Parkdale Dr., Ste. 104
Minneapolis, MN 55416
800-759-5645; 612-544-8581
FAX: 612-541-4973

X-LOCK 50

X-Lock Corp.
1 Mecca Way
Norcross, GA 30093
404-564-5545
FAX: 404-564-5528

Macintosh-based Software

FILEGUARD (V.2.75)

ASD Software, Inc.
4650 Arrow Hwy., Ste. E-6
Montclair, CA 91763
909-624-2594
FAX: 909-624-9574

INFORMATION SECURITY POLICIES MADE EASY (V.3.0)

Baseline Software
PO Box 1219
Sausalito, CA 94966
800-829-9955; 415-332-7763
FAX: 415-332-8032

ACCESS MANAGED ENVIRONMENT (V.2.1)

Casady & Greene, Inc.
22734 Portola Dr.
Salinas, CA 93908-1119
800-359-4920; 408-484-9228
FAX: 408-484-9218

CENTRAL POINT ANTI-VIRUS (V.2.0)

Central Point Software, Inc.
15220 N.W. Greenbrier Pkwy., Ste. 150
Beaverton, OR 97006
800-333-0744; 503-690-8088
Direct Sales: 800-445-4208
FAX: 503-690-8083

VFIND

CyberSoft, Inc.
210 West 12th Ave.
Conshohocken, PA 19428-1464
215-825-4748
FAX: 215-825-6785

VIREX

Datawatch Corp.
(Triangle Software Division)
3700-B Lyckan Pkwy.
Durham, NC 27707
919-490-1277
FAX: 919-490-6672

MENU MASTER MAC (V.1.4)

Electronic Learning Systems, Inc.
4131 Northwest 28th Lane, Ste. 3A
Gainesville, FL 32606-6681
800-443-7971; 904-375-0558
FAX: 904-375-5679

COP (COMPUTER OWNER PROTECTION)

IDX Technologies, Inc.
14 Research Way
Setauket, NY 11733
800-626-6863; 516-689-9866
FAX: 516-689-1419

MacSecure (V.1.7)

Learning Performance Corp.
2850 Metro Dr., Ste. 413
Minneapolis, MN 55425-1405
800-926-3279; 612-854-2730
FAX: 612-854-8975

Empower I (V.4.0.8)

Magna
332 Commercial St.
San Jose, CA 95112
408-282-0900
FAX: 408-275-9147

AntiToxin (V.2.1)

Mainstay
591-A Constitution Ave.
Camarillo, CA 93012
805-484-9400
FAX: 818-484-9428

SAM (Symantec AntiVirus for Macintosh) (V.3.5)

Symantec Corp.
10201 Torre Ave.
Cupertino, CA 95014-2132
800-441-7234; 408-253-9600
FAX: 408-252-4696

Ft. Knox (V.1.05)

Transfinite Systems Co., Inc.
PO Box N, MIT Branch PO
Cambridge, MA 02139
617-969-9570

ULTRA**SECURE** (V.1.36)

usrEZ Software
18881 Von Karman Ave., Ste. 1270
Irvine, CA 92715
714-756-5140
FAX: 714-756-8810

UNIX-based Software

VFIND

CyberSoft, Inc.
210 West 12th Ave.
Conshohocken, PA 19428-1464
215-825-4748
FAX: 215-825-6785

FORTRESS

Los Altos Technologies, Inc.
2111 Grant Rd., Ste. 100
Los Altos, CA 94024
800-999-UNIX; 415-988-4848
FAX: 415-988-4860

SECURITY AUDIT

SunSoft, Inc.
(subsidiary of Sun Microsystems, Inc.)
2550 Garcia Ave.
Mountain View, CA 94043-1100
800-227-9227; 415-460-3267
FAX: 415-336-0362

FORTRESS

Woodside Technologies, Inc.
474 Potrero Ave.
Sunnyvale, CA 94086-9406
408-733-9503
FAX: 408-732-7335

X-Lock 50 .

X-Lock Corp.
1 Mecca Way
Norcross, GA 30093
404-564-5545
FAX: 404-564-5528
Tech support: 404-475-8787

Appendix C

THE UNOFFICIAL SMILEY DICTIONARY

Wherever you go on the Internet, you will find users attempting to express emotions as they type on text-based screens. The symbols they use vary from the simple smiley face :) to much more complicated symbols such as >:-> or C=}>;*()). The symbols used vary from place to place on the Internet, and even what these symbols mean may be different, depending on which group you frequent. Still, it is fun to play around with these "emoticons," as they are frequently called (emotional icons). Here's one list compiled by Clay Spinuzzi (**spinuzzi@gab.unt.edu**) during the course of research on a thesis about Usenet and language. In fact, this list is only a portion of the information Spinuzzi has compiled. Use ftp to retrieve the file **EMOTICON.TXT** in the directory **/pub/misc** at mercury.unt.edu.

:-)	Your basic smiley. This smiley is used to inflect a sarcastic or joking statement since we can't hear voice inflection over Unix.
;-)	Winky smiley. User just made a flirtatious and/or sarcastic remark. More of a "don't hit me for what I just said" smiley.
:-(	Frowning smiley. User did not like that last statement or is upset or depressed about something.
:-I	Indifferent smiley. Better than a Frowning smiley but not quite as good as a happy smiley
:->	User just made a really biting sarcastic remark. Worse than a :-).
>:->	User just made a really devilish remark.
>;->	Winky and devil combined. A very lewd remark was just made.

Those are the basic ones...Here are some somewhat less common ones:

(-:	User is left handed
%-)	User has been staring at a green screen for 15 hours straight
:*)	User is drunk
[:]	User is a robot
8-)	User is wearing sunglasses
B:-)	Sunglasses on head
::-)	User wears normal glasses
B-)	User wears horn-rimmed glasses
8:-)	User is a little girl
:-)-8	User is a Big girl
:-{)	User has a mustache

:-{}	User wears lipstick
{:-)	User wears a toupee
}:-(	Toupee in an updraft
:-[	User is a Vampire
:-E	Bucktoothed vampire
:-F	Bucktoothed vampire with one tooth missing
:-7	User just made a wry statement
:-*	User just ate something sour
:-)~	User drools
:-~)	User has a cold
:'-(	User is crying
:'-)	User is so happy, s/he is crying
:-@	User is screaming
:-#	User wears braces
:^)	User has a broken nose
:v)	User has a broken nose, but it's the other way
:_)	User's nose is sliding off of his face
:<)	User is from an Ivy League School
:-&	User is tongue tied.
=:-)	User is a hosehead
-:-)	User is a punk rocker
-:-(	(real punk rockers don't smile)
:=)	User has two noses
+-:-)	User is the Pope or holds some other religious office
`:-)	User shaved one of his eyebrows off this morning
,:-)	Same thing...other side

l-I	User is asleep
l-O	User is yawning/snoring
:-Q	User is a smoker
:-?	User smokes a pipe
O-)	Megaton Man On Patrol! (or else, user is a scuba diver)
O :-)	User is an angel (at heart, at least)
:-P	Nyahhhh!
:-S	User just made an incoherent statement
:-D	User is laughing (at you!)
:-X	User's lips are sealed
:-C	User is really bummed
:-/	User is skeptical
C=:-)	User is a chef
@=	User is pro-nuclear war
*<:-)	User is wearing a Santa Claus Hat
:-o	Uh oh!
(8-o	It's Mr. Bill!
*:o)	And Bozo the Clown!
3:]	Pet smiley
3:[	Mean Pet smiley
d8=	Your pet beaver is wearing goggles and a hard hat.
E-:-)	User is a Ham radio operator
:-9	User is licking his/her lips
%-6	User is braindead

[:-)	User is wearing a walkman
(:I	User is an egghead
<:-I	User is a dunce
K:P	User is a little kid with a propeller beenie
@:-)	User is wearing a turban
:-0	No Yelling! (Quiet Lab)
:-:	Mutant Smiley
	The invisible smiley
.-)	User only has one eye
,-)	Ditto...but he's winking
X-(	User just died
8 :-)	User is a wizard
C=}>;*{})	Mega-Smiley... A drunk, devilish chef with a toupee in an updraft, a mustache, and a double chin

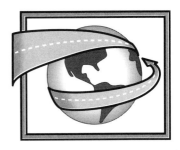

FILE TYPE REFERENCE

As you browse the Internet, you find many different types of file information. There may be program files for a particular format, text files that are compressed or grouped by one utility or another, and so on. One source for a file type reference is: **ftp nic.funet.fi**. Look for the file **README.FILETYPES** for a list of common file types used on this system. We have reproduced that list for you here as a place to start learning about file types on the Internet.

\#

\# doc/README.FILETYPES—information about meanings of various file suffixes

\#

\# Status: Draft

\# Author: staff@nic.funet.fi

\# Created: Tue Jun 15 22:16:13 EET DST 1993

\# Last modified: Thu Aug 12 08:12:15 EET DST 1993

\#

README ABOUT FILE TYPES

We use multiple file compression/packaging programs depending upon target systems. These methods are often denoted on a file name by more-or-less standardized suffix(es). On UNIX-like environments, where packaging is done with a different utility, then compressed, there may be multiple suffixes.

Sometimes there are strange hybrids of suffixes when files are intended to be able to be transported via limited name-spaces, like MS-DOS 8+3 characters.

This is NOT a list of ALL file type suffixes there are—only those that are common.

Table D.1

Suffix	Methods	Environment
.arj	ARJ compress + packing	MS-DOS
.gif	GIF-type packed (color) image	image
.gz	GNU-Zip	UNIX
.jpeg	JPEG-compressed color image	image
.jpg	--"--	image
.lha	LHA/LHARC compress + packing	multiple (Esp.Amiga)
.lhx	Variant of .lha	CBM C=64 ?
.lzh	LHA/LHARC compress + packing	multiple
.ps	PostScript -document (or program)	—
.tar	UNIX tar — "Tape ARchive" packaging	UNIX
.tgz	== .tar.gz (Esp. Linux)	—
.Z	BSD compress	UNIX
.z	GNU-Zip (old suffix, to be phased out)	UNIX
.z	SysV pack (Huffman compression)	UNIX
.zip	(PK)ZIP compress + packing	MS-DOS
.zoo	ZOO compress + packing	multiple

Note that the FTP-server at ftp.funet.fi (and some others) can unpack GNU-Zip (and BSD Compress and sysV pack) while retrieving the file. For any file with name XXX.YYY.gz, request file XXX.YYY, and automagic uncompress happens. This of course expands the data, and thus transfer times will become longer.

Places to Find Handling Programs for Above Listed Formats:

ARJ:

/pub/amiga/utilities/archivers/unarj-0.5.lha (Amiga binary)
/pub/msdos/Mirrors/zeus/utilnet/unarj230.exe (MS-DOS)
/pub/msdos/packing/archivers/arj239f.exe (MS-DOS)
/pub/msdos/packing/archivers/unarj241.exe (MS-DOS)
/pub/msdos/utilities/unix/unarj221.tar.Z (UNIX)

GIF, JPG:

Image formats, see

/pub/pics/viewers/..

That directory contains symbolic links to places which have programs per machine/operating system/...

GNU-ZIP:

/pub/amiga/utilities/archivers/gzip-1.1.2.lha (Amiga binary)
/pub/gnu/gzip-1.2.2.msdos.exe   (ready MS-DOS binary)
/pub/gnu/gzip-1.2.2.tar   (Just plain TAR, SOURCE)
/pub/gnu/gzip-1.2.2.tar.gz   (GNU-Zipped tar)
/pub/msdos/packing/compress/gzip121.zip (MS-DOS-binary)
/pub/unix/386ix/Solaris.x86/gzip (binary for Solaris 2/x86)
/pub/unix/386ix/isc/arcers/gzip (binary for ISC UNIX)
/ftp/bin/gzip   (binary for SPARC, SunOS4.1.x)

LZH/LHA:

/pub/amiga/utilities/archivers/LhA_e138.run (Amiga binary)
/pub/atari/arcers/lharc2.ttp   (ATARI binary)
/pub/atari/arcers/lzh_201l.lzh   (ATARI binary)
/pub/msdos/packing/archivers/lha213.exe (MS-DOS binary)
/pub/unix/tools/lha-lharc/lha-1.00.tar.Z (UNIX source)

SysV pack:

GNU-Zip can unpack this. Otherwise just use your favorite
SysVr3 machine.

PS

PostScript — document layout, etc. language.
Feed to your PostScript(TM) printer.

TAR-unpackers:

UNIX tar-program
/pub/amiga/utilities/archivers/tar-1.1.0 (Amiga binary)
/pub/gnu/tar-1.11.2.shar.gz   (sh(ar)-packed GNU-tar
source)
/pub/gnu/tar-1.11.2.tar.gz   (tar-packed GNU-tar source)
/pub/msdos/utilities/execomp/tar-z.zip (MS-DOS
tar+(un)compress)
/pub/msdos/utilities/execomp/tar.zip (MS-DOS tar-program)
/pub/msdos/utilities/execomp/tar2exe.zip (MS-DOS tar-
program)

BSD compress:

GNU-Zip can unpack this too.
/ftp/bin/uncompress(binary for SPARC, SunOS4.1.x)
/pub/amiga/utilities/archivers/compress-4.1.lha (Amiga binary)
/pub/msdos/packing/compress/comp430*.zip (MS-DOS
compress/)
/pub/msdos/packing/compress/decomp2.zip (uncompresses)

ZIP:

One particular format of PKZIP can be opened by the
GNU-Zip
(see GNU-Zip documents), however it is not a general case.

/pub/amiga/utilities/archivers/unzip-5.1d3.lha (Amiga binary)
/pub/atari/arcers/stzip21.lzh   (ATARI binary)
/pub/msdos/packing/zip/pkz204g.exe (MS-DOS Self-
extracting arch)
/pub/unix/tools/zip/unzip50.tar.Z (UNIX source)

ZOO:

/pub/amiga/utilities/archivers/Zoo-2.1.lha (Amiga binary)
/pub/atari/arcers/zoo*.*   (ATARI programs)
/pub/msdos/packing/zoo/zoo210.exe (MS-DOS binary)
/pub/unix/tools/zoo/zoo-2.1.tar.Z (UNIX Zoo source)

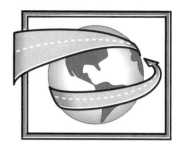

GLOSSARY

Advanced Research Projects Agency	ARPA, the government agency initially responsible for starting the Internet.
Archie	A (mostly) universal on-line searching tool that lets you find files and directories on the Internet by entering a name or description. You normally require a local client for most efficient Archie access.
ARPA	See Advanced Research Projects Agency.
ARPAnet	The beginnings of the Internet. ARPAnet was started by the Advanced Research Projects Agency (ARPA).
BITNET	Another network provider, separate from the Internet but accessible from the Internet for e-mail at least. BIT-NET users also can send information to Internet users.
BTW	By The Way. Used as an abbreviation on e-mail and real-time conversation links.
Capture File	A file managed by your terminal emulation and communications software that stores information viewed on the screen during a communications session. There are several forms of capture file. The most common is a file that captures text as it scrolls on the screen. Another is a snapshot file—a text or graphics representation of a single computer screen display.

Channel	On IRC and other communications applications, a named area where users gather to discuss specific topics.
Client	A software application that pre-processes information before sending it to a server. There are Internet clients that link to Archie, Gopher, IRC, and other facilities.
CompuServe (CIS)	CompuServe Information Service. A commercial network that provides e-mail, games, discussion, research, and other services. CompuServe users can link to the Internet via e-mail services.
CompuServe Packet Network (CPN)	An international network provided and maintained by CompuServe. It was designed primarily to service CompuServe Information Service users, but it also carries traffic for other networked services, including Internet providers such as The Well.
CSNET	Computer Science Network. Among the early networks that grew with the Internet.
DARPA	See Defense Advanced Research Projects Agency
Defense Advanced Research Projects Agency	DARPA, a later version of the Advanced Research Projects Agency (ARPA). This agency also gave its name to an early version of the Internet, the DARPA Internet.
Distributed Application	A software application that runs on multiple machines in different locations. One component may be the user interface, which is run on a local machine, while a database searching component is executed on a remote computer.
Domain	A method of identifying Internet nodes with words or abbreviations instead of numbers. The domain name system (DNS) is divided into groups for ease of management and name assignment.
Download	The process of copying a file or files from a remote computer to a local one.
DNS	Domain Name System. See Domain.

E-mail	Electronic mail. Text, graphics, sound, and photographs transmitted from one computer system to a specific user or group of users at a remote system or systems.
Electronic Mail	See E-mail.
Emoticon	A symbol used to convey emotions on a network link. Among the most popular emoticons are the smiley face :-) and the sad face :-(. Other symbols vary with the network or group.
FAQ	Frequently Asked Questions. An abbreviation used on newsgroups, conversation links, and file structures. When researching a new topic, look for files labeled FAQ for quick introductory information.
Fiber Optic	An optical technology to carry high speed communications. Optic cable is being increasingly used for network backbone links.
File Transfer Protocol	A set of communication rules that provides for error-free transfer of files across a computer-to-computer link. Among the popular communications protocols are Kermit, ZMODEM, and XMODEM.
Freenet	A network service provider that offers the service as a community or free service. Freenets often are associated with libraries, universities, and other public institutions. Freenets can be accessed through the Internet and often provide access to the Internet via a local dial-up number.
FYI	For Your Information. An e-mail and real-time link abbreviation.
Hit	In database terminology, a found record. If you search a database for files on games and you locate 23 files, your search resulted in 23 hits.
Host	A computer system that accepts local and remote logins to provide some type of computer service, such as running programs, conducting database searches, communications, and network access.

IMHO — In My Humble Opinion. An abbreviation used on e-mail and real-time computer links.

Interchange Point — A network-to-network link that provides a set of services such as e-mail to users of the linked networks.

Internet Protocol — A packetized method of transmitting information across the Internet. See also TCP/IP.

Interoperability — The ability of computer hardware and software systems from different manufacturers to work together. Interoperability takes on different forms, from complete software and hardware compatibility, to the ability simply to exchange data from specific applications.

IP — See Internet Protocol.

IRC — Internet Relay Chat. A real-time, channelized Internet service that allows multiple users to talk among themselves.

Kermit — A file transfer protocol.

Listserv — An automated application that maintains mailing lists and other data, usually on an IBM Mainframe.

Local Area Networks (LAN) — A grouping of local PCs and other computers that connects the machines via Ethernet or another networking protocol. A LAN lets the linked machines share files and printers, and exchange e-mail. Many LANs include a communications gateway that allows users to communicate with dial-up services or other networks.

Log File — A form of capture file generated and managed by your communications software. A log file captures all characters and keystrokes during a communications session.

MCI Mail — A commercial electronic mail service from MCI. MCI Mail users can exchange mail among themselves and with Internet users.

Metropolitan Area Networks — A form of local network that connects users across a metropolitan area.

Milnet — One of the early networks that derived from the original ARPAnet.

Modem	Modulator/Demodulator. An electronic device that converts a computer's digital information into analog data for transmission across a dedicated line or dial-up link. A modem also converts the transmitted analog data back into digital information for use by the computer.
Node	A computer system that serves as a host on the Internet. A node can be a minicomputer or a mainframe, a PC, Macintosh or other personal computer configured as a host. A node is connected directly to the Internet as opposed to using Internet facilities through another machine.
NSFNET	National Science Foundation Network. A network established in 1986 to tie together users with five national supercomputer centers.
Packets	Groups of data to be transmitted over a network. Packets include information for error correction in addition to the actual data being transmitted.
Peer-to-peer	A computer-to-computer network relationship that makes each computer equal in power. Peer-to-peer networks allow all computers to share resources equally, rather than having a single server through which all computers on the network must work.
Pine	A menu-driven UNIX Mail software application. Pine is available on many Internet hosts to make sending and receiving e-mail easier.
PPP	Point to Point Protocol. A software application that lets a personal computer or very small network become a full-featured node on the Internet. PPP is sometimes used instead of SLIP.
Protocol	A software utility that packages data to be transmitted over the network so the receiving computer can check for errors. Sometimes called "error free protocol." See also File Transfer Protocol, Kermit, XMODEM, and ZMODEM.

Router	A network facility that manages communications links.
Server	Computer software that manages the major part of a software system in conjunction with a remote client application. Also, a portion of a distributed application.
Service Provider	A company or other entity that provides Internet or other computer services for third parties.
Shell	A user interface that provides access to an operating system or other application.
SLIP	Serial Line Internet Protocol. Similar to PPP.
Tar	A UNIX-based application that groups multiple files into a single file for transmission over a network, or between two computers through a dial-up link. This enables the transfer of a single file when multiple files are required for an application. Tar files are frequently compressed before they are transmitted.
TCP/IP	Transmission Control Protocol/Internet Protocol. Networking data transmission protocols used on the Internet.
Telnet	A local software tool that lets you log on to remote computers. Telnet software knows how to convert domain names to Internet addresses and how to use those addresses to locate the target computer. Once your system is attached to the target, a normal logon sequence is initiated.
Text Tile	A computer file that contains only text characters, with no graphics or special symbols. A text file can be edited with most UNIX or PC editors and can be displayed on a computer screen without using a special application.
Upload	The process of transmitting a local computer file up the network link to a remote computer system.
USENET	A bulletin board network system used to exchange special interest information. USENET was around before the Internet, but now a lot of USENET traffic is carried over the Internet.

User Interfaces	A software system that presents the personality of a given operating system or application. User interfaces can be either graphics-based or text-based. Most Internet user interfaces are text-based systems.
UUCP	UNIX-to-UNIX Copy. A built-in feature of UNIX that also can be used to provide users with e-mail and file transfer access to the Internet.
Virus	A software application designed to infect existing software and cause damage. Viruses are sometimes injected into networks and computer systems to harass the users and to damage data.
W	A UNIX command that displays the user ID of everyone logged on to the local system and shows what tasks they currently are conducting. See also the **Who** command.
WAIS	Wide Area Information Servers. An Internet facility for managing and distributing a variety of data across the Internet.
Who	A UNIX command that displays the ID and other information about all the users logged on to the local system, or about a specific user when a user ID is included. See also the **W** command.
Whois	A UNIX command that displays the user ID and other information about the person whose on-line handle or nickname is supplied as an argument to the command. whois tbadgett, for example, will show registered information about user tbadgett if this user is maintained in the Internet whois server database.
Wide Area Networks (WAN)	A network connecting users from many areas that transcends cities or other geographical boundaries.
XMODEM	A file transfer protocol.
Z	A file designator in UNIX that shows that the file with which it is associated has been compressed with the COMPRESS command. You must use UNCOMPRESS to expand the file before using it.
ZMODEM	A file transfer protocol.

INDEX